SELF-GUIDED
Berlin

Current Titles in Langenscheidt's Self-Guided Series:

ALASKA
BERLIN
CANADA
EGYPT
ENGLAND
EUROPEAN CITIES
FRANCE
ISRAEL
ITALY
MEXICO

SELF-GUIDED
Berlin

*With 27 illustrations and photographs;
18 maps in color and black and white*

L

LANGENSCHEIDT PUBLISHERS, NEW YORK

Publisher:	Langenscheidt Publishers, Inc.
Managing Editor:	Lisa Checchi Ross
New text, research, rewrite, and adaptation for U.S. edition:	Donald S. Olson
U.S. Editorial Staff:	Dana Schwartz; Linda Eger
Cartography:	Eberhart von Harsdorf
Illustrations:	Vera Solymosi-Thurzó
Cover Design:	Diane Wagner
Cover Photograph:	Transmedia/D. Okon
Text Design:	Irving Perkins Associates
Production:	Ripinsky & Company
Photographs:	Donald S. Olson, Nos. 1, 2, 3, and 6; Transmedia, W. Okon, Nos. 4, 9, and 10; Gerd Schnürer, Berlin, Germany, No. 5; Transmedia, D. Okon, No. 7; action press, Ralph Succo, No. 8
Original German Text:	Frauke Burian
Original English language translation and U.S. adaptation for German edition:	Donald Arthur
Letters:	We welcome your comments and suggestions. Our address: Langenscheidt Publishers, Inc. 46-35 54th Rd. Maspeth, N.Y. 11378

Special thanks to Lufthansa Airlines, Euro-Berlin, the German National Tourist Board, and the Berlin Tourist Office for their generous assistance in the preparation of this edition.

Self-Guided Berlin *is part of the Self-Guided travel book series published by Langenscheidt Publishers, Inc.*

© 1991 by Langenscheidt Publishers, Inc.
All rights reserved under international and Pan-American copyright conventions.
Adapted and revised from *Travel Guide Berlin*, © 1987 by Polyglott-Verlag Dr. Bolte KG, München.

Manufactured in the United States of America.

10 9 8 7 6 5 4 3 2 1

ISBN: 0-88729-210-0

Contents

FOREWORD vii
Using This Guide   viii

GETTING YOUR BEARINGS 1
Location and Area   1; Landscape, Lakes, and Rivers   1;
Climate   2; Population   2; Berliners and their
Language   3; Economy   4; Architectural
Reconstruction   4; Constitution and Administration   6

CHRONOLOGY 8

ART, ARCHITECTURE, AND LITERATURE 17
Romanesque and Gothic   17; Renaissance   17;
Baroque   17; Rococo   18; Classicism and Romanticism   18; Historicism   19; 20th Century   19

16 WALKS AROUND BERLIN 25
Walk 1: Zoo District and Kurfürstendamm 25
Walk 2: Bahnhof Zoo–Ernst-Reuter-Platz–Tiergarten 33
Walk 3: Architectural Tour: Schloss Bellevue–Reichstag–
Brandenburger Tor–Kulturforum–Bauhaus Archives 40
Walk 4: Schloss Charlottenburg 48
Walk 5: Theodor-Heuss-Platz–Messegelände–ICC–
Funkturm–Olympia Stadion–Spandau 55
Walk 6: Through the Grunewald to the Wannsee 62
Walk 7: Around the Grunewaldsee 65
Walk 8: Wannsee–Düppel Forest–Pfaueninsel–Volkspark
Klein-Glienicke 67
Walk 9: Freie Universität–Dahlem-Dorf–Museen Dahlem–
Botanischer Garten 74
Walk 10: Schöneberg–Tempelhof–Neukölln 81
Walk 11: Kreuzberg 88
Walk 12: Through the Wedding and Reinickendorf
Districts 93
Walk 13: Brandenburger Tor–Under den Linden–Dom 99
Walk 14: Checkpoint Charlie–Platz der Akademie–Unter
den Linden 107
Walk 15: Museumsinsel 110
Walk 16: Alexanderplatz–Marienkirche–Rathaus–
Nikolaiviertel(–Markische Museum) 118

Contents

Other Sights to See in East Berlin — 124
Special Excursion: Potsdam–Schloss Sanssouci — 126

PRACTICAL INFORMATION — 133

Choosing When to Go 133; National Holidays 133; Average Monthly Temperatures 134; Weight, Measure, and Temperature Equivalents 134; Time Zones 135; Passport and Visa Requirements 135; Customs Entering Germany 135; Customs Returning Home 135; Embassies and Consulates 136; Getting to Berlin by Air 137; Hotels and Other Accommodations 138; Currency Regulations 141; Business Hours and Closings 141; Postage 141; Telephones 144; Traveling in Berlin 144; Driving in Germany 145; Restaurants and Cafés 146; Bars and Nightlife 148; General Sources of Information 148; Shopping 150; Clothing Sizes 150; Museums 152; Theaters 155

INDEX — 157

Foreword

If Berlin never sleeps, it's probably because this city on the Spree has witnessed more history-making events in the last century than most cities accrue in a millennium. Recent political developments only underscore Berlin's amazing volatility, energy, and capacity for change, and help to make it one of the most exciting cities in Europe.

For forty years Berlin was the hot seat of the Cold War, the epicenter of radically conflicting ideologies. For nearly thirty years West Berlin was encircled by a seemingly impenetrable concrete Wall that symbolized quite literally the separation of the two postwar German states. When Berlin celebrated its 750th birthday in 1987, Berliners could not have imagined the astonishing whirlwind of events that would engulf them just two years later.

On November 9, 1989, the East German government was forced to submit to pressure from its citizens and open the barricade that separated East from West. The world looked on in amazement as Berliners joyously embraced one another, toasted each other, and danced together on top of the Wall that had kept them apart for so long. Within a few months most of the Wall had been dismantled, Checkpoint Charlie and other border crossings had been removed, the severed subway and streetcar lines reopened, and East and West Berliners were using one currency. On October 3, 1990, Germany became one nation again. Berlin, proclaimed the new capital, experienced the immediate effects of reunification more than any other city in Germany.

Visitors to Berlin will feel these effects too—as they happen—which is why the city is a doubly exciting place to visit just now. For the first time since 1961, sights in East Berlin that were difficult to see are suddenly easy to reach. Gone are the long waits at the East Berlin crossing points, gone the obligatory currency exchange, gone the surly guards, gone the daily visa requirement and all of the restrictions that once made a trip into East Berlin uncomfortable and intimidating. Visitors to Berlin will now find that their travel horizons have been expanded immeasurably. What other city in the world offers two different environments no more than a subway stop apart? Where else can one witness the historic dismantling of an entire political culture and the rebuilding of a new society—a new *city?*

Berlin will once again become the capital of a united Germany. A flurry of new activity and cultural cooperation characterizes the city these days. For Berlin the 90s begin an era of unprecedented change; to the city's visitors, the decade offers a unique opportunity to observe history in the making.

Langenscheidt's Self-Guided Berlin puts all of this within reach of every independent traveler. Written especially for seasoned travelers, this unique guide includes extensive detailed tours of downtown Berlin and its greater metropolitan area. Travelers will find all the information they need to explore Berlin at their own pace and follow their own interests.

Self-Guided Tours

The heart of this books is its self-guided tours. Walking tours of Berlin describe all the important sites and put them in historical perspective. Extensive tours are broken up into shorter segments, should you wish to rest or resume the tour at another time. We also advise you on how best to get around to the various points of interest in each route.

Using this Guide

This travel guide helps you plan, organize, and enjoy your trip to Berlin. In "Getting Your Bearings," a brief rundown of Berlin's geography, economy, climate, population, customs, postwar reconstruction, and administration, helps to introduce travelers to the city and its people. A chapter on art, architecture, and literature, as well as a chronology provide helpful background and perspective on the sights you'll be seeing in this electrifying city.

Langenscheidt also offers a subjective guide to the most appealing sights. Our unique three-star system appears throughout the guide:

*** Worth a special trip—don't miss it!
 ** The most important sights on the tour
  * Highlights

Other sights along the way are also worth seeing, but are not necessarily as important as the starred sights.

Major sights appear in boldface for easy reference, while other notable places appear in italics. Numbers in parentheses correspond to locations on the maps.

The guide concludes with a Practical Information chapter. Sections include information designed to help you gather information you'll need before you depart for Berlin and helpful facts to know once you are there, such as information offices, local transportation, hotels, and restaurants.

Notes and Observations

Travel information, like fruit, is perishable. We've made every effort to double-check information in this guide and to keep pace with the rapid changes in Berlin. But hotels do close, museums do shut down for renovation, and place and street names may change as the city realigns itself, so check ahead wherever possible.

Special note on the Berlin text: Because Berlin is so recently reunified, we have maintained references to West Berlin and East Berlin, since the character of each side of the city is still very different. Likewise, with the fall of communism, we expect the names of many streets and buildings in East Berlin to be changed in the near future and statues of socialist leaders to be removed as Berlin acts to erase its past.

Visitors should also note that museum holdings in East and West Berlin are undergoing a major reshuffling. Although information was correct at presstime, some museum collections will be moved and others consolidated in the near future.

We welcome your comments and updates of our information. Please write us at:

Langenscheidt Publishers, Inc.
46–35 54th Road
Maspeth, New York 11378

Getting Your Bearings

Location and Area

Berlin is in the geographical center of Europe, about halfway between Moscow and Lisbon. It is on the same latitude as London, England, and Vancouver, Canada, and its longitude is the same as Naples, Italy. The city lies in the great plain of the Northern German lowlands, between the Mittelgebirge mountain range and the Baltic coast in the middle of the Mark Brandenburg on the Spree and Havel rivers. Its average elevation is between approximately 35 to 36.5 meters (115 and 120 feet) above sea level.

Berlin is Germany's largest city, encompassing about 883 square kilometers (340 square miles). Before reunification, West Berlin comprised 480 square kilometers (185 square miles), nearly 55 percent of the total area, and East Berlin 405 square kilometers (156 square miles), or about 45 percent. Larger in area than New York City, Greater Berlin would easily accommodate the cities of Atlanta, Boston, Cleveland, and San Francisco within its boundaries. Only about 40 percent of West Berlin is developed—the remainder is forests, lakes, rivers, parks, and farmlands, all of which provide ample recreational opportunities.

Landscape, Lakes, and Rivers

Located on the edge of an ancient Ice Age river valley, Berlin has very low elevations, such as the Müggelberge (9.5 meters/377 feet), the Schäferberg (8.5 meters/337 feet), the Havelberg (8 meters/318 feet), the 6.5-meter- (259-foot-) high Karlsberg, crowned by the Grunewald Tower, and the Kreuzberg (5.5 meters/217 feet). In addition, it has several "rubble mountains"—artificial hills built of rubble left after the war—all of which have been fully landscaped, equipped with various sporting facilities, and turned into popular city parks. One of them, the Teufelsberg at the Teufelsee in Grunewald, is actually Berlin's highest peak, with an elevation of 10 meters (378 feet). The hill is high enough to be used as a launching point for hang-gliders, provides a toboggan run in the winter, and is a place where city hikers get in shape for their more strenuous excursions.

The city lies on the Spree and Havel rivers. The Spree, which has its source in the Lausitz region, flows through the Great Müggel Lake inside the Berlin city limits and past both sides of the Museum Island in East Berlin before emptying into the Havel near Spandau. The Havel, in turn, forms three of the loveliest of Berlin's lakes, the Tegeler See, the Stössensee, and the Wannsee. In all, Berlin contains no less than 62 lakes and 127 other bodies of water, such as tributaries and canals—and has more bridges than Venice. Boats can be rented on many of the lakes, and several sightseeing companies offer one-day excursions on steamers that cover a picturesque circuit through the rivers, lakes, and canals.

No other large city in Germany offers so much recreation area within its city limits as does Berlin. Some of these places, such as the Wannsee Beach (easy to reach from the downtown area), the Schlachtensee, the Krumme Lanke, and the Havelchaussee, that runs along the western side of the Grunewald, can be as crowded as the Kurfürstendamm on weekends. But Berliners have some 39 square kilometers (15 square miles) of woods to wander in, and there are quiet, remote areas in the Spandau, Tegel, and Düppel forests to explore for those interested in solitude and nature. Within the central area of the city there are several large, beautifully landscaped parks such as the Tiergarten, the Botanical Gardens, and the grounds of Charlottenburg Palace. Hiking, bicycling, picnicking, and swimming are popular activities among the Berliners—and so is sunbathing.

Climate

Situated between an oceanic and a continental climate, Berlin has relatively dry weather with predominating westerly winds. Its famed "Berliner Luft" (bracing air) is a natural result of the surrounding forests, which act as an air filter. The city's annual precipitation of 23 inches is well below the national average. The average annual temperature is 49 degrees Fahrenheit (9 degrees centigrade), with 34 degrees F. (one degree C.) being the median for January and 66 degrees F. (19 degrees C.) for July.

Population

Berlin, with about 3.5 million inhabitants, is the most densely populated city in Germany. Population figures are variable at the present time, primarily because thousands of East Germans have moved to Berlin—especially the western part—since the 1989 opening of the Wall and the national borders. In addition, an estimated 100,000 foreigners living in West Berlin entered illegally and are therefore not registered in official population tallies.

The population of Berlin is a mixture of established Berliners and newcomers from other German territories, as well as large numbers of Turkish, Yugoslavian, Italian, Greek, and Polish immigrants recruited by industry and known as "Gastarbeiter" (guest workers). Many Vietnamese and Africans live in East Berlin, having been recruited as laborers or students from other Communist countries.

West Berlin's foreign population lives primarily in the districts of

Schöneberg, Neukölln, and Kreuzberg, known as "Little Istanbul" because fully 27 percent of its population is Turkish. More Turks—some 112,000 of them—live in Berlin than in any other German city. Turkish shops and restaurants give Kreuzberg an exotic, Oriental air unique to Berlin and make it a fascinating place to visit.

At last count, nearly a quarter of a million foreign nationals—over 11 percent of the total population—live in Berlin; nearly a quarter of the city's children under six years of age have non-German parents.

Berliners and their Language

The great German poet Johann Wolfgang von Goethe described the Berliners as an "audacious race" whom one could outwit only by giving as good as one got, if not a little better. He was referring to the legendary "Berliner Schnauze," or quick tongue, a trait peculiar to long-time residents of the city and one that is simultaneously feared, scorned, and admired by other Germans.

Berliners are still known for their acerbic wit, cynical attitude, and argumentativeness, and it's true that they love to mock sacred cows—especially politicians and the government—revered by the rest of the nation; but they are also direct, friendly, and more easygoing and tolerant in their acceptance of the new, the unusual, the eccentric, and the outrageous than other Germans. After all, these are people who have seen everything over the years—including the complete destruction of their city and its postwar political division—and lived to tell the tale. Their attitude is in part a result of the sophistication and frustration that comes from living in a giant metropolis with more than its share of daily problems: With all its confrontations, fears, and political anxieties, the Cold War was played out for years right here on opposite sides of a wall that separated families, friends, and countrymen, and kept the residents psychologically marooned. Thus contemporary Berlin wit is a psychological safety valve in some ways—a way to let off steam. In a less complicated sense, it's simply a colorful way to express an opinion—and a true Berliner has plenty of those.

The old Berlin dialect is now heard more often in East Berlin and blue collar West Berlin neighborhoods than on the busy shopping streets and international commercial tourist hubs. Although it's commonly regarded as the dialect of the common man, Berliners never associate their distinctive dialect with class distinctions—in fact, even the Kaiser took great pride in speaking Berlinerisch. The dialect originated in the Platt-Deutsch spoken in the Middle Ages in an area between the Harz mountains and the Elbe River and was brought to Berlin by early settlers. When High Saxon was introduced as the new "official language" in the early 16th century, the residents of Berlin adopted some of its sounds and words and created a kind of provincial argot of their own. Later on, in the late 17th and early 18th centuries, they borrowed colloquialisms from the French Huguenot refugees, and later still incorporated underworld slang and Yiddish expressions.

Economy

Berlin is the largest industrial city in Germany. In West Berlin, 40 percent of the 877,000 employed people work in the production of goods (industry, manufacturing, etc.). The largest industrial sector is the electrical industry (26 percent), followed by the engineering, machine construction, chemical, and clothing sectors. The West Berlin women's wear industry produces almost one-half of West Germany's total output. The tourist trade is the sixth largest industry in the city's economy and growing—as made evident by the sudden difficulty of finding a hotel room. More than 28 American firms have offices and production facilities in Berlin, including General Motors, Gillette, and IBM.

The economic picture is changing rapidly as a result of the monetary and political reunification of the two Germanys. Many East German companies, including dozens in East Berlin, have already found themselves unable to compete in the new free market economy and have closed down their operations. Several large multi-national corporations have already invested in East Berlin companies, and a further spate of mergers and corporate takeovers can be expected. East Germany as a whole is projecting unemployment figures somewhere around four million in the years ahead.

Numerous measures are being developed to promote employment, improve the environment, and increase cooperation on all levels to integrate the country since reunification, as well as to encourage a new emphasis on high-tech, future-oriented industries. The imminent opening of the European Common Market will offer further opportunities and challenges to the new, undivided city.

Architectural Reconstruction

Berlin's contrasting architectural styles range from early Romanesque and Gothic village churches to the ultra-modern functional buildings of the 20th century. Although World War II destroyed a significant portion of Berlin's historic architecture—only about 30 percent of the city's buildings survived—many remaining Renaissance, Baroque, Rococo, and neoclassical examples have been restored and are worthy of attention. East Berlin, with its restored Platz der Akademie, Nicholas Quarter, and Unter den Linden area, is exceptionally rich in historic buildings and will provide visitors with a good idea of prewar Berlin's architectural diversity. Charlottenburg Palace in West Berlin is another historic compendium, a splendid showcase of the Prussian Baroque, Rococo, and neoclassical styles.

Most public and cultural buildings, however, are products of the last three decades: the buildings of the Free University and the Technical University, museum buildings, and the Europa Center shopping and recreation mall in West Berlin are just a few examples. On the southern edge of the Tiergarten district, the new Culture Forum, begun in 1963, is nearing completion. Buildings here include the aggressively modern Philharmonic Hall (1963), Chamber Music Hall (1987), and State Library (1978), all designed by Hans Scharoun and constructed over the past 25 years, the Musical Instruments Museum (1984) and the Museum of Applied Arts (1985), as well as Ludwig Mies van der Rohe's National Gallery from 1968.

Residential construction in West Berlin began in 1949, most of it in publicly financed "social housing projects" that created several completely new neighborhoods. The Hansaviertel on the edge of the Tiergarten district—a result of the Interbau 57 architectural show—enjoys a better reputation than the Gropiusstadt and the Märkisches Viertel, two massive housing projects that are frequently cited as deplorable examples of depersonalized residential architecture. Today, as in many other places, the city planners of Berlin have learned by the mistakes of the past and have transferred the main thrust of their activities to the preservation and modernization of existing residential properties. The 1987 International Architectural Exhibition (IBA) was intended to show how the city center can be revitalized by "behutsame Stadterneuerung" (careful urban renewal).

In East Berlin, work began on the reconstruction and restoration of great portions of the downtown area in 1961. New government buildings were constructed on Marx-Engels-Platz (this name may change in the near future), and the Palace of the Republic was erected between 1973 and 1976 on the spot where the 16th-century Berlin Palace once stood. Between 1968 and 1970 Alexanderplatz was expanded to twice its former size, and the Television Tower was completed in 1969 to the west of the "Alex." In recent years new East Berlin housing developments were put up on Karl-Marx-Allee in Friedrichsfelde, satellite towns housing several hundred thousand people were built in Marzahn, Hohenschönhausen, and Hellersdorf, and the turn-of-the-century apartment blocks in the workers' quarter of Prenzlauer Berg were modernized. New building continues at a rapid pace in East Berlin, spurred on by the new free-market economy and ongoing reunification of the two Berlins. In the coming years Friedrichstrasse will be completely transformed, and visitors can expect to see a complete—and no doubt fascinating—urban reintegration between the two sides of the city. (See the Art, Architecture, and Literature essay for further information.)

Constitution and Administration

After the Second World War, supreme authority in Berlin was vested in a military government administered by the occupying Allied powers. The basis of the Allied authority stemmed from the London Protocol, signed

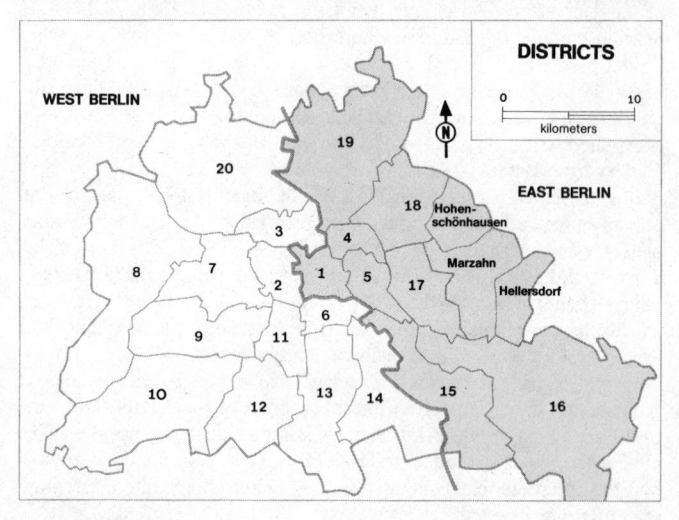

West Berlin Districts
  2. Tiergarten
  3. Wedding
  6. Kreuzberg
  7. Charlottenberg
  8. Spandau
  9. Wilmersdorf
 10. Zehlendorf
 11. Schöneberg
 12. Steglitz
 13. Tempelhof
 14. Neukölln
 20. Reinickendorf

East Berlin Districts
  1. Mitte
  4. Prenzlauer Berg
  5. Friedrichshain
 15. Treptow
 16. Köpenick
 17. Lichtenberg
 18. Wiessensee
 19. Pankow
     Marzahn
     Hohenschönhausen
     Hellersdorf

Districts 6 and 10–14 formed the American sector, Districts 2 and 7–9 the British, and Districts 3 and 20 formed the French sector.

by the United States, Britain, France, and the Soviet Union on September 12, 1944, before the war was over. In this agreement, each of the four victorious powers was allocated one zone of Hitler's capital of National Socialism. Another agreement soon followed, establishing the constitution of an Allied Control Council. After Germany's defeat in 1945, the city was divided into four sectors and an Inter-Allied Governing Authority (Kommandatura) was set up to jointly administer the Greater Berlin area. At the beginning of 1948, however, the Soviets resigned from the Allied Command; on November 30, 1948, a separate city administration was set up in the Soviet sector, thus marking the East-West division that resulted finally in the erection of the Wall in 1961.

Now that Germany is reunited, a new constitution will govern Berlin, and the Inter-Allied Governing Authority, dissolved by the four wartime Allies on September 12, 1990, is no longer a factor in the city's administration.

On the map opposite you can see the borders of the 20 districts into which the city has been divided since 1920 (between 1979 and 1986, East Berlin added three new districts).

Chronology

Archaeological finds have shown that the Berlin area was populated as far back as 8,000 B.C. Tribes of Swebians, Burgunds, and Slavic Wends fought for supremacy in the area from the first millennium B.C. to the 12th century.

1134: The Ascanian Albrecht the Bear is named Margrave of the Northern March by Emperor Lothar; as of A.D. 1150 he titles himself Margrave of Brandenburg.

ca. 1230: The Ascanian Margraves John I and Otto III found Berlin and Cölln, two trading settlements on neighboring islands in the Spree—the site of present-day Berlin.

1237: Cölln first mentioned in documents—this is the date celebrated in 1987 as Berlin's 750th anniversary. Berlin is first mentioned in 1244.

1307: Berlin and Cölln unite under mutual administration and experience prosperous growth throughout the 14th century.

1320: The Ascanian dynasty dies out and the March falls to the Wittelsbachs.

1415: Count Friedrich von Nürnberg of the house of Hohenzollern receives both the March of Brandenburg and the title of Prince Elector from Emperor Sigismund. He enters Berlin as Frederick I.

1432: Berlin and Cölln unite to become one town.

1442–1470: Elector Frederick II ends the union of Berlin and Cölln and builds a castle on the Spree. Berlin thus becomes the official residence of the Elector of Brandenburg.

1539: Elector Joachim II converts to Protestantism and introduces the Reformation to Berlin.

1618–1648: The Thirty Years' War and the black plague exact a stiff price from Berlin. The population dwindles from 12,000 to about half that number.

1640–1688: Frederick William, the "Great Elector," sets about reconstructing and redesigning the ravaged city. He brings foreign artists to Berlin, establishes trading companies, fortifies the city, and connects the Elbe and Oder rivers via the Frederick William Canal. The districts of Friedrichswerder and Dorotheenstadt come into being outside the fortress. In 1685, the Great Elector signs the Edict of Potsdam and invites the persecuted French Huguenots to settle in the Mark Brandenburg.

1701: Frederick III, Prince Elector of Brandenburg, proclaims himself Frederick I, King of Prussia. He continues his father's plans with the laying out of Friedrichstadt.

1709: The five towns—Berlin, Cölln, Friedrichswerder, Dorotheenstadt, and Friedrichstadt—are united to form one municipality and the new royal residential town of Berlin. The population reaches 56,000 in 1710.

1713–1740: King Frederick William I, the "Soldiers' King," extends the Friedrichstadt.

1740–1786: King Frederick II the Great makes Berlin into a major European capital. During his reign the population grows from 81,000 to 150,000. New cotton and silk mills go into operation about 1750, and Berlin becomes Germany's most important textile center. Starting in 1770, the "Linden" (today's Unter den Linden) is expanded into a grand boulevard. The palace of Sanssouci in Potsdam is built as Frederick the Great's summer residence. During the Seven Years' War, Berlin is attacked and occupied by the Russians and Austrians.

1786–1797: During the reign of King Frederick William II, Berlin becomes "The City of the Enlightenment." The Brandenburg Gate is completed in 1791 and becomes an emblem of the city.

1797–1840: The reign of King Frederick William III. After the collapse of the Prussian military forces in the Battle of Jena and Auerstadt, Napoleon I enters Berlin through the Brandenburg Gate on October 27, 1806, and a two-year French occupation of the city begins. In 1810 Wilhelm von Humboldt founds Berlin University (today's Humboldt University), which soon becomes one of the most important institutions of higher learning in Germany. Friedrich Ludwig Jahn, the "Father of Sports," sets up the first German athletic field on the Hasenheide in 1811. With the defeat of Napoleon I, the rebirth of Berlin begins. Schinkel, Rauch, and Lenné design a new city. The Berlin-Potsdam railroad is established in 1838, and the first horse-drawn omnibus line between Alexanderplatz and Potsdamer Platz opens a year later.

1840–1861: During the reign of King Frederick William IV, Berlin becomes one of Europe's most important industrial cities. The population in 1848 reaches 400,000.

1848: On March 18, the March Revolution breaks out and there is bloody street fighting in Berlin. Frederick William IV pledges his support for the unification of Germany and a short-lived Prussian National Assembly is convened. Frederick William IV declines the imperial crown offered him a year later by the Frankfurt Parliament.

1850: A reactionary "imposed constitution" of the Prussian government takes effect on January 31 and remains in force until November 1918.

1861–1888: During the reign of King William I, who is proclaimed German Emperor in Versailles in 1871, Berlin becomes the capital of the German Empire. Bismarck becomes Prime Minister of Prussia (1862–1890). The city's population rises to 826,000 during the peak of the Industrial Revolution (1850–1870).

1888: Emperor Frederick William III reigns only 99 days.

1888–1918: Emperor William II dismisses Bismarck in 1890. The "foundation years" bring a massive economic upswing to the city, but most of the workers are forced to live in crowded, unsanitary tenements. By 1900, Berlin's population has advanced to 1,900,000. The first subway line opens in 1902.

1914–1918: First World War: Berlin remains outside the front lines of fighting but it is increasingly difficult to keep the city stocked with food and supplies; rationing goes into effect. Hunger and war-weariness, compounded by political grievances, culminate in mass strikes in 1917 and 1918. Germany's defeat in the war marks the beginning of the end of the Prussian-German monarchy.

1918: The November Revolution ends Hohenzollern rule in Germany. Emperor William II abdicates on November 9, and Friedrich Ebert, the head of the Social Democratic Party (SPD), is named Chancellor of the Reich. Hours later, Philipp Scheidemann proclaims the "German Republic" from the Reichstag while Karl Liebknecht of the revolutionary Spartacus Union proclaims the "Free Socialist Republic." Berlin becomes the scene of fierce power struggles among conflicting political groups.

1920: Berlin is unified with its suburbs to make one single municipal unit with a population of 4,100,000. Left- and right-wing political agitation and infighting continues: a police operation against leftist radicals in January, 1920, ends with 42 dead, and the Reich government flees in the face of an attempted right-wing putsch in March. During the years of the Weimar Republic (1920–1933) the city blossoms into the political, economic, and cultural center of Germany.

Chronology 11

1921–1923: Large-scale strikes disrupt and paralyze the city. Political violence escalates and culminates in the assassination of Foreign Minister Walter Rathenau on June 24, 1922. The number of unemployed soars to 235,000 by 1923. Inflation, which had reached ludicrous proportions, is stabilized in 1923 when one new banknote (Rentenmark) is issued to replace 1,000 billion old paper marks.

1924: With the completion of Tempelhof Airport, Berlin becomes the "hub of European aviation." Berlin is now the largest industrial city on the continent, the major commercial, banking and stock exchange center, the most important railway junction, and the second-largest inland port of the German Empire.

1933: Adolf Hitler seizes power on January 30 and Josef Goebbels stages a torchlight parade through the Brandenburg Gate. After the Reichstag goes up in flames on February 27—most likely the work of Nazis—constitutional rights are suspended and totalitarianism replaces municipal self-government. The first brutal measures against the Jews, the purge of the Civil Service, and the book burning in Opernplatz (today's Bebelplatz) signal the descent of "Golden Berlin" into barbarism. Hundreds of artists, scientists, and politicians begin to emigrate. Berlin is chosen by Hitler to be the capital of a new Thousand Year Reich.

1936: The games of the XIth Olympiad are held in Berlin's new stadium, where Hitler plans to demonstrate the "Aryan" superiority of Germany's athletes. A black American, Jesse Owens, dominates the competition and wins four gold medals; Hitler storms out of the stadium.

1938: Synagogues and Jewish businesses are savagely attacked and destroyed by Nazis on November 9—the so-called "Kristallnacht"—the Night of Broken Glass.

1939–1945: World War II begins in 1939 with the German invasion of Poland. The monstrous "final solution to the Jewish question" is adopted at the Wannsee Conference in 1942. After Germany's first large-scale defeat, the National Socialists declare "total war" on February 18, 1943, in the Berlin Sports Palace. On November 23, 1943, the Allied forces begin the steady bombardment of Germany's capital city. A secret resistance group around Colonel von Stauffenberg fails in its attempt to assassinate Hitler on July 20, 1944; von Stauffenberg and 89 of his associates are executed.

Soviet troops reach Berlin on April 21, 1945; some 5,000 Russian soldiers lose their lives in the Battle of Berlin. Hitler and his mistress Eva Braun commit suicide in a bunker. The city is captured by the Red Army on May 2, 1945, and Germany capitulates on May 8, 1945, in Berlin-

Karlshorst. The city becomes the seat of the Supreme Allied Control Council on June 5. American and British troops enter Berlin on July 4, followed by French troops on August 12.

Berlin becomes a four-sector city, occupied by the four powers, the U.S., Great Britain, France, and the Soviet Union. Of the 160,000 Jews who had lived in Berlin in 1933, only 7,247 are left by war's end. Berlin's total prewar population of 4.3 million has been reduced to 2.8 million. Of the 245,000 buildings standing in Berlin before the war, 50,000 are completely destroyed or beyond repair.

1946: A democratic City Assembly comprised of the Social Democratic, Liberal, Social Unity (Communist), and Christian Democratic parties is elected—the first and last free postwar election in Berlin for 44 years.

1948: Following their March 20th resignation from the Allied Control Council and their June 16th resignation from the Allied Command, the Soviets begin their blockade of the western part of the city on June 24. Four days later, the Allies begin the Berlin Airlift: Every day almost 1,000 American and British aircraft laden with food and other supplies land at the three West Berlin airfields, Tempelhof, Gatow, and Tegel. On November 30, a separate municipal government is proclaimed in East Berlin, sealing the division of the city.

1949: After 11 months, the Soviet blockade is lifted on May 12th. On October 7, the German Democratic Republic (GDR) is founded and East Berlin declared its capital.

1950: The new democratic constitution of West Berlin goes into effect on October 1st. The first Governing Mayor is Ernst Reuter.

1953: The June 17 workers' uprising in East Berlin spreads over the whole of East Germany. Soviet military authorities declare a state of emergency, move tanks into the city, and forcibly end the revolt.

1958: On November 27 the Soviet Union issues the "Berlin Ultimatum," demanding the departure of the western powers from Berlin and the transformation of Berlin into a "demilitarized free city." The Western Allies refuse to give up their rights in West Berlin.

1959: The Four Power foreign ministers' conference meets to discuss Germany and the Berlin question. There is no agreement, but a clarification of standpoints.

1961: On August 13 the construction of the Wall begins. Units of the People's Police and National People's Army block access to the Western sectors of the city. Barbed wire and barricades divide Berlin as the concrete wall is erected; S-Bahn (metropolitan railroad) and U-Bahn (subway) connections between the two parts of the city are cut off. West Berlin becomes an island. The Western Allies limit themselves to statements protesting the blocking measures.

1963: American President John F. Kennedy visits West Berlin on June 26. In a famous speech from the balcony of Schöneberg City Hall he emphasizes American and Allied solidarity with West Berliners: "All free men, wherever they may live, are citizens of Berlin, and therefore, as a free man, I take pride in the words: Ich bin ein Berliner."

On December 17 the first Border Pass Agreement goes into effect, allowing West Berliners to visit next-of-kin in East Berlin.

1968: In June the GDR (German Democratic Republic) introduces passport controls and compulsory visas on transit routes to and from Berlin.

1971: The Allies sign the Quadripartite Agreement (also called the Four Power Agreement) in Berlin on September 3, confirming the legal and political ties between West Berlin and the Federal Republic of Germany. In December, the GDR and Federal Republic sign the intra-German agreement on transit traffic to and from Berlin on the basis of the Four Power Agreement. West Berliners can again enter East Berlin and the GDR; transit formalities are simplified. In East Berlin, Erich Honecker takes office as General Secretary of the Central Committee, replacing Walter Ulbricht.

1972: Signing of the Treaty on the Basis of Relations between the Federal Republic and the GDR.

1974: Permanent missions of the two German states open in Bonn and East Berlin; West Berlin is represented by the West German mission.

1978: The two German States agree on the construction of an expressway between Berlin and Hamburg and other cooperative improvements in communications between the two Berlins.

1979: On July 9, the western powers protest in Moscow against a law enacted on June 28 by the GDR Volkskammer (Parliament) which permits the direct election of East Berlin delegates to the Volkskammer. The Allies stress the quadripartite status of Greater Berlin, which cannot be changed by one signatory.

1980: In October, the GDR drastically increases the mandatory minimum exchange rate for Western visitors.

1983: Erich Honecker and West Berlin's Governing Mayor Richard von Weizsäcker meet in East Berlin.

1984: The GDR grants the West Berlin Public Transportation Authority (BVG) operating rights to S-Bahn lines in the western parts of the city.

1987: Both sides celebrate Berlin's 750th anniversary. Major urban renewal projects brighten up the city.

1988: Berlin is designated this year's "Cultural Capital of Europe."

1989: Ironically, East German party chief Erich Honecker proclaims that the Wall "will still exist in 50 and in 100 years, unless the reasons for its existence are eliminated." The last GDR citizen dies at the Wall trying to escape, bringing the final total to 78 since 1961.

Travel restrictions for West Berliners continue to ease. Mass demonstrations demanding freedom of travel and an end to the East German secret police (Stasi) begin in Leipzig in September.

Hungary opens its border to Austria on September 10, paving the way for a mass exodus of GDR citizens into West Germany via Hungary and Austria.

October 7 marks the GDR's 40th anniversary celebrations. Visitors from the West are denied access to East Berlin. Some 7,000 demonstrators march through the center of the GDR capital and are surrounded by police; at least 700 are temporarily arrested. Erich Honecker continues his hard-line stance against the protest movement sweeping through East Berlin, Leipzig, Dresden, Potsdam, Plauen, and Jena. A new social democratic party is founded in the GDR. Daily vigils for jailed civil rights leaders and demonstrators end with the release of most political prisoners.

Erich Honecker and other members of the Central Committee are ousted from office and the Central Committee votes in Egon Krenz as Honecker's successor, despite mass protests. The New Forum, a citizen's movement expressing distrust of the new government, becomes prominent in the demonstrations that have now taken over the entire country.

In November, artists call for a rally in support of democracy in East Germany and nearly one million GDR citizens respond in the largest demonstration since the end of World War II. The entire GDR Council of Ministers resigns, followed by the entire Politburo. Egon Krenz is confirmed as General Secretary.

On November 9, in a surprise move, the GDR opens its borders to West Berlin. Tens of thousands of Berliners freely cross from one side of the city to the other, and the Berlin Wall becomes the scene of a giant celebration; within the next two months, most of the Wall is dismantled. All GDR citizens are given complete freedom to travel. The West Berlin House of Representatives meets in a special session, and there is an emotional rally in front of West Berlin's Schöneberg Rathaus; speakers include Chancellor Helmut Kohl, Berlin's Governing Mayor Walter Momper, and former Berlin Mayor and Federal Chancellor Willy Brandt.

The first new border crossing points between West and East Berlin are opened on November 10, and the following day more than 100,000 East Berliners visit West Berlin. West Berlin's Governing Mayor Walter Momper and East Berlin's Mayor Erhard Krack meet at a new border crossing established on Potsdamer Platz. Hans Modrow becomes the GDR's new prime minister. New border crossings open the city even more. The Federal Republic's permanent mission in East Berlin is reestablished. The GDR has by now issued 5.7 million travel visas to its citizens.

A coalition government led by Hans Modrow is elected to the GDR People's Parliament. GDR citizens wait in long lines for their "welcome money": 15 marks of hard currency is available to them in East Berlin and another 100 marks in West Berlin. The Federal Republic makes further aid to the GDR dependent upon the extent of reforms. By November 23, the GDR government has ordered stricter customs controls to prevent a "selling-out" of the country.

At a rally in East Berlin in December, SED members successfully demand the resignation of Egon Krenz and the entire Politburo. At a special session of the Central Committee, Erich Honecker and other top SED functionaries are expelled from the Party and arrested on charges of misappropriation of state funds.

GDR Prime Minister Hans Modrow and a top aide to Chancellor Kohl meet in East Berlin and agree that all visa and compulsory exchange requirements for West Germans and West Berliners will cease as of January 1, 1990. A convention of the SED in East Berlin decides to develop a new constitution and to disband the State Security Service. Gregor Gysi is elected to succeed Egon Krenz.

On December 11, ambassadors of the Four Powers meet in Berlin for the first time since 1971. The Brandenburg Gate is ceremoniously opened to East and West German pedestrians on December 22, and two days later the visa and compulsory exchange requirements are officially abolished for West Germans and West Berliners. On December 31, a half million people ring in a new decade for Berlin at the Brandenburg Gate.

1990: The Allied side of Checkpoint Charlie, one of the two crossing points into East Berlin for non-German visitors since 1961, is removed in June. Several large mergers or cooperative ventures between Western and East German businesses are announced (Lufthansa, Volkswagen, and Chrysler among them).

On July 2 the two Germanys adopt a single monetary system, further simplifying access to East Berlin. The public transportation system between the two Berlins—severed since 1961—begins its reunification and borders cease to exist.

The four wartime Allies sign a document on September 12 relinquishing their occupation rights in Germany.

Germany is officially reunified on October 3 and Berlin proclaimed its new capital. In December, Helmut Kohl becomes chancellor of a united Germany in the first free nationwide elections since Adolf Hitler was named Chancellor of the Reich in 1933.

Art, Architecture, and Literature

Romanesque and Gothic

Most of the few buildings that remain from the Middle Ages were either reconstructed at a later date or destroyed in the Second World War. The simple Gothic Marienkirche (St. Mary's Church) in East Berlin—with its medieval fresco known as the "Dance of Death"—is a particularly notable example, as is the restored 15th-century Nikolaikirche (St. Nicholas's Church) in the center of the old city of Spandau. The lovely 14th-century St.-Annen-Kirche (St. Anne's Church) in Dahlem is another medieval gem.

Worthy of mention, too, are the 55 or so former village churches, most of which were begun in the 13th century. These are scattered throughout the Greater Berlin area in places like Britz, Buckow, Heiligensee, Lichterfelde, Mariendorf, Rudow, and Schmargendorf. The oldest of them is the Romanesque village church of Marienfelde, built in 1192.

Renaissance

The Ribbeck House from 1624, located in East Berlin, is the sole remaining example of the many ornate town houses and palaces built in Berlin during the Renaissance. The most significant Renaissance building in the city—the Berlin Palace of the Prussian kings—was built in 1538 by Caspar Theyss, and then torn down in 1950–1951 by the East Germans.

Baroque

The great architect and sculptor Andreas Schlüter (1664–1718) dominated Berlin's artistic life during the Baroque period. One of the most important works of sculpture from that time is his Equestrian Statue of the Great Elector, which stands today in front of Charlottenburg Palace. Schlüter was also a major contributor to the expansion of the Berlin Palace and the construction of the Zeughaus (Armory), built between 1695 and 1706 and now East Berlin's Museum of German History. Another noteworthy architect was the Swede Eosander von Göthe (ca. 1670–1695) who, together with Johann Arnold Nering (1659–1695), designed Charlottenburg Palace. Most of the churches that date from around 1700 were either destroyed or badly damaged in the war, but two beautifully reconstructed examples are the French Cathedral and German Cathedral in East Berlin's Platz der Akademie. The façade of the Ephraim Palace in East Berlin's Nicholas Quarter also dates from the Baroque period.

18 Art, Architecture, and Literature

Rococo

Berlin entered the Rococo era when Frederick the Great ascended the throne in 1740. Its most important master was Georg Wenzeslaus von Knobelsdorff (1699–1753), who built the Opera House on Unter den Linden and the palace of Sanssouci in Potsdam, redesigned the Potsdam Town Palace, and added the east wing, with its Golden Gallery—a masterwork of Prussian Rococo—to Charlottenburg Palace.

Frederick the Great brought many French artists to Berlin, among them the Belgian painter Charles André Vanloo. His court painter, Antoine Pesne (1683–1757), had been active in Berlin during the reign of Frederick I. The Danzig painter and copperplate engraver Daniel Chodowiecki made a name for himself with his realistic depictions of the age.

Frederick the Great only invited French authors to Berlin, so that a native German-speaking literary culture could not become established during his reign.

Classicism and Romanticism

Classicism made its appearance in the mid-18th century and brought forth a number of significant works of art in Berlin. The main exponents of this style were Carl Gotthard Langhans (1733–1808), who built the Brandenburg Gate, and Karl Friedrich Schinkel (1741–1841), whose outstanding buildings include the Neue Wache (New Watch) on Unter den Linden, the splendid Schauspielhaus that forms the centerpiece of East Berlin's Platz der Akademie, and the Altes Museum on East Berlin's Museum Island. Joseph Peter Lenné, the greatest landscape architect in Germany, created new gardens on Peacock Island, around the Klein-Glienicke Palace, and on the grounds of Sanssouci.

The two most important sculptors of this epoch were Gottfried Schadow (1764–1850), whose statue of *Victory* crowns the Brandenburg Gate, and his pupil Christian Daniel Rauch (1777–1857), responsible for the tombs of Queen Luise and Frederick William III in the mausoleum of Charlottenburg palace.

The landscape artist Karl Blechen (1798–1840) was the outstanding painter of the Romantic era. Berlin's Biedermeier period is typified by the works of portrait and horse painter Franz Krüger (1797–1857), architectural painter Eduard Gärtner (1801–1877), and the genre painter Theodor Hosemann (1807–1831).

At the end of the 18th century, Berlin became a literary center for the early Romantic movement. The poets Ludwig Tieck (1773–1853) and Friedrich Schlegel (1772–1829) translated the works of Shakespeare into German; other Romantic poets of the period who lived in Berlin include Adelbert von Chamisso (1771–1838), Achim von Arnim (1781–1831), and Heinrich von Kleist (1777–1831). E.T.A. Hoffmann (1776–1822) was the period's ultimate Renaissance man: attorney, writer, conductor, theater director, composer, and philosopher. His fantastic stories were the subject of Jacques Offenbach's popular opera *The Tales of Hoffmann*.

In the first quarter of the 19th century, Berlin developed its reputation as a center of German intellectualism. The brothers Wilhelm and Alexander von Humboldt, as well as Tieck, Hegel, and Heine all lived and worked in the city.

Historicism

The emergence of Berlin as a world capital in the middle of the 19th century brought about a major upsurge in architectural activity which took its inspiration for building styles from the Renaissance and Baroque periods. Schinkel's pupils Ludwig Persius (1803–1845), Friedrich Stüler (1800–1865), and Johann Heinrich Strack (1805–1880) continued to expound their master's ideas. Among Strack's many designs were the National Gallery and the Victory Column. Other buildings dating from this period include East Berlin's so-called Rotes Rathaus (Red City Hall), designed by H. F. Waesemann (1813–1879), the Reichstag building by Paul Wallot (1841–1912), and the Berlin Cathedral by J. Raschdorff (1823–1914). The latter two exemplify the massive, heavy-handed, late-19th-century style known as Wilhelmine (named after Kaisers Wilhelm I and II).

Among the sculptors, Reinhold Begas (1821–1911) set the tone for the creativity of the era with his neo-Baroque style. The most significant of Berlin's painters of this period was Adolph von Menzel (1815–1905), whose works often idealized the era of Frederick the Great.

The critical-realistic Berlin style entered literary history with the works of Willibald Alexis (1798–1871), Adolf Glassbrenner (1810–1876), and, in particular, Theodor Fontane (1819–1898), whose works remain popular today; his novels have inspired many of the New German Cinema's most highly regarded films.

20th Century

From the early years of the 20th century until the advent of the Nazis in 1933, Berlin reigned as one of the most advanced cultural capitals in the world. The "Golden Years" of the Weimar Republic (1920–1933)—a period in which government censorship was abolished—were characterized by radical experimentation and a fervid proliferation of all the arts.

20 Art, Architecture, and Literature

The year 1900 marked the beginning of the "high period" of painting in Berlin, when artists began to react against the official "historic" style of Prussian court art. The great German impressionist painter and illustrator Max Liebermann (1847–1935), the portraitist and landscape painter Lovis Corinth (1858–1925), and Max Slevogt (1868–1932), renowned for his portraiture, all lived and worked in Berlin. Other painters such as Max Beckmann (1884–1950), Wilhelm Lehmbruck, and the sculptor Ernst Barlach sought to capture something deeper and more angst-ridden than the shimmering surface of the Impressionists. These Berlin Expressionists sounded *"Der geballte Schrei"* ("the clenched scream") of their age in powerful works that often stunned their viewers. As the decade moved ahead and social conditions deteriorated, artists such as Otto Dix (1891–1969) and Georg Grosz (1893–1959) portrayed Berlin life in the 1920s with savage realism and satire. Despite the lifting of government censorship, Grosz was fined several times for "attacks on public morality," and the Nazis confiscated Dix's paintings. The much-loved illustrator Heinrich Zille (1858–1929) drew the men and women of the Berlin slums with an earthy, unsentimental understanding, while Käthe Kollwitz (1867–1945), best known for her graphics, compassionately portrayed the misery of the poor and the tenderness of motherhood. Both Zille and Kollwitz have museums in Berlin dedicated to their work, as do the "Brücke" artists who migrated to Berlin from Dresden: Ernst Ludwig Kirchner, Erich Heckel (1883–1969), Max Pechstein (1881–1955), and Karl Schmidt-Rotluff (1884–1974).

The avant-garde Berlin Dada movement celebrated the absurdities of modern life (including political life) with Dada manifestos, magazines, and performances. Richard Huelsenbeck, Walter Mehring, Raul Hausmann, Johannes Baader, and George Grosz were all part of this group that felt Expressionism had become passé. They inaugurated the short-lived but influential "Club Dada" at the Tribüne Theater in Berlin-Charlottenburg, and, with scores of other Berlin-based writers, playwrights, journalists, musicians, and cabaret-artists, often congregated at the legendary Romanisches Café on the Kurfürstendamm.

Included among the many important writers who worked in Berlin from the early 20th century through the Weimar years are Stefan Zweig (1881–1942), the Nobel laureate Thomas Mann (1875–1955) and his brother Heinrich (1871–1950), Georg Heym (1887–1912), Rainer Maria Rilke (1875–1926), Frank Wedekind (1864–1918), Stefan George (1868–1933), Robert Musil (1880–1939), Gottfried Benn (1886–1956), and Alfred Döblin (1878–1959). Döblin's *Berlin Alexanderplatz*, written in 1929, probed beneath the appearance of reality in Berlin during the two world wars and was the first novel in modern German literature to follow the stream of consciousness technique made famous by James Joyce. Christopher Isherwood, a British writer who gave English lessons while living in the city, wrote two popular novels that convey what life was like in Berlin during these years, *Goodbye to Berlin* and *Mr. Norris Changes Trains;* his work was later adapted by John van Druten into a play called *I Am A Camera,* which in turn inspired John Kander and Fred Ebb's musical and motion picture *Cabaret.*

The naturalistic plays of Gerhardt Hauptmann (1862–1946) initiated a new age of German theater which quickly found its epicenter in Berlin. By the mid-1920s, there were more than 40 legitimate theaters in the city. The legendary Austrian director Max Reinhardt staged enormous, innovative spectacles in his 3,000-seat Grosses Schauspielhaus, while Erwin Piscator toured his small repertory troupe through the slums and beer halls in an attempt to revolutionize the workers, before establishing a permanent theater on Nollendorfplatz. In terms of theatrical innovation, these two men have no peers. The Theater am Schiffbauerdamm premiered the world-famous *Threepenny Opera* by Bertolt Brecht and Kurt Weill in 1928; their later collaboration, *The Rise and Fall of the City of Mahagonny* is perhaps the most "Berlinese" of all operas.

Berlin was also the home of a thriving silent and talking film industry. In the Babelsberg studios of Universum Film AG (UFA), the largest in Europe, directors such as G.W. Pabst, Ernst Lubitsch, Josef von Sternberg, and Fritz Lang created such film classics as *The Cabinet of Doctor Caligari, Nosferatu, Metropolis, M,* and *The Blue Angel,* which established Marlene Dietrich as an international star. Other actors who worked in Berlin before migrating to Hollywood included Greta Garbo, Pola Negri, Conradt Veidt, and Peter Lorre.

Berlin's musical life provided another embarrassment of riches. Composer Richard Strauss (1864–1949) was the principal conductor of the Imperial court opera, the composer Hans Pfitzner conducted at the Theater des Westens, and Hans von Bülow and Arthur Nikisch conducted the acclaimed Berlin Philharmonic. Wilhelm Furtwängler, Otto Klemperer, Bruno Walter, and Arturo Toscanini each contributed to Berlin's reputation as a world capital of music. Alban Berg's new experimental opera *Wozzeck* was first performed at the State Opera in Berlin in 1925 under the baton of Erich Kleiber. The French composer Edgard Varèse spent five years in Berlin before the First World War, and the Italian-German composer Ferruccio Busoni was a professor of composition at the Berlin Akademie der Künste until his death in 1924. One of his great pupils was Kurt Weill.

Inspired by the visionary ideas of Walter Gropius and his Bauhaus school of design, which moved from Dessau to Berlin in 1932 before being suppressed a year later by the Nazis, architects and designers introduced a new, streamlined functionalism to Berlin architecture. The new functionalism was an attempt to reconcile art and technology in buildings, furniture, and everyday objects. The last remaining building in

22 Art, Architecture, and Literature

Berlin to typify the style is the Bewag office block built by Emil Fahrenkamp in 1930–1931. Gropius, like the Berlin-born architect Ludwig Mies van der Rohe, was forced into exile by the Nazis.

By 1933, when the Nazis took power, the "Golden Age" of Berlin was already on the wane. Countless artists who had been drawn to the exciting and innovative atmosphere that prevailed in Berlin were forced to flee: George Grosz, Thomas and Heinrich Mann, Brecht, Weill, Alfred Döblin, Erich Maria Remarque, Reinhardt, Arnold Schönberg, Bruno Walter, Otto Klemperer, and Paul Hindemith, to name just a few. On March 10, 1933, Nazi students under the leadership of Goebbels lit bonfires on Opernplatz and began to burn books that were considered "un-German." Hitler's purge of "Culture-Bolsheviks" also resulted in the burning of "degenerate art" in the Berlin National Gallery: works by the German Expressionists and modern paintings by van Gogh, Modigliani, Gris, Munch, Schwitters, and Klee were all lost. Self-conscious and uninspired Fascist architecture—the Olympic Stadium and the Air Transport Ministry in East Berlin are two surviving examples—replaced the modern Bauhaus style. By 1945 and the end of Hitler's Thousand Year Reich, everything that had made Berlin a world capital of art, architecture, and culture lay in heaps of smoldering rubble. The rebuilding and restoration of Berlin continues to this day.

One result of the conflicting postwar ideologies between East and West is that the two halves of the city reveal very different architectural and urban aesthetics. In East Berlin, the difference is especially noticeable in the area around the vast square of Alexanderplatz, where many of the postwar buildings that date from the 1950s and 1960s have a faceless anonymity. Soviet influence has been pervasive since the end of the war, and visitors should remember that East Berlin did not have the massive influx of subsidies for rebuilding that West Berlin enjoyed; also, the East German political philosophy eschewed the kind of aggressively modern, commercial, private-use buildings that began to spring up in West Berlin after the war. A new trend in East Berlin architecture began in the 1970s, when buildings such as the Palace of the Republic were erected using great quantities of copper-colored reflective glass. The newest buildings—the Dom Hotel near the Platz der Akademie, for example—indicate that East Berlin is now in the process of visually upgrading and actively changing its urban face. With the advent of a new free market economy and the reunification of the two Berlins, visitors can expect to see many changes in the years to come.

The architectural scene in West Berlin was very different after the war. Starting with the Interbau Exhibition in 1957, West Berlin became the site of numerous modern buildings designed by internationally-known architects. The exiled Bauhaus architects Walter Gropius and Ludwig Mies van der Rohe returned to the city—the last building Gropius designed was the Bauhaus Museum, while Mies van der Rohe was responsible for the National Gallery. Hans Scharoun, who designed the Philharmonic Hall, the Chamber Music Hall, and the State Library in the Kulturforum, has also played a major role in West Berlin's postwar rebuilding efforts.

German artists, attracted by generous subsidies and the city's reputation as Germany's most liberal and lively center for the arts, flocked to West Berlin after the war and continue to do so today. Of the hundreds of contemporary painters and sculptors whose work has gone well beyond the Berlin city limits, mention can be made of Peter Sorge, Wolfgang Petrick, Hans-Jürgen Diehl, Ulrich Baehr, and Arwed Gorella—the "Berlin Realists"—as well as Johannes Grutzke, Manfred Bluth, Gerd Winner, Peter Foeller, the sculptor Joachim Schmettau, and the husband-and-wife team of Matschinsky-Denninghoff, whose immense pieces can be found on many Berlin streets.

The Berlin literary scene is an active one, and the city is home to such outstanding writers as Gunter Grass, Peter Schneider, Sarah Kirsch, and Elisabeth Plessen. Stefan Heym, Christa Wolf, and the dramatist Heiner Müller live in East Berlin. The great playwright Bertolt Brecht returned to East Berlin after the war to found the Berliner Ensemble, which remains one of Berlin's most provocative theaters.

The city's three opera houses—West Berlin's Deutsche Oper and East Berlin's Staatsoper and Komische Oper—all enjoy international reputations, as does the famed Berlin Philharmonic, conducted for years by Herbert von Karajan and now under the leadership of Claudio Abbado.

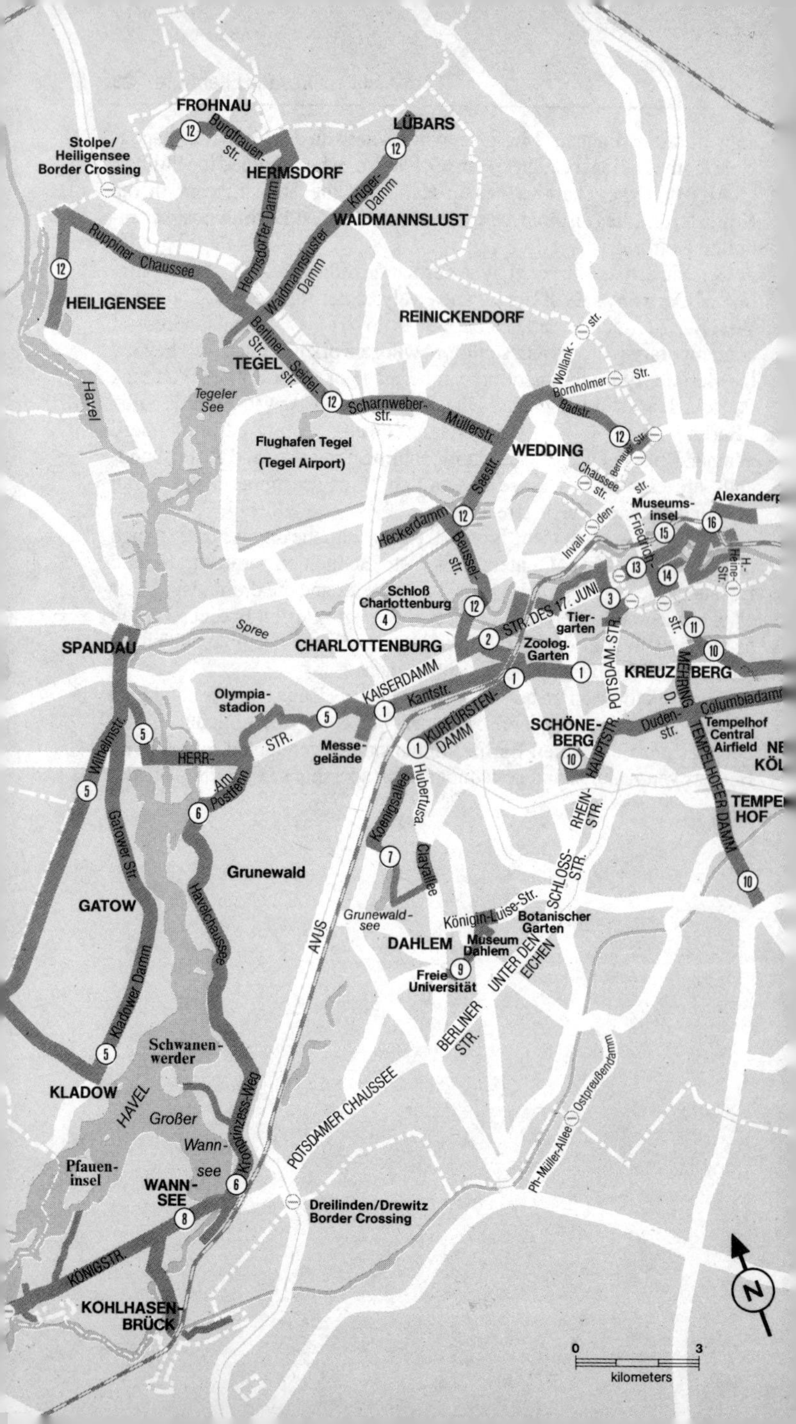
FROHNAU
LÜBARS
Stolpe/
Heiligensee
Border Crossing
HERMSDORF
WAIDMANNSLUST
HEILIGENSEE
REINICKENDORF
TEGEL
Tegeler See
Flughafen Tegel
(Tegel Airport)
WEDDING
Museums-
insel
Alexanderp
Schloß
Charlottenburg
SPANDAU
CHARLOTTENBURG
Spree
Tier-
garten
Zoolog.
Garten
KREUZBERG
Olympia-
stadion
Messe-
gelände
SCHÖNE-
BERG
Tempelhof
Central
Airfield
TEMPE
HOF
Grunewald
GATOW
Grunewald-
see
DAHLEM
Botanischer
Garten
Museum
Dahlem
Freie
Universität
Schwanen-
werder
KLADOW
HAVEL
Großer
Wann-
see
Pfauen-
insel
WANN-
SEE
KOHLHASEN-
BRÜCK
Dreilinden/Drewitz
Border Crossing
Havel
Burgfrauen-
str.
Ruppiner Chaussee
Hermsdorfer Damm
Waidmannsluster
Damm
Krüger-
Damm
Berliner
Str.
Seidel-
str.
Scharnweber-
str.
Müllerstr.
Wollank-
str.
Bornholmer
Str.
Badstr.
Bernauer Str.
Chaussee
str.
Saestr.
Heckerdamm
Beussel-
str.
Invali-
den-
str.
Friedrich-
str.
H.-
Heine-
Str.
STR. DES 17. JUNI
KAISERDAMM
Kantstr.
KURFÜRSTEN-
DAMM
POTSDAM. STR.
MEHRING
D.
Columbiadamm
Duden-
str.
HAUPTSTR.
TEMPELHOFER DAMM
HERR-
STR.
Am
Postfenn
Wilhelmstr.
Gatower Str.
Havelchaussee
Koenigsallee
Hubertusa.
Clayallee
Königin-Luise-Str.
RHEIN-
STR.
SCHLOSS-
STR.
UNTER DEN
EICHEN
BERLINER
STR.
AVUS
Kladower Damm
Kronprinzess.-Weg
POTSDAMER CHAUSSEE
Ostpreußendamm
Ph.-Müller-Allee
KÖNIGSTR.
N
0
3
kilometers

16 Walks around Berlin

See map opposite.

Berlin encompasses an enormous metropolitan area with an incredibly diverse array of sites and activities. To facilitate your visit, we have designed a system of 16 "walks" through Berlin's most important areas—East and West—to help you organize your visit. The city's excellent public transportation system makes getting around easy, and we have recommended train and bus routes whenever possible since many of our tours take in large sections of the city (see map on pages 142–143). In addition to the walks, we have included a section describing other sights to see in East Berlin, as well as an excursion to the historic city of Potsdam and the magnificent Sanssouci Palace.

Although Berlin has become one city again, we have maintained references to West and East Berlin for geographic purposes throughout our text. Likewise, as vestiges of the Communist regime begin to disappear in East Berlin, you may find that the names of some of the streets and buildings in Walks 13–16 have been changed, and that statues and memorials to Communist leaders no longer stand.

WALK 1: Zoo District and *Kurfürstendamm

See map on page 26.

This walk will introduce you to the exciting heart of Berlin. No visitor can leave the city without a stroll along the Kurfürstendamm, its most famous boulevard. This walk will also introduce you to one of the greatest zoos and aquariums in the world, take you to the landmark Memorial Church, give you a glimpse of the first shopping mall in Europe, and then lead you down various intriguing side streets where shopping is a temptation and café-sitting is a must.

The walk begins at **Bahnhof Zoologischer Garten** (Bahnhof Zoo, for short), the city's main train station, where you can also catch the U-Bahn (subway) or S-Bahn (elevated train), and the last stop of several bus lines. You'll find a post office here and an office of the Berlin *Verkehrsamt* (Tourists' Bureau), where you can pick up general information brochures on events going on around the city.

Just outside the main entrance, on the corner of Hardenberg Strasse, there is a currency exchange (open Monday–Saturday 8:00 A.M.–9:00 P.M.; Sundays 10:00 A.M.–6:00 P.M.). A *BVG information office* (open daily 10:00 A.M.–6:00 P.M.), where you can get information on the city's transportation system and buy special tickets (see page 144), is located across the street in an attractive new pavilion on Hardenbergplatz.

There are two entrances to the **Zoologischer Garten** [1]: the *Löwentor* (Lion's Gate), right across Hardenbergplatz from the train station; or the dramatic *Elefantentor* (Elephant Gate), which you can get to by walking down Hardenberg Strasse to Budapester Strasse and then following Budapester Strasse to the impressive entrance. Built in 1899, and destroyed in World War II, the Elefantentor was recently reconstructed according to original designs. The street entrance to the aquarium lies a few steps farther.

**Zoologischer Garten

(Open daily from 9:00 A.M.–6:00 P.M. Admission DM 7.50; children ages 3–15 DM 4. Combination zoo and aquarium ticket DM 11.50 for adults, DM 6 for children.)

The history of Berlin's Zoological Gardens dates back to 1841, when the Prussian King Friedrich Wilhelm IV presented his large "Pheasantry" and collection of animals from Peacock Island (see page 70) to the citizens of the city for a public zoo. When it officially opened in 1844, it was the first zoo in Germany and the ninth in the world. By 1939 it had become one of the most important zoos in the world, with a collection of about 4,000 mammals and birds and 750 species of reptiles, amphibians, fish and invertebrates in its famous aquarium. The zoo was repeatedly hit in the heavy bombing raids of World War II, however, and became a combat zone in the last days of the war. Only 91 animals survived, the most famous being "Knautschke," a hippo born in 1943.

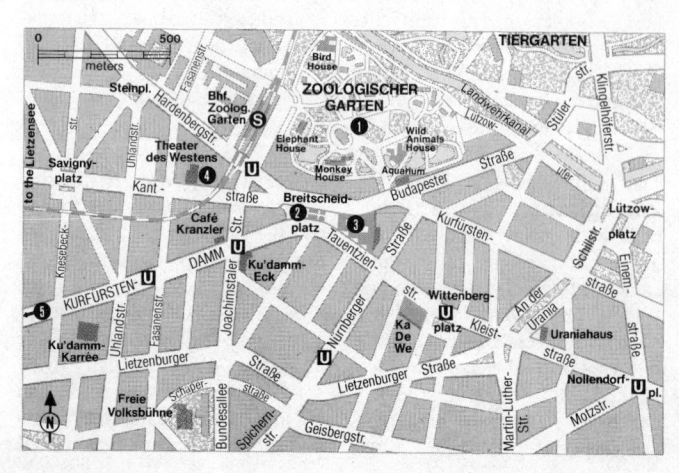

Since that time the zoo has been completely reconstructed and modernized, featuring open-air enclosures. With about 16,400 animals representing some 1,761 different species, it can again claim to house one of the most extensive animal collections in the world. One of the prime objectives of the modern zoo is to aid conservation by breeding endangered species. The Berlin Zoo has been particularly successful in this effort.

The zoo covers some 82 parklike acres; so, unless you have a lot of time to stroll, you'd do well to pick out those animals and exhibits you most want to see and plan your viewing itinerary accordingly. Zoo maps and sign posts help you to find your way around easily.

"Bao Bao," the giant male panda, tops the list of visitors' favorites. A gift from the People's Republic of China, this rare creature—now the meaningful symbol of the World Wildlife Fund—came to the zoo in 1980; he lives in a wing of the *Wild Animal House,* close to the Elephant Gate. Here you'll also find his cousin, the lesser panda, as well as leopards, lynxes, bobcats, jaguars, lions, and Siberian tigers, with only a pane of glass between you and them. Peek into the dim recesses of *The Nocturnal Animal House* for a moonlit glimpse of aardvarks, Australian phalangers, fruit-eating honey gliders, huge-eyed loris from Southeast Asia, and many other night-hunting species. The zoo has a remarkable collection of primates—chimpanzees, African gorillas, orangutans, and gibbons—in its *Ape House.* Next door, in the *Monkey House,* you'll find macaques, mandrills, and more long-armed gibbons. The Monkey House is connected to the *Tropical Animal House,* where you can see exotic primate species found in tropical and subtropical forests.

Other zoo highlights include the *Elephant House,* where several African and Asian elephants, the largest land mammals in the world, reside; the herd of giraffes in the mosquelike *Antelope House* (constructed in 1872 and the oldest building in the zoo); the *Rhino and Tapir House,* where you'll see Indian, black, and square-lipped rhinoceri; and the large *Polar Bear Enclosure,* where these solitary creatures swim and doze in the sun. The *Sea Lion and Penguin Rocks* are always popular, as is the neighboring *Hippopotamus House,* with its heated indoor and outdoor pools. One of the largest

Russian Log Building in the Zoo

and most attractive buildings in the zoo is the *Bird House,* with a walk-through aviary and dozens of species of brilliantly colored birds from all over the world. But take your pick: this is only a sampling of dozens of options.

The zoo also features a restaurant, a children's zoo and playground, and a special "Photo Opportunity Area" where children can get close to baby animals and pose for pictures with them.

If you are already in the zoo and have purchased a combination ticket, you can enter the aquarium directly across from the lion enclosure; an enormous life-sized statue of an iguanodon, a giant lizard that has been extinct for some 90 million years, stands guard over the entrance. The street entrance is just beyond the Elephant Gate on Budapester Strasse.

**Aquarium

(Open daily from 9:00 A.M.–6:00 P.M. Admission DM 7 for adults, DM 3.50 for children.)

Europe's largest, and one of the best known in the world, the Berlin Aquarium was first inaugurated in 1913 and once again in 1952, following major repair work of World War II damage. It was handsomely expanded in 1980. Some 12,000 fishes, frogs, snakes, crocodiles, tortoises, insects, and invertebrates from all over the world swim, slither, and glide through natural habitats on three fascinating floors. You'll see gorgeously colored tropical rarities such as the Picasso fish, the queen trigger fish, and the odd, fox-face rabbit fish. Other tanks contain the stuff of underwater nightmares: sharks, piranhas, Moray eels, enormous shovel-nosed sturgeons, paddlefish, sting rays, and primitive lungfish. Some of the most beautiful tanks are filled with delicate sea anemones gently waving in the currents; the jellyfish *(Aurelia aurita),* moving through the water like tiny transparent umbrellas, are particularly fascinating. The reptiles are located on the second floor. Here you'll find Komodo monitors, iguanas, basilisk lizards, giant frogs, crocodiles, alligators, turtles, and giant tortoises, as well as an enormous variety of snakes, including the emerald and tiger pythons, cobras, anacondas, boa constrictors, mambas, rattlesnakes, and vipers. The third floor is devoted to insects. Spiders, scorpions, centipedes, ants, beetles, crickets—as well as several varieties of everyone's favorite insect, the cockroach.

Leave the zoo and aquarium by the Elephant Gate on Budapester Strasse. To your left you'll see the impressive curved façade of the new *Grundkredit-Bank.* Turn right and head back down Budapester Strasse. You'll pass the conspicuous blue dome of *Das Panorama Berlin,* where the multivision spectacle "Destination Berlin" is projected on a wrap-around screen (daily from 11:00

A.M.–10:00 P.M.; screenings every 60 minutes; admission DM 10). At Budapester Strasse 42, you'll find the two-story exhibition hall and cafeteria of the *Staatliche Kunsthalle Berlin* (State Art Gallery), which primarily exhibits contemporary art. You'll have no trouble recognizing Berlin's most famous landmark, the *Kaiser-Wilhelm-Gedächtniskirche* [2], across the street. Cross the street here to *Breitscheidplatz* and have a look at Joachim Schmettau's intriguing red-granite *"Weltkügel-Brunnen" fountain*, nicknamed "Wasserklops" (water meatball), which began flowing in 1983 and serves as a focal point for this busy pedestrian area. Café tables are set up on the side of the fountain that abuts the Europa-Center; the other side serves mostly as a hang-out for teenagers. A curved stairway leads down to a passageway into the Europa-Center. The area around the fountain is busy far into the night, attracting sidewalk musicians, clowns, artists, skateboarders, street vendors, and young people from all over the world.

Emperor William Memorial Church

*Kaiser-Wilhelm-Gedächtniskirche

Berlin's most famous landmark, the ruined tower of the Emperor William Memorial church on Breitscheidplatz is now a memorial to World War II. The church, originally intended both to pay lavish homage to the emperor's memory and to commemorate the establishment of the German Empire in 1871, was constructed in ponderous neo-Romanesque style between 1891–1895 from plans by Franz Schwechten. At the end of the war only a ruined shell remained. This was preserved as a symbol of the ravages of war, and a new church complex designed by Egon Eiermann was constructed around it between 1959 and 1961. A permanent exhibition, showing the history of the church, the remaining fragments of mosaic and relief work, and a model of the surrounding area before the war's devastation has been set up in the old church, which the iconoclastic Berliners call "der hohle Zahn" (the decayed tooth). The new complex consists of an octagonal central church with walls inlaid with deep blue stained glass made in Chartres, with a golden statue of Christ dramatically suspended in front of it. A small chapel and a hexagonal church tower complete the complex. There are frequent organ recitals in the octagonal church, and also productions of religious drama such as Hugo von Hoffmansthal's version of the medieval morality play "Everyman." The buildings are perhaps more mysteriously attractive after dark, when the internally lit stained glass in the newer structures glows deep blue and red and the neon-gold clock faces on the old ruined tower tick off the minutes between sunset and sunrise.

Europa-Center

When it first opened in 1965, the Europa-Center [3] was considered the epitome of indoor shopping sophistication—and back then it was. In the meantime, however, most of us have come to take shopping malls for granted, and the malls themselves have become more and more lavish. For this reason, you might find parts of the Europa-Center a bit on the tacky side, but it's still a good place to shop, eat, and explore, with some 100 stores, bars, restaurants, and cafés, as well as five movie theaters, the city's largest sauna, and the popular satirical political cabaret "Die Stachelschweine" (The Porcupines). The main shopping area contains the unusual 13-meter- (43-foot-) high *"Uhr der fliessenden Zeit"* (Clock of Flowing Time), designed by the French physicist Bernard Gitton. With their usual irreverence, the Berliners have dubbed this water clock, with its neon-colored liquids, the "fruit juice machine." The Europa-Center complex includes a 20-story office building with an *observation deck at the top, the Palace Hotel, and, with an entrance on Budapester Strasse, the *Spielbank Berlin* gambling casino, where you can play roulette, baccarat, and blackjack from 3:00 P.M. to 3:00 A.M. Next door to it is the main office of the *Berlin Verkehrsamt* (Tourists' Bureau), where you can reserve hotel and pension rooms and gather up a stack of information about events in the city (open daily 7:30 A.M.–10:30 P.M.).

A bench-filled promenade behind the Gedächtniskirche planted with pink-flowering chestnut trees will take you to the beginning of Kantstrasse, which, along with its continuation, Neue Kantstrasse, cuts through the Charlottenburg district, the 25-acre Lietzenseepark, ending at the Messedamm and the International Congress Center (see page 57). Walk down Kantstrasse, passing under the S-Bahn tracks. The large white building on your right is the well-known *Theater des Westens* (Theater of the West)[4] (see page 156), built in 1896 and renovated in 1978; today it stages Berlin's musicals and operettas. There is a ticket booth across the street for advance sales, as well as the pre-performance box office in the lobby.

Continue down Kantstrasse to **Savignyplatz,** one of the city's many little parks and a prime residential area. Around the outer edge of the park (Kantstrasse cuts through the middle of it) there are wonderful wisteria arbors, each with a bench, and in the center there are pleasant green lawns surrounded by a beautiful border of perennials. Linden trees provide shade, while the white lilac blossoms perfume the air in springtime. Climbing yellow and purple clematis mingle with the wisteria. Take some time to explore the surrounding area, which is filled with book stores, taverns, and sidewalk restaurants, some of them tucked under the arches of the S-Bahn. It reminds many people of St. Germain des Prés in Paris. The *Bücherbogen* book store at Stadtbahnbogen 593 (under the S-Bahn) has a wide selection of art and photography books, novels, and art and film-related magazines. The world-famous *Prinz Eisenherz Bookshop*, at Bleibtreustrasse 52, features an outstanding selection of international literature concentrating on homosexual themes. To get there, continue on Kantstrasse for one block to Bleibtreustrasse and turn right.

If you want to stroll through Lietzenseepark at this point or visit the International Congress Center, the Number 94 bus on Kantstrasse will take you there. Otherwise, head south from Savignyplatz on Knesebeckstrasse until you get to the main street of Berlin's shopping district, ***Kurfürstendamm.**

Strolling down the bustling "Ku'damm," as the street is nicknamed, you will find yourself rubbing elbows with both locals and visitors from every part of the world. This famous boulevard began its existence in 1542 as a log road, built to make it easy for the Prince-Electors (Kurfürsten) to reach their hunting lodge in the Grunewald; it was extended in the 1880s by Bismarck, who wanted it to rival the Champs-Elysées in Paris. From the turn of the century until the Second World War, the Ku'damm was the most brilliant, lively, and elegant street in this part of Berlin, filled with legendary cafés and renowned for its nightlife. After the war, and the division of the city, it became West Berlin's most famous commercial thoroughfare. It's still *the* place to sit and people watch, so if a café takes your fancy along the way, don't hesitate to stop there and linger over a coffee or a beer.

Head east on the Kurfürstendamm, back in the direction of the Gedächtniskirche. On your right, just past Knesebeckstrasse, are two theaters specializing in old-fashioned drawing-room comedies, the *Komödie* and the *Theater am Kurfürstendamm*. In the opposite direction, you will find the *Schaubühne* [5] on Lehniner Platz, located in the restored Mendelssohn building, which offers more ambitious performances. Continue east up the Ku'damm to the elegantly restored Fasanenstrasse and turn right.

The villa at No. 23 is the home of *Literaturhaus Berlin*, which has frequent exhibitions devoted to literary figures and events. It includes a lovely outdoor garden café with a fountain splashing in the middle of a verdant lawn, an upstairs restaurant in the Wintergarten, and a fine, small bookstore on the lower level called *Kohlhaas & Company*. Next door at No. 24, the *Käthe-Kollwitz-Museum* (open daily except Tuesdays 11:00 A.M.–6:00 P.M.; admission fee DM 6) contains an important collection of drawings, sculptures, and graphics by this popular German artist who worked in Berlin. The *Villa Grisebach* at Fasanenstrasse 25 gives you an idea of one type of Berlin's pre-war architecture; today it houses an art auction house and the contemporary *Galerie Pels-Leusden*. Continuing down Fasanenstrasse, you'll pass chic restaurants and expensive art and antique galleries. There are also several entrances marked "Fasanen Passage." Duck into any one of them and you'll find a hidden but very upscale shopping arcade with exclusive shops, bars, and the *Fasanerie Restaurant*, which also bills itself as a Viennese coffee house.

If you are still in a shopping mood, you can go through this passage back to Uhland Strasse, the next street over, and cross the street to the *Ku'damm-Karree*, another shopping mall. From here, walk back up to the Ku'damm and turn right. At the busy corner of Ku'damm and Joachimstaler Strasse is the *Café Kranzler*, an elegant, old-style pastry shop and a popular spot to stop for a coffee, an ice cream, or one of their scores of delectable homemade baked goods. *Joe am Ku'damm,* across the street, is hopping from morning to night and appeals to a younger crowd. Another shopping mall, the *Ku'damm Eck,* complete with a wax museum, is located diagonally across the street from the Café Kranzler.

Continue east on the Ku'damm, passing the Gedächtniskirche and the Europa-Center. The Kurfürstendamm now becomes Tauentzien Strasse, another one of Berlin's principal shopping streets. Several large department stores line the blocks leading to **Wittenbergplatz** in the Schöneberg district. The most famous store—in fact, the largest department store on the continent, with an inventory of some quarter million items—is the *Kaufhaus des Westens* (known as KaDeWe), built just after the turn of the century. If you have the time, head for the sixth floor food emporium (Feinschmecker-Etage), a gourmet's paradise that outdistances even the Food Halls at Harrod's. If it is edible or drinkable, it will be here, and several specialty food counters, including elegant lobster and oyster bars, provide on-the-spot dining and drinking.

Step into the beautifully restored *U-Bahn station* at Wittenbergplatz, just outside KaDeWe, for a glimpse of how a Berlin subway station looked at the turn of the century. You can also get transport information or purchase special tickets here. Then, if you're still in a walking (or shopping) mood, continue down Kleist Strasse to the *Nollendorfplatz U-Bahn station* where an unusual flea market is held in old subway cars in a disused part of the elevated railway station (open daily except Tuesdays from 11:00 A.M.–7:00 P.M.). Original drawings that evoke old Berlin's "Milljöh" (neighborhood atmosphere) are on exhibit in the small *Zille Museum* (same opening hours as the flea market). From Nollendorfplatz you can catch the U-Bahn or a bus to take you to your next destination.

WALK 2: Bahnhof Zoo–Ernst-Reuter-Platz–*Tiergarten

See map on page 34.

Berlin is a city of surprising contrasts, and this walk will highlight many of them for you. Along the way, architecture buffs will see examples of Berlin's pre-war buildings and be able to compare them with buildings and entire sections that were specially constructed by world-renowned architects after the havoc of World War II. You'll pass through Berlin's student quarter and skirt along the edge of the city's most beautiful park on your way to the impressive Victory Column. Give yourself at least a day for this itinerary.

The point of departure for this walking tour is again the *Bahnhof Zoo*. Turn up Hardenbergstrasse toward the northwest, passing under the S-Bahn tracks. Turn right on the first street you come to, Jebenstrasse, which runs along the rear of the railroad station. Note the ornate pre-war portal on the cream-colored *Evangelischer Oberkirchenrat* (Protestant High Consistory) at No. 3.

At No. 2 you will find the **Kunstbibliothek mit dem Museum für Architektur, Modebild und Grafik Design** [6] (Art Library with the Museum of Architecture, Fashion Illustration and Graphic Design). *(Hours Monday, Thursday 1:00–9:00 P.M.; Tuesday, Wednesday, Friday 9:00 A.M.–5:00 P.M. Materials available upon request.)*

The Art Library contains some 180,000 volumes dealing with all aspects of the fine arts and contains the *Lipperheid Costume Library*, the *Graphics Collection*, with sketches and engravings from the Gothic era to the present, the *Grisebach Collection*, dealing with the history of European art book printing, and the *Applied Art and Poster Collection*. Special exhibitions take place regularly.

Return to Hardenbergstrasse and turn right. The first large pre-war building immediately on your right is the *Bundesverwaltungsgericht* (Federal Civil Court).

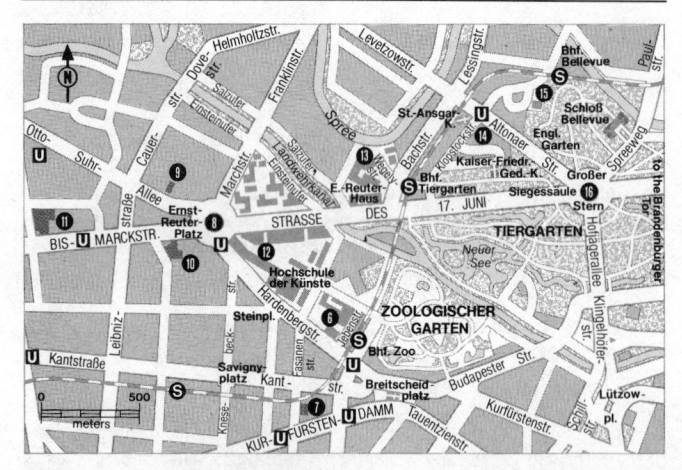

Across the street at 22–24 is the U.S. Cultural Center, **Amerika-Haus Berlin** with extensive library, research, and periodical services—a good place to know about if you are spending any amount of time in Berlin. The Center puts on frequent exhibitions, lectures, and readings by American artists, scholars, and writers (*library hours: Monday, Wednesday, Friday 11:30 A.M.– 5:30 P.M.; Tuesday, Thursday 11:30 A.M.–8:00 P.M.*). Next to it is the office of the *Deutsche Bundesbahn* (German Federal Railroad), where you can make train reservations. Farther on, set back from the street at Hardenbergstrasse 20 is the **Informationszentrum Berlin** and the offices and library of **The British Council.** The attractive Informationszentrum on the second floor is an excellent source of free Berlin-related materials (*hours Monday–Friday 8:00 A.M.–7:00 P.M.; Saturday 8:00 A.M.–4:00 P.M.*), while the British Centre on the first floor provides a good library (membership fee), an excellent British film series, as well as concerts, readings, and lectures (*library hours: Monday, Wednesday, Friday noon–6:00 P.M.; Tuesday, Thursday noon–8:00 P.M.*).

Continue along Hardenbergstrasse to Fasanenstrasse. On your right, at the corner of Hardenbergstrasse and Fasanenstrasse, the **Hochschule der Künste** (Arts' Academy), built in 1902, will give you an idea of the imperial style of old Berlin. The curriculum here includes music, drama, fine arts, design, architecture, and music education. Exhibitions and concerts are held frequently. If you have the time, enter the building, head straight back through the foyer (the sculpture, called "Concerto," is by Hans Uhlmann), and you'll find a peaceful inner courtyard filled with birch, linden, chestnut trees, and singing birds—it's well worth a visit.

Now turn left down Fasanenstrasse for a short detour. At No. 79/80, just beyond the S-Bahn tracks, is the **Jüdisches Gemeindehaus** [7]. The Jewish Community Center was built on the site of the former synagogue destroyed by the Nazis in the infamous pogrom euphemistically called "Kristallnacht" ("Night of Broken Glass") in 1938. The original portal of the old synagogue frames the entrance of the new building, and an elaborate memorial column made from the remains of the old building has been set up on one side of it. Today this is a gathering place for Berlin's Jewish community, which numbers about 6,500 and is the largest in Germany. Before the Hitler era, Berlin was home to some 170,000 Jews. In the lobby there are photographs of the original house of worship and its destruction, as well as a collection of elaborate Chanukah menorah candelabras, household items used in the Sabbath ritual, prayer books, Passover seder dishes, ram's horn shofars for high holy days, and silver and ivory mezuzim, or prayer scrolls. A building next door is now being restored for use as the Gemeindehaus' new center.

Across the street is the *Zille-Hof flea market*, where you can find everything from used clothing and linens to busts of Frederick the Great and Bismarck. It is open every day except Sunday from 8:30 A.M.–5:30 P.M. The market is decorated with reproductions of the work of Heinrich Zille, famous for his evocative, unsentimental drawings of life among Berlin's urban proletariat in the 1920s and 1930s.

Head back to Hardenbergstrasse and turn left. A block away, on *Steinplatz*, a memorial to the victims of Fascism has been created from stones recovered from the burnt Fasanenstrasse synagogue. A second memorial pays tribute to the victims of Stalinism. Steinplatz is the heart of the Charlottenburg district's student quarter. Here you will find several bookshops, cafés, and a *Bote & Bock* music store.

As you continue up Hardenbergstrasse, you'll see a fascinating pre-war villa at No. 9, now used as a showroom for Steinway pianos, and the new and very elegant *Goethe-Institut* (the German Cultural Institute) directly beside it, with a small back courtyard garden with a fountain. At the corner of Hardenbergstrasse and Knesebeckstrasse stands one of Berlin's major classical repertory theaters, the *Renaissance Theater* (see page 156). The charming "Duck Fountain," designed in 1911 by August Gaul, stands in front of it. Across the street is the block-long *Kiepert Bookstore*, with an art poster gallery and an enormous selection of books on every imaginable topic. The *Travel Store* (separate entrance on Knesebeckstrasse) is a must for anyone with a passion for maps or travel books. You might also want to check out its extensive Berlin section. Just around the corner on Schillerstrasse is another example of pre-war architecture, the *Schiller-Oberschule Charlottenburg* (Schiller Secondary School), built between 1911 and 1913, which has a fanciful portal.

The eclectic mixture of buildings across the street from the school marks the beginning of the **Technische Universität** [12]. With a total student population of over 100,000, Berlin is considered the largest "university city" in Germany. About 32,000 of these students are enrolled at the Technical University (TU). Located in the Charlottenburg district since 1884, the TU started life in 1879 as the Königlich-Technische Hochschule (Royal School of Science and Engineering), a small academy for construction and industry. Steadily enlarged over the following decades, it now boasts some 22 departments and virtually forms a small city along the east side of Hardenbergstrasse up to Ernst-Reuter-Platz and down the Strasse des 17. Juni to the Landwehrkanal.

Ernst-Reuter-Platz [8] is located at the end of Hardenbergstrasse, surrounded by modern office buildings and a traffic circle. This impressive square, dating back to the 1950s, was named for Ernst Reuter, West Berlin's first postwar governing mayor (1950–1953), and before that, the last mayor of all Berlin. Five of Charlottenburg's major thoroughfares converge here, and bicycle traffic along the peripheries can be almost as heavy as the constant swirl of cars in the streets. As a piece of early postwar urban landscaping, the square is fairly impressive. The flags of many nations flutter in the breeze while 41 fountains send their spray aloft and perform graceful gyrations. The surrounding office towers, among them the 22-story Telefunken building, the 9-story IBM building, and the Eternit building, are good examples of functional, postwar German architecture. The newer buildings of the Technical University along Hardenbergstrasse and the Strasse des 17. Juni are perhaps more interesting.

If you're interested in a brief theater detour, walk left (clockwise) from Hardenbergstrasse around the circle and you'll come to Bismarck Strasse. A block to your left you'll find the *Schiller-Theater* [10], an impressive building dating from 1951. This is one of Berlin's leading dramatic theaters, performing classic and modern plays in repertory (see page 156). Two blocks farther down Bismarck Strasse, on the north side of the street, is the long windowless façade of the ***Deutsche Oper Berlin** [11], designed by Fritz Bornemann and opened in 1961. The façade is made of concrete panels inlaid with colored stones. An abstract sculpture, created by Hans Uhlmann in 1961, stands in front. The Deutsche Oper Berlin, among Europe's most prestigious opera houses, boasts a first-rate international resident ensemble (including the largest American contingent outside the United States), which has been supplemented over the years by regular guest appearances by such operatic greats as tenors Placido Domingo and James King. King, incidentally, is a Kansas boy, who got his start at the Deutsche Oper Berlin. The company's repertoire is encyclopedic, ranging from definitive productions of the standard classics to adventurous stagings of everything from Renaissance opera to modern works specially commissioned for this company (see page 155).

Return to Ernst-Reuter-Platz and continue clockwise to Otto-Suhr-Allee where, just up the street at No. 18 you will find the small, popular *Tribüne Theater* [9] (see page 156). Continuing clockwise around the square you'll come to March Strasse with Bernhard Heiliger's 1963 memorial to Ernst Reuter, the 5-meter- (17-foot-) high sculpted *"Flame."* The inscription in front is a quotation from Ernst Reuter: "Friede kann nur in Freiheit bestehen" (Peace can only endure in freedom).

You may wish to end this portion of the walking tour at Ernst-Reuter-Platz, continuing from here another time. There is a U-Bahn station here and buses on four of the five streets leading to the square. There is, however, no city bus or public transportation that goes down the Strasse des 17. Juni, the next portion of the walk.

The nearly 3-km.- (2-mile-) long *Strasse des 17. Juni*, running east from Ernst-Reuter-Platz and ending at the Brandenburg Gate, will no doubt figure prominently in future ceremonial events now that the two halves of Berlin have been reunited. Formerly called Charlottenburger Chaussee, the street was part of the great East-West axis route through the city up until the time the Wall was put up. The present name commemorates the 1953 workers' uprising in East Berlin.

As you head down the Strasse des 17. Juni you'll see the Siegessäule (Victory Column) ahead of you. New and old buildings of the Technical University line both sides of the street as far as the *Landwehr Kanal,* which you cross via the *Charlottenburger Brücke* (Charlottenburg Bridge), built in 1907. Next to it is the *Charlottenburger Tor* (1905), symbolic gates with bronze statues of King Frederick I and his wife, Queen Sophie Charlotte (for whom the district— once the wealthiest town in Prussia—is named). The canal, some 10 km. (6 miles) long, was dug in the 19th century and was once an important shipping route.

On the left side of the street, once you cross the bridge, you'll see the *Ernst-Reuter-Haus* (Ernst Reuter House), where the Senate Library, the German Institute of Urban Studies, and the Berlin Representation to the Assembly of German Cities have their homes. On weekends a popular *Trödelmarkt* (flea market) is held in front of it.

Just beyond the Ernst Reuter House, leading off westward from the Tiergarten S-Bahn station, is Wegelystrasse; at No. 1 you will find the **Staatliche Porzellan- manufaktur** [13]. The State Porcelain Factory originated here in 1751, when W. C. Wegely established the Berlin Porcelain Factory. It was purchased by Frederick the Great on behalf of the Prussian State in 1763 and its products still bear the blue scepter of Brandenburg as their trademark. The exhibition rooms contain an impressive assortment of rococo pieces. (There is a factory sales room at Kurfürstendamm 205. *Hours for exhibition and salesroom: Monday–Friday 9:00 A.M.–6:00 P.M.; Saturday 9:00 A.M.–2:00 P.M.*)

The vast expanse of greenery all around you as you continue down Strasse des 17. Juni is the famed Berlin *Tiergarten. Tiergarten is the name of the district of Berlin you have just entered, as well as the name of this magnificent inner city park. In the 16th century, the area served as a game preserve and exclusive hunting grounds for the Prince Electors of Brandenburg. Frederick II opened the park to all classes of society in 1742. About a hundred years later the landscape designer Peter Joseph Lenné (1789–1866, also responsible for the landscaping on Peacock Island, see page 70) transformed the 3-km.-long, 1-km.-wide (2-mile-long, half-mile-wide) Tiergarten into the picturesque site it is today, full of shady paths, as well as lakes and streams crossed by small bridges. During the last days of the Second World War, the park was the scene of fierce fighting, and by war's end it had been reduced to a wasteland. Its few remaining trees were cut down for fuel, and the land was parceled out in plots for growing vegetables. Reforestation efforts symbolically began when Mayor Ernst Reuter planted the first linden tree in 1949. Since then, over a million trees and shrubs have been planted. By now they have come to full maturity, making the Tiergarten Berlin's pride once again. About 40 species of birds— including owls and nightingales—use the park as their breeding grounds. Thirty-two km. (20 miles) of paths lead to such pleasure spots as the *New Lake* (created in 1841), where you can linger at a café, rent a rowboat, or stroll in the charming *Rose Garden,* with its restored pergola, and the *English Garden,* which was sponsored by England's Queen Elizabeth II and filled with trees donated from British royal parks.

At the northern edge of the Tiergarten, between the Tiergarten and Bellevue S-Bahn stations and reached by turning left on Altonaer Strasse, is a pioneering example of postwar urban renewal, the **Hansaviertel** [14]. It is difficult to imagine how much of Berlin was destroyed in the Second World War, but no area was as totally decimated as the Hansaviertel. Completely evacuated, it lay in ruins for years. As part of the

1957 international architectural exhibition known as Interbau 57, 48 noted architects from 13 countries (Walter Gropius, Alvar Aalto, and Oscar Niemeyer among them) helped in the reconstruction of the Hansaviertel by designing a model housing project. Many different types of buildings were constructed here, from one-family houses to skyscrapers. Two churches were also built: the Protestant *Kaiser-Friedrich Gedächtniskirche* (Emperor Frederick Memorial Church) and the Roman Catholic *St.-Ansgar-Kirche* (St. Ansgar's Church), with bells donated by Konrad Adenauer. There is also a school, a library, shops, restaurants, and an internationally renowned children's theater *(Gripstheater)*. If you are interested in architecture, you'll find a plaque on each building bearing the name of the architects.

Just south of the Bellevue S-Bahn station on Hanseatenweg you'll find the **Akademie der Künste** (Arts' Academy) [15]. Dedicated in 1960, this modern building, designed by Berlin architect Werner Düttman, contains an exhibition hall, a studio building with a theater, and a building housing art studios and conference rooms. In the forecourt is a statue by the British artist Henry Moore called "Woman Reclining," which dates from 1956. One of Berlin's most important cultural centers, the academy was established in 1954 to succeed the Prussian Academy of Arts, founded by Frederick III in 1696. There are frequent art, architecture, music, literature, and theater exhibitions here.

Victory Column

Continue back down Altonaer Strasse past the English Garden to the *Grosser Stern* (Great Star) on Strasse des 17. Juni. Four major streets converge here, and in the center stands one of Berlin's best-known landmarks, the **Siegessäule** [16]. *(Observation platform open April–October, Tuesday–Sunday from 9:00 A.M.– 6:00 P.M.; Monday 1:00–6:00 P.M.; closed in winter.)* The 67-meter- (223-foot-) high Victory Column, designed by Friedrich Drake, was built between 1865 and 1873 to commemorate Prussia's military defeat of Denmark (1864), Austria (1866), and France (1870–1871). Dubbed "Gold-Else" by the Berliners, it first stood in what is today's Platz der Republik (in front of the Reichstag Building). It was moved to its present location in 1938 by

Hitler, who wanted it as a focal point for the parade grounds of his new German "world capital." A granite pedestal with four patriotic reliefs (the last of which, removed by the Allies in 1945, was returned from Paris for Berlin's 750th birthday celebration in 1987) supports a round 16-columned substructure with glass mosaics depicting Germany's 19th-century wars of liberation and unification. A freshly regilded statue of Victoria crowns the monument. The spiral staircase will take you up to a magnificent panoramic *view of the entire city.

From the Victory Column, you may wish to continue directly down to the *Brandenburger Tor* (Brandenburg Gate, see page 43, Walk 3, for description) at the end of the Strasse des 17. Juni. Otherwise, you can catch a northbound No. 16 bus to either the Hansaplatz U-Bahn station or the Bellevue S-Bahn station.

WALK 3: Architectural Tour: Schloss Bellevue– *Reichstag–*Brandenburger Tor– *Kulturforum– *Bauhaus Archives

See map opposite.

This walking tour will give you a superb historical overview of Berlin's architecture from the palaces and monuments of the late 18th Century up to the most important contemporary buildings of the present day. You'll be able to stroll where the Berlin Wall once stood and make stops at the superb museums that fill the Kulturforum. It's a long walk filled with an abundance of riches. To give yourself sufficient time in the museums, you may wish to break the walk up into two or more days.

The walk begins at the *Bellevue S-Bahn station* where a leafy path behind the station leads to the *Spree-Ufer*. Follow this lovely, quiet lane along the river bank— you'll share it with an occasional jogger or bicyclist, and, if the day is sunny, you'll see the inevitable Berlin sun worshipers in all states of dress and undress stretched out in the grass—to busy Spreeweg. Set back on a rich green lawn and framed by chestnut trees on your right, is the beautifully restored, elegant pale yellow façade of **Schloss Bellevue** [17].

Bellevue Palace, the official Berlin residence of West Germany's Federal President (and now President of all Germany) since 1959, was built in 1785 by Daniel Philipp Boumann for Prince August Ferdinand, Frederick the Great's youngest brother. The interior was designed by Carl Gotthard Langhans. Prince Ferdinand used the neoclassical palace as a summer residence, entertaining guests like Friedrich Schiller. Various Hohenzollern princes resided here up until the First World War. During the Hitler regime high-ranking guests of the Reich (including Vyacheslav Molotov, Soviet Secretary of State for Foreign Affairs, and Yosuke Matsuoka, his Japanese counterpart) stayed in the palace. Badly damaged in the bombings of Berlin, renovations began in 1954. (Grounds open to the public when the Federal President is not in residence.)

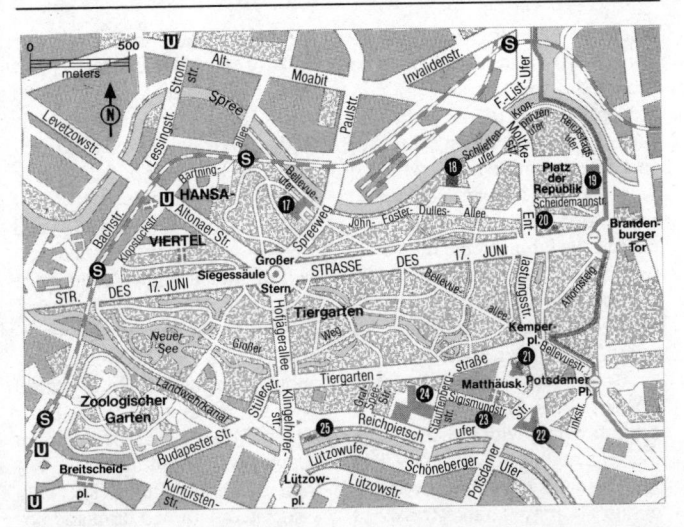

Cross the Spreeweg and continue down John-Foster-Dulles-Allee (an alternative is to take the No. 69 bus, which runs down this street as far as the Reichstag and makes stops along the way). You'll soon come to *Grossfürstenplatz* where a restored fountain splashes amidst a semicircular hedge containing badly damaged but mysteriously evocative statues of the *Vier Deutsche Strömen* (Four German Rivers) sculpted by different artists between 1860 and 1870. Photographs on an information board show the area as it was after the war—yet another grim reminder of Hitler's legacy to Berlin.

Ahead, and to your left, the path continues along the Spree, passing a ticket office for boat tours, and leads to the **Kongresshalle** [18]. America's contribution to the Interbau 57 exhibition (see page 38) was this building with a cantilevered concrete roof set amid reflecting pools. Constructed in 14 months from designs by Hugh Stubbins, the Kongresshalle was considered one of the most "daring" buildings in Europe in 1957. Irreverent Berliners immediately dubbed it "the pregnant oyster" because of its shape. The oyster collapsed in 1980 and was reopened seven years later. It is now known as *Haus der Kulturen der Welt* (House of World Cultures) and features an ambitious program of events (conferences, concerts, lectures, and film) highlighting various artistic trends in countries around the world.

Continue on to the *Carillon,* housed in a slender 42-meter (140-foot) black marble tower with red and blue interior trim—a superb model of functional design. With 68 bells weighing some 60 metric tons, this is the largest carillon in Europe and the fourth largest in the world. It plays for five minutes twice daily at noon and at 6:00 P.M.

As you continue down John-Foster-Dulles-Allee you'll pass a sculpture park with modern stone pieces standing in a grassy field like remnants from some neolithic culture. Cross Moltkestrasse at Scheidemannstrasse and you will be in the vast, historically significant *Platz der Republik*. The Siegessäule (Victory Column) now located at the Grosser Stern originally stood here, when the area was known as Königsplatz. The west side of the square, now totally empty, was once the site of the Kroll Opera House, where conductor Otto Klemperer, director Carl Ebert, designer Adolphe Appia, and their eminent associates made operatic history in the 1920s with their innovative productions. Following the Reichstag fire of 1933 (by which time many of Germany's greatest artists had fled or were forced out of the country), the building was taken over for meetings of Hitler's rubber-stamp parliament. The Kroll Opera House was demolished in 1951.

Directly before you, in front of the rapidly diminishing remains of the Berlin Wall, is the massive bulk of the ***Reichstag** [19]. *(Hours Tuesday–Sunday 10:00 A.M.–5:00 P.M.; free admission as well as free information that explains the workings of the German government.)* Designed by Paul Wallot and built between 1884 and 1894 in a pompous, domed version of Italian High Renaissance style, the Reichstag was the seat of parliament during the Wilhelminian Empire and the Weimar Republic. During the First World War, the inscription "Dem Deutschen Volke" (To the German People) was added above the entrance. The building is especially associated with two dramatic political events: On November 9, 1918, Philipp Scheidemann, a Social Democrat and Member of Parliament, proclaimed the Republic from one of the corner windows, and in February of 1933, the building was mysteriously set ablaze by arsons—probably the Nazis, although this has never been unequivocally established. The fire was, in any case, an excuse for Hitler's National Socialist Party to persecute and imprison a host of political opponents. Allied air attacks during the Second World War left the Reichstag in ruins. During the years 1957–1971, the building was reconstructed, minus its original dome. Today, the meeting and conference rooms are available to the parties and committees of the German Federal Parliament. The first session of the new united German Parliament was held here on October 3, 1990. If you have time, visit the important permanent exhibition here called *"Fragen an die deutsche Geschichte"* (Questions addressed to German History). The show is in German, but you can rent a portable cassette-tour in English or buy the English-language edition of the catalog, which explains everything (the same catalog, by the way, is now used as a standard textbook in German history courses). To enter you must cut around to the far left side of the building. There is a good restaurant inside, as well as a self-service cafeteria and a gift shop.

If you wish, you may end this part of the walking tour here—the No. 69 bus will take you back to Bahnhof Zoo. Otherwise, continue the walk by heading behind the Reichstag building. This entire area could now be called "Souvenir Strasse," because it is usually filled with tables at which vendors sell bits of the Berlin Wall, Communist medals, military caps, memorabilia from the Soviet army, and so on. As the two Berlins continue their unification over the coming years, there will be many changes around here, and no doubt a great deal of new building and urban renewal. The Wall itself, once such a prominently grim feature, is now gone.

Follow "Souvenir Strasse" behind the Reichstag south to what has been Berlin's most symbolic monument for the last two hundred years, the **Brandenburger Tor** (Brandenburg Gate). Centuries before the Wall dividing the two Berlins was erected in 1961, another wall circled the city, and in 1734 this became the site of one of 18 city gates set into it. After Prussia had become a major European power under Frederick the Great, his successor, Frederick William II, commissioned the construction of a worthy terminating point for Unter den Linden, the city's new grand boulevard. Modeling his design on the Propylaea, the great entrance hall to the Acropolis, architect Carl Gotthard Langhans created his masterpiece, the new Brandenburg Gate, constructed between 1788 and 1791. Gottfried Schadow designed the Quadriga, completed in 1793, a four-horse copper chariot drawn by the omnipresent goddess Victoria to sit atop the gate, and which will be re-installed in 1991 to mark the gate's 200th anniversary. Napoleon had the Quadriga removed and brought to Paris in 1806 as a symbol of his triumph, but Marshall Blücher brought it back to Berlin in 1814 following the wars of independence. In the 19th and 20th centuries, the Brandenburg Gate was the scene of huge military parades, triumphal marches, and glittering receptions. The revolutionary events of 1848 and 1918 also saw the Gate used as a kind of symbolic gathering place. World War II bombing attacks badly damaged the Gate and totally destroyed the Quadriga. East Berlin was responsible for the restoration of the Gate between 1956 and 1958. The Quadriga and Victoria were recast from the original molds in West Berlin and returned to their positions—

although this time facing the opposite direction, that is, toward East Berlin. Traffic continued to flow through the Gate until 1961, when the grand boulevard passing through it was severed by the Wall. Caught in the crossfire of East-West politics, for nearly thirty years the Gate stood forlorn and isolated, a symbol of division and discord rather than triumph. Then, just before Christmas 1989, the Gate was reopened as a pedestrian crossing point for German citizens on both sides of the Wall, an event celebrated euphorically by all Berliners. Now that the last remnants of the Wall have been removed from the front, the two Berlins dramatically meet again at this spot, and the entire area will soon be undergoing a major urban transformation.

Directly west from the Brandenburg Gate on the Strasse des 17. Juni is the *Sowjetisches Ehrenmal* (Soviet Monument) [20], built to commemorate the liberation of the city by the Red Army, followed by the U.S., British, and French troops, in 1945. Flanked by Russian tanks, the monument was built in the shape of a wide gate of honor.

You'll see history being made—or dismantled—as you continue from the Brandenburg Gate south towards Potsdamer Platz. The Tiergarten is to your right, and you can walk where the Wall once stood. The empty area to your left, beyond the fence, was a no-man's-land guarded and patrolled by East German soldiers with machine guns and guard dogs. In the distance is East Berlin's last major housing project. The open land all around here is now suddenly worth billions, and will be completely changed over the coming years as new buildings go up (a new Berlin headquarters for Mercedes is already planned for Potsdamer Platz). Following this route along the Tiergarten, you'll come to a wide open field where you can see the rising swell of the *Philharmonie* (Philharmonic Hall) to your right. To its left is the recently opened *Staatsbibliothek* (State Library).

Cut across the field, turn right on busy Bellevuestrasse, and cross Entlasstungstrasse with its murderous traffic (a result of the opening of Potsdamer Platz to motor traffic) to reach the buildings of Berlin's Kulturforum.

*Kulturforum

When completed, the area will be a cultural center of international importance, the home of several outstanding museums and concert halls. Inevitably, politics has now entered into the final plans for the site. The original plan, as envisioned by Hans Scharoun, met with some resistance, and an alternative design by a Viennese architect named Hans Hollein has now won the backing of the Berlin Senate. Some buildings in the complex were completed thirty years ago, but others are still under construction, and the overall result can be a little disorienting.

The oldest member of the Kulturforum, located at its north

Philharmonic Hall and Reichstag Building

eastern corner, is the world-renowned ***Philharmonie** [21]. Home base of one of the world's greatest orchestras, the Berlin Philharmonic, the Philharmonic Hall was designed by Hans Scharoun and constructed between 1960 and 1963. The controversy surrounding this bold octagonal building with its metallic-looking, ochre-colored skin and wave-like roofline has long since subsided, and the most important feature—the acoustics—was never called into question: The sound in the 2,200 seat hall is excellent. The orchestra is seated in the center of the hall, with the seats rising up all around it. The Berlin Philharmonic has counted some of the world's greatest conductors as its musical director, an elite that included Wilhelm Furtwängler and Herbert von Karajan. After Karajan's death, Claudio Abbado was named Principal Conductor in 1990. To one side of the Philharmonie is a newer addition to the Kulturforum, the 1,000-seat *Kammermusiksaal* (Chamber Music Hall), another futuristic Scharoun design. It was opened in 1988.

Of special interest to music lovers is a small gem of a museum next to the Philharmonie on Tiergartenstrasse, the new ***Musikinstrumenten-Museum** (Museum of Musical Instruments). Scharoun and Edgar Wisniewski were responsible for the design of this showcase of musical instruments from earliest times on. The loving craftsmanship evident in most of the instruments makes visitors long to hear how they sound in performance. *(Hours Tuesday–Friday 9:00 A.M.–5:00 P.M.; Saturday and Sunday 10:00 A.M.– 5:00 P.M.; closed Monday; admission free.)*

Continue down Tiergartenstrasse to reach another superlative new museum (opened in 1985) in the Kulturforum complex. The red-brick ***Kunstgewerbemuseum** (Museum of Applied Arts) originated in a private foundation in 1867 and contains, despite war losses, an extraordinary range of European applied arts in exhibits of the highest quality. Nine departments display collections ranging from gold reliquaries of the Early Middle Ages to the wildest fashion designs of the present day. Don't miss the sumptuous room hung with *Gobelin tapestries*, where the magnificent **Lüneburger Ratssilber* (Lüneburg Town Hall Silver Plate) glows in glass cases, the golden ***"Guelph Cross"* and renowned *Domed Reliquary,* and the exquisitely crafted gold and silver contents of the *"Pommersche Kunstschrank"* on the upper floor. Art Deco fans will swoon over the collection of deco furniture, glass, and clothing. The *Information Gallery* provides visitors with explanations, both of the craft methods, and the historical contexts in which they developed over the centuries. This is also an excellent place to take a lunch or coffee break. There is a handsomely designed cafeteria with outdoor tables overlooking the Philharmonic. *(Hours Tuesday–Sunday 9:00 A.M.–5:00 P.M.; closed Monday; admission free.)*

To continue the architectural tour, return to Matthäuskirchstrasse to one side of the Museum of Applied Arts and follow it toward the church. You'll pass a construction site on your right: When completed this new building will house the newly reunified European Collections of the *Gemäldegalerien* (Painting Galleries) in East and West Berlin, the reconstituted *Skulpturengalerie* (Sculpture Gallery), and the *Küpferstichkabinett* (Department of Prints and Drawings) currently housed in the Dahlem museum complex (see page 77).

The *Matthäuskirche* (St. Matthew's Church) ahead of you, built in 1846 from designs by August Stüler and restored in 1958, is the only "old" building in the aggressively modern Kulturforum. It has been interestingly incorporated into the overall scheme.

Walk around to the right of the church and you will find yourself across the street from yet another major museum, the **Nationalgalerie** [23]. *(Hours Tuesday–Sunday 9:00 A.M.–5:00 P.M.; closed Mondays; admission free.)* This celebrated building by Ludwig Mies van der Rohe, the proponent of "less is more," with its enormous expanse of glass windows and utterly simple symmetry, stands in sharp contrast to the architectural complexities of Scharoun's neighboring Philharmonic Hall. The National Gallery, dedicated in 1968, contains an outstanding collection of 19th- and 20th-century painting and sculpture on its lower floor. (The upper floor is used for temporary exhibitions.) German Romanticism is well represented in works by Adolph von Menzel (including *The Flute Concerto*) and the group known as the Germans in Rome: Hans von Marees *(The Rowers)*, Anselm Feuerbach, and Arnold Böcklin *(Island of the Dead)*. Included among the 19th-century French paintings are Gustave Courbet's *The Wave,* three major Édouard Manets, and landscapes and portraits by Claude Monet, Pierre Bonnard, and Auguste Renoir. Max Liebermann, Max Slevogt, and a remarkable series of paintings by Lovis Corinth highlight the German Impressionist group. Works by Ferdinand Hodler and Edvard Munch *(Life Frieze for Max Reinhardt's Chamber Theatre)* lead to compelling examples of the group known as "Die Brücke" (The Bridge), composed of Ernst Ludwig Kirchner, Karl Schmidt-Rotluff, Erich Heckel, Otto Mueller, and Emil Nolde. Works from Picasso's various periods, as well as canvases by Juan Gris and Fernand Léger may be seen in the central room, which opens out to the Sculpture Garden (jazz concerts in the summer). There is a Dada room, a fine collection of paintings by Oskar Kokoschka, Max Beckmann, Otto Dix, two bitter and brilliant oils by George Grosz, as well as paintings from the Bauhaus and Surrealist schools (Max Ernst, Giorgio de Chirico, René Magritte, Salvador Dalí, Joan Miró). American abstract painting is represented by Mark Rothko, Frank Stella, and Barnett Newman, while Anselm Kiefer, A. R. Penck, and Georg Baselitz exemplify more recent examples of German work. With plans underway to reassemble all the art collections in East and West Germany, some changes in the holdings of this museum are inevitable.

Stroll around the outdoor sculpture plaza surrounding the National Gallery for a good view of the surrounding area. Across the street (Potsdamer Strasse) is the **Staatsbibliothek** [22], another unmistakable Scharoun building. Built between 1967 and 1978, the State Library is Germany's central academic library, and contains other special sections (music, special collections, a picture archive, autographs) of international importance. Over 3.5 million books, covering all areas of scholarship, are housed here, and the library subscribes to some 30,000 current periodicals. There are frequent exhibitions, and a concert hall. (*Hours Monday–Friday 9:00 A.M.–9:00 P.M.; Saturday 9:00 A.M.–1:00 P.M.*)

*

For the final portion of this architectural walking tour, head down the Reichspietsufer to the left of the entrance to the National Gallery. To your right you'll see a new pink-and-blue-striped, Italian-inspired building by James Stirling, completed in 1990, which is incorporated into the prewar building used for the *Wissenschaftszentrum Berlin für Sozialforschung* (Academic Center for Social Research). Beyond it, just before Stauffenbergstrasse, is the *Bewag Building,* an often overlooked office block that is, in fact, one of Berlin's most important architectural landmarks. With its clean lines and surfaces the Bewag looks as though it might have been built in the 1970s, but it was, in fact, built in 1930–1931 from designs by Emil Fahrenkamp. In the 1920s, Berlin pioneered the simple, functional style this building represents.

At No. 13/14 Stauffenbergstrasse is the courtyard of the one-time military Supreme Command Headquarters (the "Bendler Block") which is now the *Gedenkstätte Deutscher Widerstand* (Memorial to the German Resistance), placed here in 1953. It was here that Colonel Claus, Count von Stauffenberg and several other officers formed a secret military group opposed to Hitler, which culminated in an unsuccessful attempt on Hitler's life. Stauffenberg and the officers involved in the plot were hauled before a drumhead court-martial and shot on the night of July 20, 1944, in what is now the memorial courtyard. An exhibition called "Resistance to National Socialism" is located in Stauffenberg's office suite adjacent to the memorial.

Cross Stauffenbergstrasse and continue along the canal-side path. Once this area of Tiergarten was a diplomatic district filled with expensive villas, such as the neoclassical Greek-style *Villa von der Heydt,* formerly the Chinese embassy, located adjacent to the attractive orange-and-black pedestrians-only *Herkulesbrücke* (Hercules Bridge), which crosses the Landwehrkanal. At this point Reichpietschufer becomes Vonder-Heydt-Strasse. The next building you come to, and the final destination of this architectural tour of the city, is the ***Bauhaus-Archiv/Museum für Gestaltung** [25].

One of the last works of the great Berlin-born architect Walter Gropius, the Bauhaus Archives and Museum for Design was completed in 1979. Its extensive collections cover a period from the late 19th century to the present day, but focus primarily on the history of the Bauhaus, an art school founded in 1919 at Weimar by a group of progressive teachers and students seeking to amalgamate the fields of art, technology, and science. The Bauhaus moved to Dessau, and then to Berlin, before it disbanded in 1933. (A new Bauhaus was founded in 1937 in Chicago.) Walter Gropius, Josef Albers, Ludwig Mies van der Rohe, Paul Klee, László Moholy-Nagy, Vassily Kandinsky, Marcel Breuer, and Johannes Itten are some of the artists who were trained or taught at this famous school of architecture, applied and graphic arts. The museum contains prime examples of all their work. There's a pleasant cafeteria to one side of the entrance. *(Open daily except Tuesdays 11:00 A.M. – 5:00 P.M.; admission fee.)*

WALK 4: *Schloss Charlottenburg

See map on page 50.

Charlottenburg, the largest and most beautiful palace in Berlin, also happens to be part of an outstanding museum complex. This walk covers the palace and its beautifully laid-out grounds, and stops in briefly at each of the six small museums. It's a full day's outing, and art-lovers may want to return to savor the treasures at a more leisurely pace.

To reach Charlottenburg Palace by public transportation, take the U-Bahn to *Richard-Wagner-Platz* or *Sophie-Charlotte-Platz;* bus numbers 9, 54, 62, and 74 also serve the area. The walk begins on

Charlottenburg Palace

Spandauer Damm directly in front of Charlottenburg Palace [26].

*Schloss Charlottenburg

The original central section of Charlottenburg Palace, without wings or dome, was built between 1695 and 1699 as a small chalet for the Electress and first Prussian Queen, Sophie Charlotte, the wife of King Frederick I. Arnold Nering was the first architect of what was then known as Lietzenburg Palace. The palace was considerably enlarged between 1701 and 1712 from plans by the Swedish-born royal master builder Eosander von Göthe, who created the high central dome over the main building and the orangerie on the west side. His plan for a new east wing was one of the first projects undertaken by Frederick the Great on his accession to the throne in 1740. The construction was carried out by Georg Wenzeslaus von Knobelsdorff (who also built the Staatsoper) on commission from the new king. A huge fire broke out in 1746 during the birthday celebrations for the Queen Mother, Sophie Dorothea, and a much worse mishap occurred in 1760, when the united Austrians and Russians entered Charlottenburg and thoroughly sacked and demolished it. Rebuilding and renovations dragged on for several years. Between 1788 and 1790, Frederick William II had Carl Langhans build a palace theater and the charming Belvedere tea house in the park (Langhans was additionally responsible for the interior design of Schloss Bellevue). Although he had a summer villa at Heiligensee and a romantic palace on Pfaueninsel (see page 70), the king, like most of his predecessors, felt most strongly drawn to Charlottenburg. Langhans's theater, where plays by Goethe and Schiller were performed, played an important cultural role in recognizing the merits of German literature (as opposed to the French bias of Frederick the Great). From 1795 on the theater was opened to all citizens. The last royal building constructed here is the free-standing Schinkel Pavillon to the east of the garden terrace, a summer house designed for Frederick William III in 1825 by Karl Friedrich Schinkel and modelled after the Villa Reale Chiatamone in Naples. After its destruction in 1943, the palace was carefully restored and is used today for the official receptions of Berlin's Governing Mayor.

As you approach the front entrance of the palace through the forecourt you'll see Andreas Schlüter's ****Reiterstandbild des Grossen Kurfürsten** (Equestrian Statue of the Great Elector), cast in one piece in 1700 and considered the most important Baroque statue of its kind. The statue formerly stood on the Lange Brücke (Long Bridge) near the (now-demolished) Berliner Schloss (Berlin Palace) in East Berlin; it was placed here in 1952.

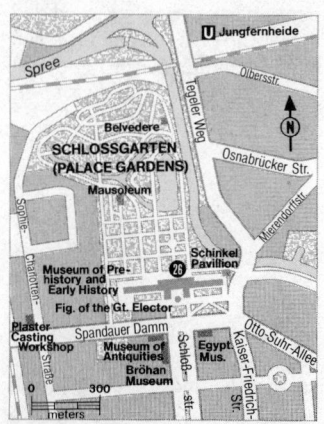

Enter the palace if you want to tour the ***Historical Rooms.** *(Hours Tuesday–Sunday 9:00 A.M.–5:00 P.M.; closed Monday; admission fee.)* You can only see them on a guided tour, given in German. Don't let this deter you, however. The rooms are a marvel to look at, even if you don't understand German (you can purchase a detailed guide to the palace in English at the ticket kiosk). The best bargain is a *Sammelkarte* (multiple ticket, DM 6) which allows you to tour the historical rooms, the Knobelsdorff Wing, the Schinkel Pavillon, the Belvedere, and the Mausoleum. Otherwise you'll have to pay a separate admission for each. You are required to put on enormous felt overshoes for the guided tour to protect the wood floors. These may be a bit awkward at first, but you'll soon find yourself skating along.

The rooms featured on the tour are the ground floor of the central Nering section of the palace and in the Eosander wing, and include the *Frederick I* and *Sophie Charlotte rooms,* decorated primarily in the "Chinese" taste of the period. You'll be guided through the panelled gallery, where important receptions are held, see dressing rooms in red, bedrooms in blue, mirrored rooms, a "play room," and Frederick I's bed chamber with its sunken marble bath off to one side—a sensation for 1700.

Wall coverings include damask and Chinese silk; there are Gobelin tapestries, Chinese porcelains, and dozens of paintings and royal portraits, including several by the French artist Antoine Pesne, whom Frederick I brought to the Prussian court after 1710. Look for the portraits of Sophie Charlotte over the doors in the "Glass Bed Chamber" and the "Red-braid Room." The plump, double-chinned Queen of Prussia, for whom the first palace was built, was responsible for elevating the intellectual life of the Court by subsidizing music, philosophy, and theology—she even conducted an opera performance or two. The tour ends with a special highlight, the elegant *Porcelain Cabinet, where a vast collection of porcelain (more than 1,000 pieces)—most of it Chinese—fills every niche from floor to ceiling.

You may now visit the rooms on the upper floor of Knobelsdorff's "New Wing" on your own—if anything, these are even more sumptuous than the ones featured on the guided tour. To get to the rooms, turn left as you leave the tour entrance hall and walk to the adjacent wing of the palace. The ground floor is the new home of the *Galerie der Romantik* (Gallery of Romantic Art); once you are in the vestibule, head upstairs via the *Stair Hall*, completed by von Göthe in about 1704. The cantilevered staircase was probably the first of its kind in Germany. On the upper level you'll find the luxurious *private quarters of Frederick the Great*, with *paintings by the king's favorite French artist, Antoine Watteau—the largest collection of Watteau works outside of France. The enormous *White Hall* with its concave ceiling was once the king's throne room as well as his private dining room, but save some of your awe for the fabulous Rococo *Golden Gallery* just beyond it. The complex gilded ornamentation in Knobelsdorff's grand ballroom gleams against green stucco-marble walls, meant to harmonize with the green of the palace gardens.

There are several other rooms to explore here—including the pink bedroom of Queen Luise—before you head back downstairs for a visit to the **Galerie der Romantik.** *(Hours 9:00 A.M.–5:00 P.M. daily; closed Mondays; admission free.)*

Works of the Romantic and Biedermeier periods will be housed here in the New Wing's Gallery of Romantic Art until their removal (probably in 1991) to the National Gallery on Museum Island. The artistic development of that master of German Romanticism, Caspar David Friedrich, can be observed in the two rooms devoted entirely to his work. An outstanding landscape artist who favored brooding landscapes, in which human figures proved insignificant against the enormous backdrop of nature, you can trace his work from the early *The Monk by the Sea* and *Abbey in an Oak Wood* (1808–1810) to the tranquil imagery of his late years as seen in *Riesengebirge* (Giant

Mountains, 1835). Other interesting displays include the visionary landscapes, filled with imaginary architecture, by the Prussian architect Karl Friedrich Schinkel (whose Neue Wache building is part of Walk 13 and who designed the next building in this tour). Also on display are paintings showing Berlin in the early 19th century, and David's famous portrait of Napoleon crossing the St. Bernhard Pass.

Turn left as you leave the New Wing and follow the façade of the building around the corner. To your right, set off by itself, stands the **Schinkel Pavillon.** Designed by Schinkel in 1824 for Frederick William III, this graceful, compact building is also known as the Villa am Meer (Villa by the Sea) because it was modeled after the Villa Reale Chiatamone in Naples, where the King had stayed in 1822. Eventually this pavilion became his personal residence. The rooms, evenly grouped around a center stairwell, contain sculptures, 19th-century paintings, period furnishings, and china. Upstairs, two interesting triptychs painted by Eduard Gärtner in 1834 show panoramic views of Berlin as seen from the roof of the Werdersche Kirche. There are also some rare paintings by Schinkel.

The walk now becomes a garden stroll. From the Schinkel Pavillon you can follow a shady path along the Spree River all the way to the Belvedere, or walk through the formally-landscaped Baroque gardens directly behind the palace. Sophie Charlotte was much taken with Lenôtre's garden design at Versailles and managed to obtain the services of Lenôtre's pupil, Simon Goudeau, to landscape the grounds of Charlottenburg. Starting his work in 1697, Goudeau created the first French Baroque garden in Germany. Since that time, the gardens have been through several major alterations. Garden design during the Romantic period eschewed the stiff geometrical patterns of formal gardens in favor of "natural" English landscapes with wide vistas filled with follies, grottos, and "ruins" that created a rustic effect. With this in mind, winding paths were arranged through the once strictly formal gardens, flower beds were scattered decoratively around the palace grounds, and a peaceful, romantic island was created.

Continue north, past the lake (or along the river) to reach the **Belvedere.** Set back in a grassy meadow surrounded on three sides by old trees, the graceful white-and-turquoise Belvedere presents an undeniably picturesque sight. Designed by Carl Langhans in 1788 as a tea house with an open view to the Jungfernheide forest on the opposite side of the riverbank, it is today the home of the *Berliner Porzellan collection* (Berlin Porcelain Collection). Even if you've already had your fill of porcelain, you can climb to the top floor for a view over the gardens with the palace in the distance.

From the Belvedere, head back

down the canal-side path to your right. You'll stroll past lush meadows and, if the day is sunny, inevitably see a nude sunbather or two. Oak, linden, and chestnut trees shade the path, and ducks swim and forage in the water. Cross the first bridge you come to, then follow the path down to the first intersection, where you turn left. Continue a short distance until you come to a shady avenue of pines, turn left again, and you'll be at the **Mausoleum.**

King Frederick William III drew the first design for this temple-like building, which he had built as a final resting place for Queen Luise immediately after her death in 1810. Heinrich Gentz and Karl Friedrich Schinkel were responsible for the actual execution of the king's design. The mausoleum is set back behind a circular gravel entrance planted with purple rhododendrons. The melancholic Queen Luise no doubt would have loved the dim interior, where four red-brown jasper columns separate the two rooms. The marble tomb effigies of Queen Luise (1776–1810) and King Frederick William III (1770–1840) are by C. D. Rauch. In 1894, the sarcophagi of Emperor William I (1797–1888) and his wife, Queen Augusta Victoria (1811–1890) were also placed here.

Follow the pine avenue south from the Mausoleum until you reach the back of Langhans' former theater building, now the **Museum für Vor- und Frühgeschichte.** The Museum of Prehistory and Early History suffered heavy losses in the Second World War—some of Heinrich Schliemann's finds from Troy among them—but its five well-organized rooms still afford some remarkable insights into the history of human civilization from the Pleistocene Era to the High Middle Ages. Of special interest is the *Gold Treasury from Troy* in Room 4 and the splendid *Kaisermosaiken* (Imperial Mosaics) from the church of San Vitale in Ravenna. There are helpful dioramas and displays throughout. It seems likely that most of the material here will eventually be incorporated into the collections on Museum Island. *(Hours 9:00 A.M.–5:00 P.M. daily; closed Friday; admission free.)*

As you come out of the museum, the former orangerie is to your left. To the south, in the old barracks, there are a café and restaurant, where you might want to rest and have a snack before continuing your walk. You leave the palace grounds at this point and cross the Spandauer Damm to get to the museums on the other side. You'll also find other "time-out" alternatives—two neighboring restaurants with outdoor tables—at the corner of Spandauer Damm and Nithackstrasse, to the left of the Egyptian Museum.

The next two museums on the tour flank Schloss-Strasse, and were once the barracks of the palace's *Garde du Corps*. F. A. Stüler, a pupil of Schinkel's, designed them, and they were built in neoclassical style between 1851

Bust of Queen Nefertiti

and 1859. Between them, on the center island, is a statue of Albrecht, Prince of Prussia (1809–1872).

To your left is the justly popular *Ägyptisches Museum. *(Hours 9:00 A.M.–5:00 P.M. daily; closed Friday; admission free.)* The special pleasure of this museum lies not only in its outstanding collection, but also in its beautifully designed rooms and manageable size. The art and artifacts from the Nile Valley on display here range from 4500 B.C. to the time of the Roman Empire. Don't miss the fabulous ***limestone bust of Queen Nefertiti* (ca. 1350 B.C.) found in 1912 near Tell-el-Amarna and dramatically displayed in a dark room; the riveting beauty of the queen's face and profile are no doubt idealized, but even the one missing eye adds a haunting touch of mysterious glamour. Another treasure is the tiny *Head of Queen Teje* (or Tiyi) carved from boxwood about 1370 B.C. With her inward-looking eyes and petulant lips, the chief wife of Amenhotep III (and mother-in-law of Nefertiti) looks permanently displeased. The **Green Head* from ca. 600–330 B.C. is a major late period Egyptian sculpture, and the **Kalabasha Gate,* on the lower level, was a gift from Egypt's late President Anwar el-Sadat. Check out the mummy cases on this lower level. In the far end of the room, to the right, is one that some say looks remarkably like Mikhail Gorbachev! Note that this collection will soon be moved to the Pergamon Museum on Museum Island.

Across Schloss-Strasse you will find the *Antikenmuseum, yet another fine museum in the Charlottenburg complex and one that will also be moved to Museum Island. The collection of the Museum of Greek and Roman Antiquities includes world-famous works of antique decorative art, particularly pottery from Ancient Greece and Italy, Greek, Etruscan, and Roman statuettes and implements, ivory carvings, glassware, objects in precious stone, jewelry from the Mediterranean region, gold and silver treasures, mummy portraits from Roman Egypt, wood and stone sarcophagi, and a small number of marble sculptures. The *Schatzkammer* (Treasury) with the Hildesheim silver (1st century B.C.–1st century A.D.) is in the basement. The museum also contains the sculpted *Portrait of*

Queen Cleopatra VII of Egypt (69–30 B.C.), the only known contemporary portrait of this legendary figure. *(Hours 9:00 A.M.–5:00 P.M. daily; closed Fridays; admission free.)*

Beside the Museum of Antiquities is a place that lovers of Art Nouveau and Art Deco will not want to miss, the often overlooked and uncrowded ***Bröhan Museum.** Formerly a private collection, the Bröhan has been open to the public only since October, 1983, and as such is a private museum not officially affiliated with all the other museums in the Charlottenburg complex. The display features about 1,600 objects—paintings, sculptures, graphics, furniture, glass, silverware, applied arts, and industrial designs—from the period between 1889 and 1939. Design aficionados will not be disappointed, especially when they see the **Suite Emile-Jacques Ruhlmann.* Set up as a completely decorated suite from a luxurious private residence from the 1920s and 1930s, it contains period furniture, objects from the *Wiener Werkstätte* (Vienna Workshop), porcelains, and paintings. *(Hours 10:00 A.M.–6:00 P.M. daily; closed Monday; admission DM 3.)*

From here, you turn left down Spandauer Damm, and walk to Sophie-Charlotten-Strasse, where the *Gipsformerei der Staatlichen Museen* is located at No. 17/18. The Plaster Casting Workshop of the State Museums displays and sells plaster copies of well-known sculptures, reliefs, and vases from museums in Germany and around the world—including some you may have seen on your walking tour of Charlottenburg. *(Hours Monday–Friday 9:00 A.M.–4:00 P.M.; Wednesday 9:00 A.M.–6:00 P.M.)*

WALK 5: Theodor-Heuss-Platz–Messegelände–*ICC–*Funkturm–*Olympia Stadion–*Spandau

See map on page 57.

Berlin is an enormous city, and although we call this a walk, it actually covers too much territory to be covered comfortably on foot. Plan to travel parts of the route by car, U-Bahn, bus, or taxi. The itinerary covers Berlin's impressive Exhibition and Fairgrounds, the futuristic International Congress Center (perhaps your daily stop if you're in town for a conference), the landmark Broadcasting Tower, going on to the famous Olympic Stadium, and concluding in the charming streets of Spandau, a distinctive historical village incorporated into the city of Berlin.

The point of departure for this route is *Theodor-Heuss-Platz,* a major traffic intersection for vehicles going through western Charlottenburg. The simplest way to get here is by U-Bahn or the No. 94

bus from Bahnhof Zoologischer Garten. In the center of the square there is a fountain with an enclosed flame that was originally lit by Theodor Heuss, West Germany's first Federal President after World War II. The symbolic flame was to burn until the two Germanys were completely reunified—an event that became reality in late 1990. It remains to be seen if the flame will now be extinguished or continue to burn as a reminder of the city's divided past. On Masurenallee, to the south of the square, stand the *Sender Freies Berlin* (Radio Free Berlin) television broadcasting center and the blue-and-black lined brick *Haus des Rundfunks* (Broadcasting House), built in 1931 from designs by Hans Poelzig. Constructed with all of its studios facing an interior courtyard, Broadcasting House is one of the most modern broadcasting centers in Europe.

Walk down Masurenallee to *Hammarskjöldplatz*, where you'll see the enormous expanse of the **Ausstellungs- und Messegelände.** The Exhibition and Fair Grounds contain 24 large, interconnected halls measuring some 85,050 square meters (945,000 square feet). Upwards of 25 major trade fairs and exhibitions are held here annually, including "Green Week," a giant food and agricultural fair, and the "International Fashion Fair." In the center of the halls is the oval *Sommergarten* (Summer Garden), with a terrace restaurant known as

Exhibition Grounds with Broadcasting Tower

the "Palace at the Broadcasting Tower."

Continue down Hammarskjöldplatz to the ***Funkturm** [27], the landmark that dominates West Charlottenburg. Berliners have a special fondness for this historic 150-meter- (500-foot-) high steel broadcasting tower, which they have nicknamed "Langer Lulatsch" ("Long Louie"). Reminiscent of the Eiffel Tower, the Funkturm was put on line in 1926, on the occasion of the Third Deutsche Funkausstellung (German Broadcasting Exhibition), and transmitted the world's first television program in 1932. Today its antenna equipment is used by Berlin's police and fire department. Take the elevator to the **observation platform* (open daily 10:00 A.M.–midnight) for a magnificent view of the surrounding area. If you're hungry and feeling in an elevated mood, you can eat in the *Funkturmrestaurant,* perched at 55 meters (182 feet). At the foot of the tower, communications enthusiasts will find the interesting *Deutsches Rundfunkmuseum* (German Broadcasting Museum). *(Hours Daily 10:00 A.M.–5:00 P.M.; closed Tuesday; admission fee.)*

Now walk down to the covered bridge that crosses Messedamm providing access to one of Berlin's most amazing contemporary buildings, the ***International Congress Center (ICC)**. A monumental sculpture—appropriately entitled "Man Builds His City"—by French sculptor Jean Ipousteguy stands in front of this city-sized conference center, completed in 1979 at a cost of some one billion marks. With its silver-grey aluminum panels and shiplike design, the building is somewhat overwhelming at first. A view of the foyer (entrance on Neue Kantstrasse) is a bit more welcoming. There are 80 halls, conference, and work rooms here, the largest of which can accommodate 8,000 people. The ICC is used for national and international meetings, congresses, and political conventions as well as ballet performances, concerts, and other cultural events.

Cross Messedamm over the bridge and head south to the *Deutschlandhalle* [28], built in 1935 and restored after the war. Large-scale events, such as iceshows, rock concerts, and bicycle races, take place here. The once-famous car-racing track known as the *Avus* begins across Messedamm. Now part of the Berlin Autobahn, the Avus heads straight southwest for 10 km. (6 miles), cutting across the Grunewald and ending at Nikolassee. Formula One races were held here in the past, and you might think they're still taking place, given the speed of today's drivers. It's currently the only section of the highway with no designated speed limit.

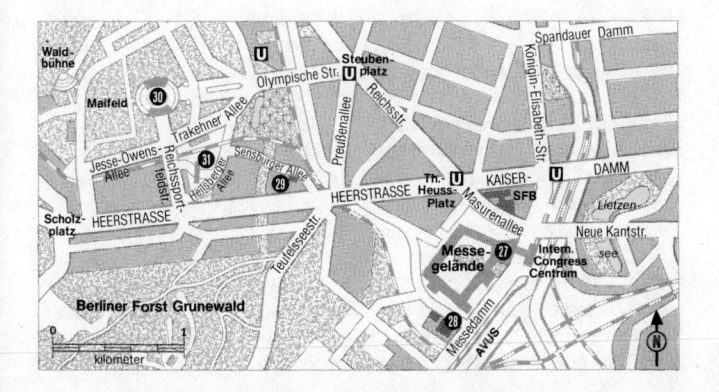

At this point you may want to return to the Theodor-Heuss-Platz U-Bahn, which is two stops away from the Olympic Stadium. You can also catch the special *Ausflugslinie* (excursion bus)—recognizable by its conspicuous triangle—that winds up to Trakehner Allee in front of the stadium.

A pedestrian alternative route to the stadium, recommended only for serious art lovers, is to head up behind the Messegelände complex on Jaffestrasse to Wandalenallee, which will take you to Heerstrasse. Cross Heerstrasse and head west to Sensburger Allee where you will find the **Georg-Kolbe-Museum** [29] at No. 25. Today the former home and workshop of the celebrated sculptor and graphic artist Georg Kolbe (1877–1947) exhibits 180 of his bronze sculptures, sketches, and drawings, providing an excellent overview of his career. The highlight here is the nearby *Georg-Kolbe-Grove,* an outdoor sculpture garden with several of Kolbe's larger-than-life-size bronzes including "Kneeling Figure," "Falling Figure," "Dionysus," and "Mars and Venus." *(Hours Tuesday–Sunday 10:00 A.M.–5:00 P.M.; admission fee.)*

If you're walking from the Georg-Kolbe-Museum to the Olympic Stadium, you can follow Sensburger Allee to Heilsberger Allee and turn left to visit the 17-story *Corbusier-Haus* at *Heilsberger Dreieck.* Europe's largest apartment building, housing more than 1,500 residents in 527 apartments, was built in 1957 as the Swiss architect Le Corbusier's contribution to the Interbau '57 architecture exhibition (see also the description of the Hansaviertel, page 38, which was built at the same time). It was patterned after his visionary "Shining City" project in Marseilles. From here you can turn back up Heilsberger Allee, which will take you to *Olympischer Platz* and the Olympic stadium. Visitors arriving on the Olympia-Stadion U-Bahn can walk south to Olympischer Platz. On the other side of the square stands the ***Olympia Stadion** [30]. *(Open daily from 8:00 A.M. to twilight, admission fee for entrance to the stadium.)*

The former Third Reich-era sports arena, seating some 90,000 spectators, was designed by Werner March and built for the Games of the XIth Olympiad in 1936. Adolf Hitler saw these Olympic Games as a glorious opportunity to prove his theory of the superiority of the Nordic races. However, when a black American track star named Jesse Owens won the first of his four gold medals, Hitler stormed out of the stadium and never returned. (A nearby street to the south of the stadium is named for Owens, who died in 1981.) Albert Speer, Hitler's official architect for Berlin, designed spectacular stadium light shows—forerunners of today's laser extravaganzas—for events like Mussolini's 1937 visit to the capital. The main stadium, which was part of Hitler's megalomaniacal scheme for a glorified Berlin, filled with exaggeratedly oversized buildings, is an enormous oval, some 300 meters (984 feet) long and 230 meters (754 feet) wide. Colossal statues of idealized Nordic athletes (very similar to the ones Mussolini had sculpted for Rome's EUR) stand outside the gates. The sports complex includes a swimming stadium, a hockey stadium, tennis courts, and an equestrian arena. Walk through the Marathon Gate if you want to see the *Maifeld parade grounds,* which hold some 500,000 spectators. The 77-meter- (250-foot-) high bell tower on the west side of the grounds was reconstructed in 1962 and given a new four-and-a-half metric ton bell (the old cracked bell stands at the south gate). An elevator will take you upstairs for a panoramic view. Adjoining the Maifeld to the west is the *Waldbühne,* a popular outdoor concert arena.

If you arrived at the stadium by U-Bahn or bus and are interested in seeing *Corbusier-Haus* (see description above), you can walk there via Reichssportfeld. You now have several public transportation options to get to Spandau and the last portion of this itinerary. If you'd like some pleasant sightseeing along the way, take the No. 94 bus going west on Heerstrasse to Pichelsdorfer Strasse, and change there to the northbound No. 34 or 97. Get off at *Falkenseer-Platz,* the square closest to Altstadt Spandau. Another alternative is to take the U-Bahn at Olympia Stadion one stop to *Ruhleben,* where you can catch the No. 54 bus on Charlottenburger Chaussee. This will also take you to *Falkenseer-Platz.* You can get there quicker by taking the U-Bahn all the way, catching it at Olympia Stadion and transferring at Bismarck Strasse to the U7 line. Get off at Altstadt Spandau. However you choose to get there, our next stop is the village of Spandau.

*Spandau

See map on page 60.

Located at the junction of the Spree and Havel rivers, Spandau received its town charter as early as 1232, which makes it older than the original settlements of Berlin-Cölln. It remained an independent municipality up until 1920, vigorously resisting its incorporation into greater Berlin. The only authentic (that is, not entirely rebuilt after World War II) old city anywhere in Berlin, Spandau has managed to preserve much of its village character, especially in the lovely corner known as the *Kolk,* where 18th- and 19th-century houses line the cobblestone streets. Interestingly enough, though, Spandau is also Berlin's largest industrial area. It is the Berlin headquarters of Siemens, the giant multi-national electrical firm, the Reuter power station, and BMW's motorbike division. The northwesternmost corner of the district is taken up by the large *Spandau City Forest.*

Spandauers feel special, less a part of Berlin than the inhabitants of any other district. Many of them stay here their entire lives, even though Spandau was linked to downtown Berlin by U-Bahn in 1984. For a resident of Spandau, "going to Berlin" means a special trip, and not necessarily a pleasant one.

Our tour of Spandau begins just south of the Altstadt Spandau U-Bahn station. Here, at *Reformationsplatz*, the town's historic center, is the brick **Nikolaikirche** (St. Nicholas Church) [32]. Built mostly in the first half of the 15th century, the church is the last preserved example of brick Gothic architecture in Berlin, and one of the oldest Gothic churches in the March. The late-19th-century *Monument to Elector Joachim II*, a bronze statue by Encke commemorating the Elector's conversion to Protestantism (hence the name of the square) in 1539, stands with Schinkel's 1816 *War Memorial* in front of the church. In the restored *interior there is a painted limestone *Renaissance altar*, donated to the church by Rochus, Count of Lynar, who was responsible for the completion of the Spandau Citadel in 1594; a late-14th-century *bronze baptismal font;* and, on the north wall of the nave, a *crucifixion scene* dating from 1540.

Stroll around the lovely cobblestone *Reformationsplatz*—in warm weather there are outdoor tables at the Altstadt-Café to the right of the church—and the Kolk, the area north of *Am Juliusturm*. This is the oldest part of Spandau, and it's sometimes hard to believe you're in the same city that houses such futuristic buildings as the ICC. Stroll up Behnitz to *Möllentordamm* where there's a small viewing platform for watching the busy boat traffic in the *Schleuse Spandau* (Spandau Sluice). Every year some 35,000 sailing vessels use this lock, which links the Upper and Lower Havel. Plans are underway to enlarge it.

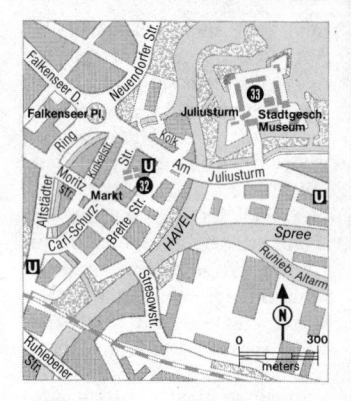

Now return to Am Juliusturm and follow it east, across the Havel, to the park on the other side. On your left, you'll come to a path that leads across a narrow canal to the **Spandauer Zitadelle** [33]. The moated Spandau Citadel, considered a masterpiece of 16th-century Italian fortress construction, was begun in 1557 to plans by the Italian architect Chiaramella de Gandino. The four pointed bastions represented a new concept in fortress construction at the time. Gandino designed the gatehouse and the "King" and "Queen" bastions.

Work on what was meant to be an "impregnable modern fortress" continued in 1578 under Count Rochus von Lynar, who was responsible for the "Crown Prince" and "Brandenburg" bastions. Mighty brick walls surround the remains of the 16th-century Spandau Fortress and the 32-meter- (105-foot-) high *Juliusturm* (Julius Tower), which dates back to the 13th century, when the Brandenburg nobility resided here in the *Palas* (Knight's Hall). After the Franco-Prussian War of 1870–1871, reparation payments from France, totalling some 120 million gold marks, were stored in the tower (the walls are 2.3 meters/8 feet thick). The gold was returned to the French in 1919 after Germany's defeat in the First World War. Through the years, the castle also served as the Prussian state prison, where revolutionaries and political opponents of the government were incarcerated. A wooden staircase spirals up to an

Spandau Citadel

observation platform atop the tower for an excellent view of the countryside, with its abundance of forests and lakes. The most elegant structure in the fortress is the Palas, where concerts and art exhibitions are sometimes held. The large Gothic hall inside was reconstructed in 1981. The *Kommandantenhaus* (Commander's House), to your right as you enter the *Heimatmuseum Spandau*, features occasional exhibitions. On Friday, Saturday, and Sunday evenings visitors can also enjoy a candlelight dinner, complete with medieval minstrels, in the popular *Castle Restaurant*—but reservations are a must. *(Hours for the Citadel, Tuesday–Friday 9:00 A.M.–5:00 P.M.; Saturday and Sunday 10:00 A.M.–5:00 P.M.; closed Monday; admission fee. Castle restaurant open from 6:00 P.M. daily except Saturday and Sunday, when it is open from 11:30 A.M. To reserve for the special candlelit minstrel dinners on Friday, Saturday, and Sunday evenings call 334-2106 after 2:00 P.M.)*

The quickest way back to downtown Berlin from the Citadel is by the U-Bahn at Altstadt Spandau. Drivers have another possible return route. Drive south from Falkenseer-Platz all the way to Heerstrasse (the street changes its name several times along the way: Altstädter Ring becomes Kloster-Strasse, which becomes Wilhelm Strasse, which becomes Gatower Strasse), turn right and then left at the next intersection, which is

Wilhelm Strasse. The area was the location of the *Allied Military Prison* (Wilhelm Strasse 21–24) where Nazis convicted of war crimes at the 1946 Nürnberg trials were imprisoned. Its best known inmate was Rudolf Hess, Hitler's one-time deputy, who was the only prisoner for twenty-one years (maintaining the one-inmate prison amounted to one million marks annually). After Hess died in 1987, the prison was quickly demolished. By following Heerstrasse east you can return to the heart of Berlin.

WALK 6: Through the *Grunewald to the Wannsee

See map opposite.

Berlin is a city that mixes its cultural sophistication with a healthy love of the outdoors. Nature is never far away here, what with fully 40 percent of the city covered with lakes and wooded areas. Hiking, bicycling, sailing, and swimming are popular recreational activities. This itinerary will guide you to some special areas in the Grunewald Forest.

There are a number of ways to get to the Grunewald, but to enjoy the western portion of the forest as described below, we recommend taking a special excursion bus *(Ausfluglinie)* and getting out at one of its stops to walk part of the route. You can catch the excursion bus, identified by a triangle, at *Scholzplatz* on Heerstrasse (the No. 94 bus will take you there, or you can catch the excursion bus outside the Theodor-Heuss U-Bahn station. From here, however, it first winds past the Olympic Stadium before heading towards the Grunewald). The fare is 1 DM unless you have a special "Umweltkarte" (weekly pass), in which case you simply show your card. By car, take Heerstrasse to Scholzplatz and turn left onto the road Am Postfenn. This will take you as far as the Havel, but at this point you will have to find a parking space because the connecting Havelchaussee is closed to car traffic. You can walk into the Grunewald from here, of course, or you can catch the *Ausfluglinie* (excursion bus) which follows the Havelchaussee.

The *Grunewald

The 40-square-km. (15-square-mile) Grunewald forest, Berlin's largest uninterrupted wooded area, is part of the Wilmersdorf and Zehlendorf districts. From Heerstrasse it stretches some 9 km. (6 miles) south to the popular *Wannsee*. The **Havelchaussee,* the Grunewald's western border, winds past several picturesque bays and beaches along the Havel River, while the forest's eastern border is roughly marked off by four lakes: *Schlachtensee, Krumme Lanke, Grunewaldsee,* and *Hundekehlesee*. Within this great green expanse, there are hundreds of hiking trails and bike paths. A few fens, moors, and smaller lakes—*Teufelsee* and *Teufelsfenn*, for example—are under government protection as nature sanctuaries and are not open to the public. The Grunewald suffered badly in the Second World War, when it lost some 44 percent of its trees. After the war, about 24 million new deciduous and evergreen trees were planted, and these have now matured, making the forest one of the Berliners' favorite areas for excursions and Sunday walks.

The Havelchaussee leads south, skirting the shores of the *Jürgenlanke Bay*, with the *Halbinsel*

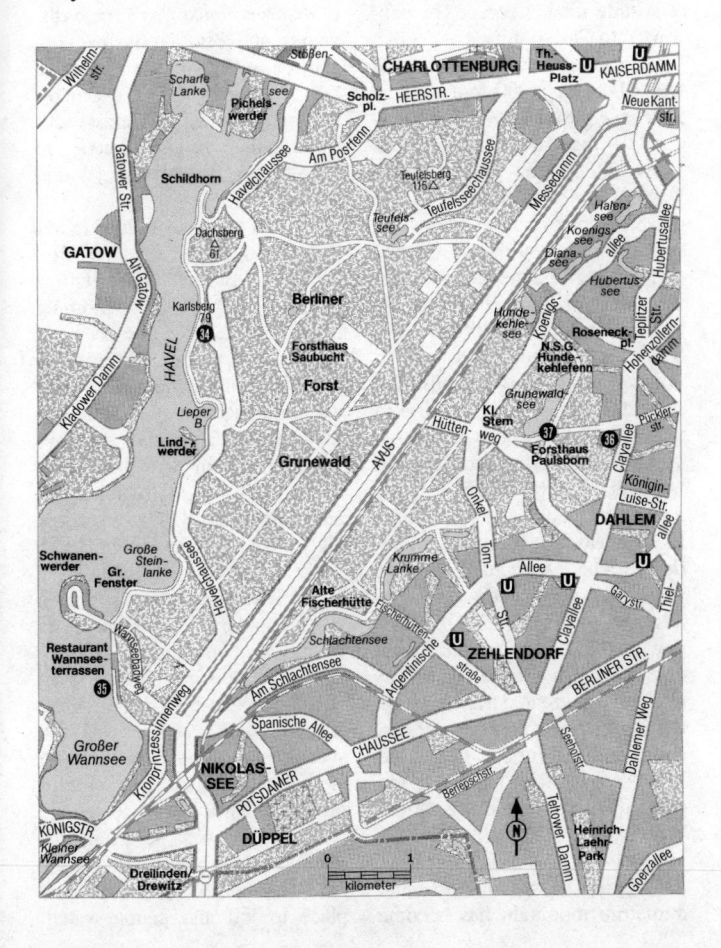

Schildhorn (Schildhorn Peninsula) on the other side. On a small promontory, there is a curious *sandstone pillar* embellished with a shield and a cross to commemorate Jaczo, the last of the Slavonic Wend princes. Jaczo managed to save himself from the murderous intentions of Albrecht the Bear by swimming along this peninsula. In gratitude for his escape, he converted to Christianity.

The road now leads around the 61-meter- (200-foot-) high *Dachsberg* to the 79-meter- (260-foot-) high *Karlsberg,* a hill crowned by the **Grunewaldturm** (Grunewald Tower) [34]. In 1898, Franz Schwechten was commissioned by the Teltow district to erect this neogothic tower in memory of Emperor William I. It is made of red Markish brick. The excursion bus stops here, so you may want to hop out and climb up to the observation platform to get a magnificent *panoramic view of West Berlin from Spandau to Potsdam. In the distance, to the northeast, you'll see what looks like curious Russian church domes. These are actually parts of the radar station on the *Teufelsberg,* at 116 meters (383 feet) one of the highest points in the city. Only in Berlin: the Teufelsberg was created from some 25 million cubic meters (33 million cubic yards) of rubble after World War II, covered with topsoil, and planted with trees and vegetation. With its toboggan run and two ski jumps (with tows and machines for making snow), this artificial miniature mountain has become Berlin's winter sports center. If you want a meal, the Grunewaldturm restaurant makes for a pleasant stop.

The Havelchaussee returns to the banks of the Havel at *Lieper Bay,* where a ferry boat makes a short run to the attractive island of *Lindwerder.* The road now runs parallel with the shore down to the *Grosse Steinlanke Bay,* crosses the woods, and joins Kronprinzessinnenweg at the southern curve of the *Avus* (see page 57). Get off the excursion bus at Wannseebadweg, which leads directly to **Strandbad Wannsee** (Wannsee Beach) [35].

This large-scale outdoor swimming area is often called the "Berlin Lido." Before this stretch of beach opened in 1907, swimming in any of the lakes and rivers of Berlin was prohibited. An expanded public swimming resort was built between 1927 and 1930 to give the Berliners, many of whom lived in wretched tenements, a chance for lakeside rest and recreation. In the years of the city's division, when West Berlin was virtually an island within the GDR, Wannsee became even more popular as an escape from the city, and on a sunny day today up to 30,000 people come to stretch out side-by-side beside the waters of the Havel. People still swim here, but pollution from East Berlin's waterways has created problems. Until that is cleared up, it's probably best to avoid the temptation to take a dip. In any case, the beach remains a great place to loll and people-watch.

There are nudist areas if you wish to sunbathe *au naturel*. The view from the thatch-roofed Wannseeterrassen Restaurant just outside the swimming area is one of the most pleasant in town.

If you follow Wannseebadweg beyond the beach, you will come to the island of *Schwanenwerder*, connected by causeway to the mainland. Colorado's Aspen Institute, an organization that promotes improved relations between business executives on both sides of the Atlantic, has its Berlin headquarters on the island. Shortly before you reach the causeway a footpath to the right leads to the *Grosses Fenster* (Big Window), from which you have a view across the Havel all the way to Spandau.

Returning to the downtown area is easy from here: You can take the excursion bus back along the same route, or follow Wannseebadweg to Spanische Allee and the Nikolassee S-Bahn station.

If you are up for some hiking, however, we recommend following Am Schlachtensee up to the path leading to the shores of *Schlachtensee*. Follow the winding lakeside walk up through *Paul-Ernst-Park*, past several small swimming areas, to the popular "Alte Fischerhütte" restaurant on the northern tip of the lake. Here you can sit and eat, or enjoy a beer or coffee and observe the Berliners on holiday (you can also rent rowboats). The smaller *Krumme Lanke*, equally picturesque, is just to the north and circled by a walk along its shores. The two lakes are separated by Fischerhüttenstrasse. When you've finished your stroll, take Fischerhüttenstrasse to Argentinische Allee, where you'll find the Krumme Lanke U-Bahn station. Before heading back, you might want to visit the art gallery known as *"Haus am Waldsee"* at Argentinische Allee 30.

WALK 7: All Around the Grunewaldsee

See map on page 63.

This walk provides a further exploration of Berlin's great forest-park known as the Grunewald. There is less territory covered than in the previous itinerary, and stops along the way include an art museum devoted to expressionist paintings and an historic hunting lodge. The walk takes you past several of the Grunewald's small lakes before ending up at the Kurfürstendamm.

The easiest way to get to the starting point of this walk is to take the No. 19 or 29 bus down the Kurfürstendamm and get off at *Roseneck*. From here, walk south along Clayallee (named for General Lucius D. Clay, the Military Governor of the U.S. zone of occupation in Germany who oversaw the Berlin Airlift) to Pücklerstrasse. You can also take the No. 50 bus from Roseneck to Pücklerstrasse. Turn right on Pücklerstrasse and then left on Fohlenweg to reach Bussardsteig and the **Brücke-Museum** [36].

This very interesting museum on the edge of the Grunewald was opened in 1967 on the initiative of the painter Karl Schmidt-Rotluff, who was then 83 years old, and, along with Erich Heckel, one of the last surviving members of the group of Expressionist artists who called themselves "Die Brücke." Founded in Dresden in 1905, the group later migrated to Berlin. Schmidt-Rotluff and Heckel donated their own works to the museum, as well as their personal collections of work by other "Brücke" artists, such as Emil Nolde, Max Pechstein, and Ernst Ludwig Kirchner. Other artists associated with the group whose work is represented here, include Max Kaus, Emy Roder, and Otto Herbig. *(Hours Daily 11:00 A.M.–5:00 P.M.; closed Tuesdays; admission fee.)*

Grunewald Hunting Lodge

From the museum, continue down a footpath to *Grunewaldsee* (Grunewald Lake). Beside the lake you'll find the ***Jagdschloss Grunewald** [37]. The entire Grunewald forest derives its name from this hunting lodge, which was originally called "Zum grünen Walde" ("At the Green Woods"). Built in Renaissance style in 1542 by Caspar Theyss for Elector Joachim II, the architect Rochus von Lynar added a farm building and stables about 50 years later. Further alterations were made around 1700, and additional farm buildings were added in 1770 during the reign of Frederick the Great. The interior decoration dates mainly from the time of King Frederick I. Kings Frederick William II and William III both used the lodge as a place to get away from court life. Baroque furniture, porcelain, hunting trophies, and hunting and animal illustrations from the 17th and 18th centuries fill the small rooms on the ground floor. The upper floor features paintings by German, Dutch, and Flemish masters—including works by Blomaert, Bruyn, Bol, Jordaens, Rubens, and Cranach the Elder. *(Hours daily 10:00 A.M.–5:00 P.M.; closed Monday; admission fee.)*

After visiting the hunting lodge you can stop for lunch or refreshments at the old Forsthaus Paulsborn, to the left of the lodge entrance, or at the Chalet Suisse, to your left on your way back to Clayallee.

To continue this tour, stroll down along the banks of the

Grunewald Lake. Paths on either side will take you to the adjoining *Hundekehlefenn nature preserve* and up to the Koenigsallee, which cuts across the elegant suburb of Grunewald and eventually connects with the Kurfürstendamm. You'll pass a chain of small lakes as you walk north out of the forest on Koenigsallee (an alternative is to catch the No. 19 bus, which runs along Koenigsallee to the Kurfürstendamm): To your left is *Dianasee* (Diana Lake) and *Koenigssee* (Kings Lake); to your right is *Herthasee,* beyond which lies *Hubertussee.* At the corner of Wallottstrasse and Koenigsallee is a *Memorial to Foreign Minister Walter Rathenau.* Rathenau, the only Jewish government minister during the short-lived Weimar Republic, was murdered here on June 24, 1922—one of the first overt acts of the Nazi terror which would soon overwhelm the entire nation. Continue up Koenigsallee. Another small lake, *Halensee,* is to your left. Just beyond is the beginning of the Kurfürstendamm, where the No. 19, 29, or 69 bus will take you back downtown.

WALK 8: Wannsee–Düppel Forest– *Pfaueninsel– *Volkspark Klein-Glienicke

See map on page 68.

This walk in the extreme southwest section of West Berlin offers glorious forest and lake scenery as well as an abundance of intriguing historical buildings, monuments, and landscaped gardens. Plan to devote the major portion of your time to an unhurried stroll through the lovely Pfaueninsel (Peacock Island). It's worth a special trip. The walk ends in one of Berlin's most beautifully landscaped waterside gardens.

To get to Wannsee and the starting point of this itinerary, take the S-Bahn from Bahnhof Zoo and get out at the *Wannsee station.* If you want to drive to Peacock Island, turn right off Kronprinzessinnenweg into Königstrasse; shortly before you get to *Volkspark Glienicke,* Nikolskoer Weg goes off to the right, taking you to a parking area near the ferry dock.

Before you reach Wannsee Station on the S-Bahn you'll pass clusters of vans and little houses inches away from the tracks, where Berliners with a few feet of grass and a tiny plot of soil indulge in their dreams of nature. These allotment communities are called *Schrebergärten* after the man (Schreber) who, back in the 19th century, came up with the idea of giving unused land to city people for cultivation. If you arrive at Wannsee on a weekend or holiday, you'll see all kinds of people heading out for an excursion, from grannies with canes and stout

68 Walk 8

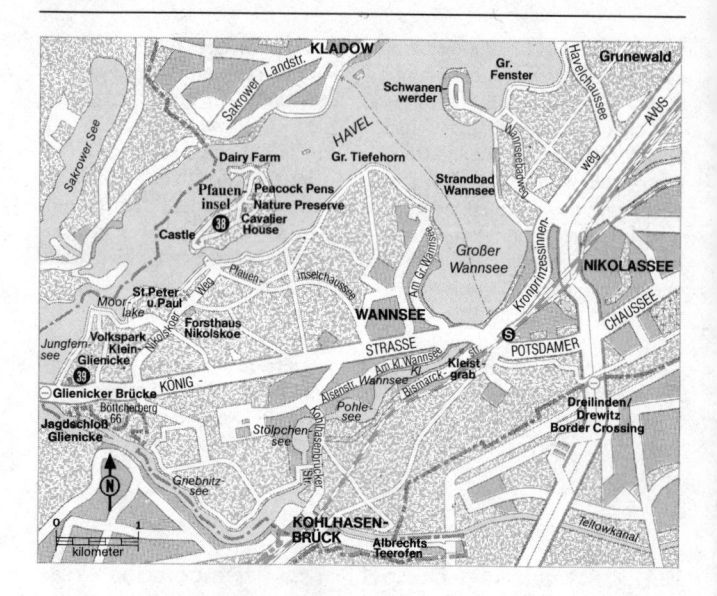

walking shoes to chic young women wearing miniskirts and jewelled sandals to beer-bellied men in shorts, all of them making off on foot or bicycle towards the lake. Since the opening of the Wall, people can easily go to Potsdam from here as well, either by bus or S-Bahn (see page 127).

Across the street from the station there is a hilltop park with a magnificent *view of the *Grosser Wannsee*, a 761-acre bay on the Havel with a chain of smaller lakes attached to it: *Kleiner Wannsee, Pohlesee, Stölpchensee,* and *Griebnitzsee*. Walk straight down the street in front of the station and you'll soon see the shimmering expanse of the Grosser Wannsee, usually full of sailboats, to your right. The tour boat esplanade and ticket office is located here. You can choose from a variety of boat rides across the lakes (some of which stop at Peacock Island). Farther off to your right you'll see *Wannsee Beach* (see page 64), where up to 30,000 Berliners stretch out and worship the sun on warm days.

If you only want to visit Peacock Island, catch the No. 66 bus across the street from Wannsee station, or the special *Ausfluglinie* (excursion bus) marked with a triangle. Both will take you to the ferry. If you want to walk around **Kleiner Wannsee** and the smaller lakes, there is a pleasant promenade, planted with willow trees and roses, that follows the shore of the Grosser Wannsee and winds around under a bridge to take you there. Literature lovers can pay tribute to the great German poet and playwright Heinrich von Kleist (1777–1811) by visiting his grave on the banks of the Kleiner Wannsee. A path just off Bismarckstrasse leads to the spot where the 33-year-old writer took his life in a strange suicide pact with a woman named Henriette Vogel, who was terminally ill (probably with cancer) and had begged her friend to put an end to her misery. A line from Kleist's *Der Prinz von Homburg* is inscribed on the red stone marker: "Now, oh immortality, you are wholly mine."

For a long scenic walk around the Grosser Wannsee and on to Peacock Island, stay on the top level of the promenade, cross the *Wannseebrücke*, and turn right on Am Grossen Wannsee. (A shorter and less scenic alternative to this is to walk or take the No. 66 bus down Königstrasse to Pfaueninselchaussee, where you can get out and walk through the Düppel Forest to the Peacock Island ferry.) Am Grossen Wannsee leads past small villas, apartment buildings, spas, private hospitals, and sailing clubs. Stay right at the next intersection. About 1.5 km. (1 mile) along you'll see an eccentric, turn-of-the-century brick villa with towers to your right; it is now used as a youth home. The villas on your left give you an idea of what life in this exclusive and very expensive area can be like. At No. 56/58, just before the Heckeshorn Hospital, you'll see a tall gate, usually guarded by soldiers. Half-hidden down a drive, and not open to the public, is the *Wannsee-Haus*, a villa that once belonged to the SS and where the infamous "Wannsee Conference" that determined the heinous "final solution" to the "Jewish question" was held in 1942. The villa is used occasionally for international conferences, and there are plans to turn it into a memorial to the victims of the Holocaust.

Slightly farther on is the *Haus Sans Souci* restaurant, with dining tables set up on a lawn overlooking the lake. To one side there's a snack stand where you can get a sausage and a drink and sit at a table above the lake, or you can go down to a lower level for lakeside table service. Directly across from you at this point is the sandy *Wannsee Beach*. In the center of the snack area is a copy of an enormous *stone lion* made by the Danish sculptor Hermann von Bissen in 1850 when the Danes conquered Schleswig-Holstein. When the Prussians conquered the same region in 1864, they brought the lion to Berlin, and eventually moved it here. The original was returned to the Danes by the Americans in 1945.

You can get down to the lakeside promenade here, or walk farther on past more villas to a blue pedestrian sign and a path leading off to the right. Follow this to a little sandy beach, turn left, and now you can simply enjoy a long scenic walk along the banks of the Havel. The quiet outskirts of the Düppel

Forest surround you. Cottonwoods line the shore, scenting the air in springtime, and frogs croak in the reeds. There are strollers and bicyclists and several small beaches where children play in the sand and paddle in the water. This path takes you to the dock where the ferry embarks for *Pfaueninsel* (Peacock Island) [38].

*Pfaueninsel

(The grounds are open daily to visitors from 8:00 A.M.–8:00 P.M. The ferry runs from 9:00 A.M.–5:00 P.M. in March and October; 8:00 A.M.–6:00 P.M. in April and September; 8:00 A.M.–8:00 P.M. from May through August, and 10:00 A.M.–4:00 P.M. from November through February.)

This justly popular and very beautiful excursion site mixes history and enjoyment in equal parts. Peacock Island, about 1,500 meters (1 mile) long and 500 meters (one-third of a mile) wide, is a protected nature preserve filled with charming echoes of Berlin's imperial past. In the 17th century the island was known as Kaninchenwerder (Rabbit Islet) because Frederick William, the Great Elector, bred rabbits on the western end of the island. The Great Elector presented the island to a famous alchemist named Joseph Kunckel in 1685 in hopes that he would be able to make gold here. A laboratory was built where Kunckel produced—instead of gold—a variation of ruby glass, then a much-treasured item. The alchemist eventually fell out of favor and was taken on by King Carl XI of Sweden. When Frederick William II bought the island from the Potsdam Orphanage in 1783, giant oak trees already filled most of the grounds and were then supplemented with several hundred more—many of these old trees still stand, contributing to the special character of the island today. Frederick William II, succumbing to the "world-weariness" that was popular at the time, wanted the island to be a kind of exotic fantasy world, evoking a place untouched by civilization. He camped out here under Middle-Eastern tents and had the court carpenter, Johann Gottlieb Brendel, construct a special palace in the style of a Roman ruin on the western end of the island for his mistress, Wilhelmine Encke, who later became the Countess von Lichtenau. The theatrically-minded king also had a dairy built in this "ruined" style, and imported the peacocks which gave the island its new name. After Frederick William II's death in 1797, the island passed to his penurious successor, Frederick William III, who often came to the palace with Queen Luise. Under Frederick William III, the grounds gradually evolved into the romantic landscape visitors see today. In 1822, Peter Joseph Lenné, the greatest garden architect in Germany, was called in to begin this transformation process. New paths were laid out, special gardens planted, and foreign trees were introduced to enrich the forms and add to the shades of foliage. At this time, too, the island developed into a private zoo, with enclosures built for apes, Chinese pigs, kangaroos, bears, llamas, and exotic birds. The entire menagerie was turned over to the public by Frederick William IV in 1841 and formed the basis for the first Berlin Zoological Gardens. The island itself, with its animal houses, was open to the public twice a week. Unlike so much of Berlin, Peacock Island, with its small palace, marvelous grounds, and curious assortment of buildings, suffered little damage in World War II. This makes it one of the few "authentic" historical environments in all of Berlin, and it has been placed on UNESCO's cultural heritage list.

Begin your tour of Peacock Island at the startlingly white **Palace** (*hours Tuesday–Sunday, 10:00 A.M.–5:00 P.M.; closed Mondays and from 1 November through 31 March; admission fee*), built between 1794 and 1797 in the form of a ruined Roman villa. The façade and bridge connecting the two towers were originally made of wood and later replaced by concrete and wrought iron. A painted vista in the recess of the western façade presents a "view" of a medieval castle gateway and portcullis opening up into the countryside. The well-preserved palace interior provides an intriguing glimpse into the tastes of the late 18th century, when Frederick William II enjoyed rural retreats here with his mistress, Countess von Lichtenau. The *"Otaheite Cabinet"* (Tahitian Room) is particularly interesting. This is where the King, eager to escape the artificiality of European civilization, had murals painted to mimic the interior of a bamboo hut.

Peacocks still strut freely about the island, filling the air with their strident cries. You might encounter one or two in the charming *Biedermeier Garden* to one side of the palace. On the waterfront north of the palace, is the former *kitchen,* built of brick in 1794–1795. Take the path leading south behind the palace and bear left to find the *Rose Garden,* where Frederick III had 5,000 roses planted in 1821. The path leading back north offers views of the palace, the Havel and, across a large meadow, the *dairy.* The path veers to the east and passes the *Jacob Well* on the left, designed by Brendel, the original architect of

Castle on Peacock Island

the palace; the ruins of the Temple of the Sun in Rome served as his model.

At this point you meet up with the main northeasterly path leading into the grove; if you follow a bend in the path the impressive *Cavalier House* soon comes into view. The façade of a late Gothic house in Danzig, purchased by the Crown Prince in 1823, was removed and placed on the front of a building constructed here in 1804. After a short walk on the main path through the woods, you will arrive at the low-lying *spawning meadow*. You can get to the picturesque **dairy** to the north by following the bend in the main path. This curious late-18th-century building, resembling a small Gothic church, helped add to the theatrical fantasy of living a simple country life. Frederick II and his Countess could sip milk in a small dairy parlor on the ground floor. The nearby *cow stall,* built in 1802, is also in Gothic style.

From the dairy, the path follows the waterfront and crosses back over the spawning ditch. In the distance, set against a forest backdrop, you can see the somber **Memorial Temple for Queen Luise.** Schinkel designed its sandstone façade in 1810, basing it on a drawing made by Frederick William III. It actually formed the original front of Queen Luise's mausoleum in the grounds of Charlottenburg Palace (see page 53), and was moved here when a new granite façade was added at Charlottenburg. There is a plaster cast of a marble bust of Luise by Christian Daniel Rauch in the open hall. Continue down the lakeside path. Johann Kunckel's laboratory was built in a glade here in 1685. A Gothic iron bridge crosses over to a small island. A restored bridge farther on leads to a fork in the path that takes you to the *aviary,* part of the original menagerie installed on the island by Frederick William III. Following the lakeside path, which now goes back south, you will pass the thatch-roofed *Winter House for Migratory Birds,* built in 1828. To your left, you can see the *Steam Engine House* which pumped irrigation water to the highest point on the island. There is a cast-iron fountain on top of the hill.

Follow the upper path along the bank past a wooden, cube-shaped structure built in 1819 and known as *The Slide.* The path will take you back to the Rose Garden and down to the ferry. The covered dock you can see from the water is called the *Frigate Shed.* It was built in 1833 to house a miniature frigate presented to Frederick William III by the King of England.

Before pressing on, you may wish to have an alfresco lunch or a beer at the *Wirtshaus zur Pfaueninsel.*

*

If you're ready to return to the city, you can catch the special *Ausfluglinie* (excursion bus) or the No. 66 bus back to the Wannsee S-Bahn station; if you don't feel like walking there, the excursion bus will carry you on to Nikolskoe.

Walkers simply follow the waterside path.

Perched high above the Havel, **Nikolskoe** presents one of the loveliest panoramas in Berlin. The first authentically Russian *Blockhaus* (Log Building) was built here in 1819 by Frederick William III for his daughter, Charlotte, the future Russian Czarina (wife of Czar Nicholas I), at a time when the alliance between Prussia and Russia was cemented by marriage. The original blockhouse eventually burned down and was replaced by the present facsimile, which is now a popular country restaurant with a magnificent dining terrace overlooking the Havel. Down a short path you'll find the lovely **Church of Saints Peter and Paul,** completed in 1837. In front of the church, which is built of a light-colored brick with a high porch and green-colored onion dome, there is a *viewpoint looking out over the Havel to Spandau. The taped *Glockenspiel* (carillon) plays hourly between Easter and Ascension Day from 10:00 A.M.– 9:00 P.M.

Hardy walkers can carry on by foot from Nikolskoe to reach the final destination of this itinerary, *Volkspark Klein-Glienicke;* if you take the excursion bus, get out at Königstrasse, where you'll find the entrance gates to **Schloss Klein-Glienicke** [39].

The gates of this lovely villa are guarded by two gilded griffins and wide gravel paths lead into the beautifully landscaped grounds of the *Volkspark Klein-Glienicke.* Near the entrance, set back from a fountain with water spewing from the mouths of gilded lions, is the villa itself (not open to the public). Originally a manor house, it was converted in 1826–1828 by the architect Schinkel into an Italian-style summer residence for Prince Karl, the son of Queen Luise (and brother of Frederick William III). Fragments of antique sculpture and architectural remnants collected by the Prince on a trip to Italy are incorporated into the walls of the buildings. Peter Joseph Lenné, the landscape architect responsible for the renovation of the Peacock Island grounds, also designed the 222-acre Volkspark, which was laid out at the beginning of the 19th century. Today, giant sprinklers keep the lawns emerald green, and gardeners are busy everywhere, clipping and tending flower beds and shrubbery. Roam around here for a look at the curious assortment of buildings, especially the *casino,* with its inset fragments of sculpture and colonnade looking out over the Havel, and Schinkel's remarkable *Great Curiosity,* a circular observation terrace built so that Prince Karl and his guests could watch traffic go by on the great road to Potsdam. From here you can see the *Glienicker Brücke,* the middle of which served as the border between East and West Berlin and the site of various prisoner exchanges between the two countries (U-2 pilot Gary Powers and Soviet-Jewish human rights activist Anatoly Shcharansky among them). In a park on the opposite side of Königstrasse is the *Jagd-*

schloss Glienicke (Glienicke Hunting Lodge, not open to the public), first used in the 17th century by the Great Elector and rebuilt in 1854 in the French-Baroque style for Prince Karl. Conferences and conventions are now held there.

From here, the No. 6 bus on Königstrasse, or the special excursion bus, will return you to the Wannsee station S-Bahn.

WALK 9: Freie Universität–Dahlem-Dorf– ***Museen Dahlem–*Botanischer Garten

See map opposite.

Dahlem is one of Berlin's handsomest districts, and this walk will provide you with a well-rounded introduction to it. Plan to devote the major portion of your time to the fabulous Dahlem Museum complex, where seven superb collections are currently housed in beautifully designed quarters. The Painting Gallery alone is worth a special trip. The walk ends in Berlin's renowned botanical gardens.

The tour begins at the *Oskar-Helene-Heim U-Bahn station*. Cross Clayallee and take Garystrasse, just to your right, into Dahlem. There's a park to your left, and the area is filled with detached houses and apartment buildings. The walk will eventually lead to *Dahlem-Dorf*, the old village of Dahlem with its historic buildings. The area around here has a pleasant suburban quality, and provides you with a glimpse of Berlin life outside the downtown area.

Continue down Garystrasse past a charming square planted with birch trees. Close by, on your left, are the buildings of the **Freie Universität** [40].

Founded in 1948, after the division of the city, as an alternative to the increasingly politicized Humboldt University in the Eastern Sector, the Free University has a student body numbering about 60,000 (all of them pursuing graduate studies—Germans receive their "liberal arts" education in high school). Its buildings, many of them former mansions, are scattered throughout the quiet streets of the Dahlem district. Funds from America's Ford Foundation helped to get the Free University started.

It was here at the Free University that the "student revolution" began in the late 1960s. Praised by many as the first step in a cleansing process that restructured German society, denounced by others as the first step down the road to anarchy, or worse yet, the cradle of the terrorism that swept the nation in the decades that followed—the truth lies somewhere between. For all the anarchy and chaos it produced, the student movement of the Sixties established the right of all Germans to question and protest the philosophies and actions of all forms of authority, a right that had been denied them in the past.

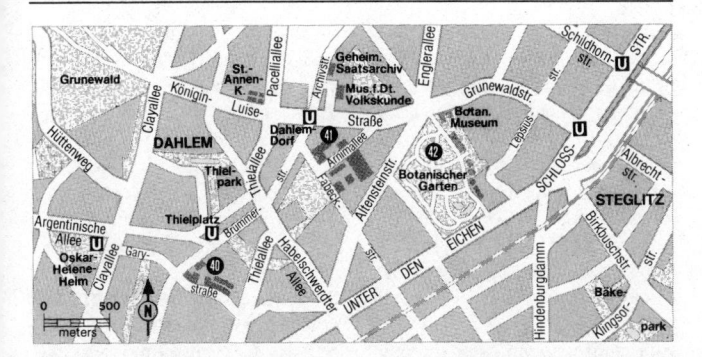

After you cross Ihnestrasse, you'll see the university library on your left, with the university's main building, the *Henry-Ford-Bau* (Henry Ford Building) attached to it. The two buildings, constructed between 1950 and 1954 with funds from the Ford Foundation, were the Free University's first modern buildings. The *Archiv zur Geschichte der Max-Planck-Gesellschaft* (Max Planck Society Historical Archives) is in a large, elegant villa surrounded by a white picket fence across from these buildings. Max Planck and Albert Einstein were among the many physicists who worked in a Dahlem-based research institute in the years of the Weimar Republic. Ultimately, they both won Nobel Prizes.

Continue on Garystrasse past more garden villas, all housing various Free University institutes. You may want to wander down one or two of the side streets here to gain a better impression of life in Dahlem.

Turn left at Thielallee. The large cream-colored building at No. 63 on your left, with a turreted roof that looks like a Prussian soldier's helmet, is the *Otto-Hahn-Bau,* the old chemistry institute where Otto Hahn and his colleagues, Fritz Strassman and Lise Meitner, ushered in the atomic age with trail-blazing work which led to the splitting of the first uranium atom in 1938. Just beyond this, you'll pass a pleasant leafy park. All the villas around here are part of the Free University.

At Habelschwerdter Allee you'll see the student *Mensa* or dining hall. It's a good idea to cross the street here and catch the No. 1 bus to the U-Bahn Dahlem-Dorf station (2 stops). You can also walk to the next point of the tour by following Thielallee to Königin-Luise-Strasse and turning right.

Dahlem-Dorf

The history of Dahlem Village stretches back some 750 years, and a few restored buildings in the area around the thatch-roofed *Dahlem-Dorf U-Bahn station* still give us some idea of the rural character that once prevailed here. From the U-Bahn station, cross the street and walk left, back down Königin-Luise-Strasse. The small *manor house* across from the subway station, built in 1679, is headquarters for the Freunde der Domäne Dahlem (Friends of the Dahlem Domain), a group that helps preserve some of the village's old character. A few yards to your right you can enter the cobbled area of the **Domäne Dahlem Landgut und Museum** (Dahlem Country Estate and Museum) where there's a farm yard, a stable, and a small museum. Outdoor craft fairs are sometimes set up here on weekends. *(Hours Daily except Tuesday 10:00 A.M.–6:00 P.M.)* Across the street is the historic *Alter Krug* inn, a lovely garden restaurant. Continue down Königin-Luise-Strasse, passing garden stores, to Pacelli-Allee, where you cross to enter the grounds of the beautifully reconstructed 14th-century **St.-Annen-Kirche** (St. Anne's Church). The tidy, flower-filled churchyard of this medieval brick-and-stone gem, one of the oldest churches in Berlin, is a gardener's paradise. The historian Friedrich Meinecke (1862–1954), first Rector of the Free University, is buried here, as is the animal sculptor August Gaul (1869–1921) and a number of important German actors.

Now head back to the U-Bahn station. If you're in the mood for casual dining, the *Luise,* a half block away at Königin-Luise-Strasse 40, provides a large outdoor dining area. Try this place if you have children with you. There's a flock of hungry, fearless, and charming sparrows that will come to your outdoor table at the slightest hint of a free crumb.

If you cross Königin-Luise-Strasse and turn left on a street called Im Winkel, you'll come to the interesting **Museum für Deutsche Völkerkunde** (Museum of German Ethnology), devoted to the popular culture of German-speaking Central Europe from the 16th century to the present day. On view in this new museum (opened in 1976) are objects unknown to our high-tech age but in everyday use during the pre- and early industrial era. Period furniture and folk costumes supplement the collection of household implements. *(Hours Tuesday–Saturday 9:00 A.M.–5:00 P.M.; closed Monday; admission free.)*

Im Winkel leads to Archivstrasse where the sinister-sounding *Geheimes Staatsarchiv Preussischer Kulturbesitz* (Secret Prussian State Cultural Heritage Archive) is housed at No. 12. With its collection of historical documents, certificates, files, records, and autographs, this museum no doubt contains fascinating insights into eight centuries of Prussian official life. (Reading room hours: Monday, Wednesday, Thursday, Friday 8:00 A.M.–3:30 P.M.; Tuesday 8:00 A.M.–7:30 P.M.)

Return to Königin-Luise-Strasse, cross the street, and continue on to Takustrasse, where you'll turn right, and right again on Lansstrasse to reach the Dahlem Museums [41].

***Museen Dahlem

(Hours Tuesday–Friday 9:00 A.M.–5:00 P.M.; Saturday and Sunday 10:00 A.M.–5:00 P.M.; admission free.)

Even in its current state of reorganization, there are enough treasures in this complex of museums to keep serious art lovers busy for a week, so it might be a good idea to decide in advance what you most want to see and allocate your time accordingly. Illustrated information sheets, available for 10 pfennigs in every section of the Dahlem Museums, help to highlight those works of special merit or interest, and taped tours are also available. The museums in Dahlem formerly belonged to the Prussian state and are administered today by the Stiftung Preussischer Kulturbesitz (Prussian Cultural Heritage Foundation), which is now in the process of amalgamating the separate collections in East and West Berlin. Seven collections of world importance form the basis of the museum complex at Dahlem, although these will be changing in the near future: the ***Gemäldegalerie (Painting Gallery), the **Skulpturengalerie mit Frühchristlich-Byzantischer Sammlung* (Sculpture Gallery with Early Christian and Byzantine Collection), the ***Kupferstichkabinett* (Department of Prints and Drawings), the *Museum für Indische Kunst* (Museum of East Indian Art), the *Museum für Islamische Kunst* (Museum of Islamic Art), the *Museum für Ostasiatische Kunst* (Museum of Far Eastern Art), and the **Museum für Völkerkunde* (Ethnological Museum).

Bear in mind that sometime in 1991 the justly famous Painting Gallery and Sculpture Collection will be moved to a new building in the Kulturforum (see page 44). As part of the new planning scheme, Dahlem will receive the holdings of the Ethnological Museum, and the museums of Indian and Far Eastern art now held in East Berlin, as well as some 45,000 objects from the Ethnological Museum in Leipzig. The description of the Dahlem collections below was correct at presstime, but changes are expected to occur throughout 1991.

If your time is limited, you would do well to start in the *****Gemäldegalerie** (Painting Gallery), where first class works from nearly every major European school up to 1800 are represented. The emphasis here is on Italian, medieval German and Dutch art, as well as 17th-century Dutch painting. Among the Italian works (Rooms 109a to 112) are several masterpieces, including Raphael's *Virgin and Child with the Infant St. John* (1505), Bronzino's *Portrait of Ugolino Martelli* (1540), Veronese's *Dead Christ*, Titian's *Venus and the Organ Player* and *Girl With a Platter of Fruit* (c. 1555), Tintoretto's *Virgin and Child* (c.

1570–1575), Giorgione's *Portrait of a Young Man* (1505–1506), and Correggio's *Leda and the Swan* (c. 1531–1532). You'll also see important works by Giotto, Mantegna, Botticelli, and several *Venetian scenes* by Tiepolo and Canaletto. Among the Early Netherlands Paintings (Rooms 143 to 150), look for Jan van Eyck's *Portrait of Giovanni Arnolfini* (c. 1440), Rogier van der Weyden's *Portrait of a Woman with a White Headdress* (c. 1435) and *Middelburg Altarpiece* (c. 1445), Jan Gossaert's *Portrait of a Nobleman* (c. 1530), Hieronymus Bosch's *St. John on Patmos* (c. 1490), and Pieter Brueghel the Elder's *The Netherlands Proverbs* (1559). One of the largest **Rembrandt* collections in the world is on display in the Dutch section, and includes self-portraits and portraits of the artist's wife Saskia. The authenticity of the world-renowned *Man with a Golden Helmet*, formerly attributed to Rembrandt, has lately been the subject of much discussion. The painting—worth looking at no matter who the artist (or artists)—is now tagged as a work from "Rembrandt's Circle." In addition to all these riches there are works by Albrecht Dürer, Albrecht Altdorfer, Lucas Cranach the Elder (*Fountain of Youth*), and Hans Holbein. If you're ready for more, continue on to the collection of French masters, where you can gaze at works by Nicolas Poussin, Claude Lorrain, and *Watteau. And don't forget the Spanish school with El Greco's *Mater Do-

"Man with the Golden Helmet"

lorosa*, and works by Goya and Velázquez.

Located in rooms next to the Painting Gallery, the **Skulpturengalerie mit Frühchristlich-Byzantischer Sammlung** (Sculpture Gallery) is divided into four large departments. The works here were originally part of the "Kunstkammer" (Chamber of Art) brought together by the Great Elector, and thus formed the original nucleus for what grew to become the vast collections of the Berlin Museums. A superb group of *ivories can be found in the Early Christian and Byzantine collection on the ground floor, with works dating from the 4th to the 6th centuries. One particularly noteworthy piece is the mid-6th-century *diptych of Christ and Mary,* executed in Constantinople. Outstanding among the pieces in the Early and High Middle Ages collection are the *Christ and St. John* group from 1320, the 15th-century *Mother of God* from Dangolsheim, and the *Madonna of the Protective Cloak,* which dates from about 1480. Be sure to visit what is popularly called the *Riemenschneider Room*, containing *figures from the Munnerstadt Altar* carved by Tilman Riemenschneider in 1490–1491. Works from the Renaissance, Baroque, and Rococo periods are also located here. The Italian collection on the upper floor has a *Madonna* by Presbyter Martinus (1199), a *marble relief by Donatello*, the famous *Pazzi Madonna*, and Antonio Canova's *Dancer*, dating from 1809–1812.

The **Küpferstichkabinett** (Department of Prints and Drawings) houses one of the greatest collections of graphic art in Europe. It includes about 25,000 masterpieces of drawing executed prior to 1800, illuminated manuscripts from the 10th to the 16th centuries, artists' sketchbooks, illustrated books from the 15th to 20th centuries, and an estimated 380,000 prints. By 1992 the entire Department will be moved to new premises in the Kulturforum (see page 44)—which is good news for the collection, of course, but not so good for visitors with a hankering to see this magnificent collection now. Because the Department is preparing to move, they have undertaken extensive preservation procedures. This, and a simple lack of space, have necessitated the closing of most of the former exhibition rooms. Successive exhibitions, showing selected works from the collection, are now located in a gallery next to the study room.

The *Museum für Völkerkunde (Ethnological Museum) at Dahlem is the largest museum in West Berlin and one of the leading museums of its kind in all of Europe. Its several sections include a wide range of collections—all of them displayed for maximum dramatic impact—from the pre-Columbian cultures of *Central and South America* (ceramics, stone sculptures, textiles, and the *Gold Room*), Oceania and Australia (cult objects, boats, costumes), the *Far East* (Tang ceramics, Chinese oracle bones), *South Asia* (shadow-play and marionette figures from India, Thailand, Java, and Bali, ritual sculptures, textiles, jewelry, and weapons), and *Africa* (terracottas, bronzes, masks, and sculptures). A special *Children's Museum* provides children and teenagers with information on non-European cultures, and a *Museum for the Blind* has special exhibitions with captions and catalogs in Braille and pieces from the museum's collections that can be felt. There's also a bank of headphones set up to let you hear authentic "Musik der Völker" (Folk Music), recordings from the Archives of the Department of Ethnomusicology that represent various musical traditions of the world.

Opened in 1971, the **Museum für Indische Kunst** (Museum of East Indian Art) contains the most important collection of Indian art in Germany. The three exhibition spaces—devoted to the *Indian collection*, the *Turfan Collection from Central Asia*, and *Indonesian art*—are filled with beautifully crafted bronzes, carvings, paintings, and fabrics spanning a period of almost four thousand years. The special attractions here are the unique 6th- to 10th-century *frescoes, the finest of their kind, depicting the life of Buddha, and Buddhist stone reliefs and sculptures from the 1st century A.D.

The **Museum für Islamische Kunst** (Museum of Islamic Art), opened in 1969, features splendid examples of Muslim art from India to Spain. Highlights include pre-Islamic art from Yemen, a prayer-niche with calligraphic friezes from a 16th-century Persian mosque, tile panels from the Mongol palace in Northern Iran, a 14th-century wooden cupola from the Alhambra, and a marvelous ceiling fresco from mid-19th-century Persia. In addition, there are carpets, exquisite miniatures, and religious objects made of glass, metal, gold, silver, ivory, and paper.

Established in 1906, the **Museum für Ostasiatische Kunst** (Museum of Far Eastern Art) moved its varied collections to Dahlem in 1970. Works on view, exhibited chronologically, date from the 3rd century B.C. to the present day and represent the cultures of *China, Mongolia, Korea,* and *Japan.* The renowned collection of Japanese and Chinese painting, calligraphy, and woodblock printing is especially interesting, but there are also exquisite objects crafted from stone, bronze, wood, ivory, lacquer, ceramics, and porcelain.

Once you've finished feasting your eyes on the treasures of the Dahlem Museums, head back to Königin-Luise-Strasse, turn right, and walk the short distance to Altensteinstrasse where you'll see the brick entrance gates to the Botanical Garden [42].

*Botanischer Garten

(Open daily March 9:00 A.M.– 5:00 P.M., April 9:00 A.M.–7:00 P.M., May–August 9:00 A.M.– 8:00 P.M., September 9:00 A.M.– 7:00 P.M., October 9:00 A.M.– 5:00 P.M., November–February 9:00 A.M.– 4:00 P.M., admission fee.)

On no account should plant lovers miss the 104-acre Botanical Gardens, one of the most extensive in Europe. It was founded in 1679 and laid out here in Dahlem between 1897 and 1903. Over 18,000 plant and tree species fill the beautifully landscaped grounds. To your left, immediately upon entering, stands the *Botanical Museum.* It contains interesting dioramas of various plant regions in Germany, displays on the history and use of plants, and exhibitions of fossil plant and rock specimens. If this is a little too specialized for you, you can skip the museum and wander instead down the main path to the *Schaugewächshäuser* (Greenhouse Displays). A left here takes you to the prickly world of the *Cactus House.* The central portion of the building features aquatic plants in aquariums. Climb the stairs to reach the steamy *Grosses Tropenhaus* (Large Tropical House), where a dense jungle of tropical foliage flourishes in the humid air. To your left as you step back outside you'll see the turn-of-the-century *Victoria-Regina-Haus* (Queen Victoria House) rising up like a glass cathedral, where exotic swamp and water plants are cultivated. Something is always blooming in the *Orchid House,* with its 120 varieties of orchids. The *Palm House* is also worth a visit. But if the day is beautiful, you may simply want to stroll through the marvelous *Freigelände* (open-air gardens) and enjoy the overall picture. Flora from various temperate zones of the earth are planted and marked along winding fragrant paths filled with the singing of birds. There are any number of walks you can take here, but the main path in front of the glass palace will lead you to a café and snack stand at the garden's opposite entrance on Unter den Eichen.

If you leave by the gate on Unter den Eichen, you also leave Dahlem and enter the district of Steglitz. The No. 48 bus across the street will take you back into the city as far as the Kulturforum (see page 44). To catch the S-Bahn, cross the street and walk to your right to *Asternplatz,* turn left down Enzianstrasse, and you'll come to Botanischer Garten station.

WALK 10: Schöneberg– Tempelhof–Neukölln

See map on page 82.

In the first nine tours of this guide we covered all the major "must-see" sights in West Berlin. The following three tours strike out a bit farther afield to show you some of those out-of-the-way places that will add to your understanding and appreciation of this vast, fascinating, and ever-changing city. Since the route covers a fair distance, having a car will substantially cut down the time it takes to get from one point to the next, but we've included instructions to make it easy for you to follow the route via bus and subway. This itinerary covers the districts of Schöneberg and Neukölln, and includes stops at places as historically diverse as the Schöneberg City Hall, where John F. Kennedy delivered his "Ich bin ein Berliner" speech, Tempelhof Airport, scene of the Berlin Airlift, and an 18th-century Bohemian "village" in the heart of the Neukölln district.

There are two possible starting points for this itinerary. For the first, take the U-Bahn to the Kurfürstenstrasse station. The station is in the middle of Potsdamer Strasse, which is a study in contrasts. Here you're likely to find antique shops and artists' studios cheek-by-jowl with inexpensive ethnic snack bars and some of the more sleazy establishments that form a part of every major city. The proximity of the infamous Wall made this street a kind of symbol of this town's feistiness; it's residents made sure their voices were heard loud and clear on the other side during times of stress. To the north, Potsdamer Strasse leads directly to the *National Gallery,* the *State Library,* and the *Philharmonic Hall* (see Walk 3). To the south, as it heads through downtown Schöneberg to the Friedenau section, it becomes Hauptstrasse, filled with exclusive 19th-century villas, and then Rheinstrasse.

Friedenau, founded in 1871 as a suitably countrified roost for rich Prussian officials and retirees, remains a peaceful neighborhood, where the mansions, gardens, and leafy squares serve as reminders of its genteel past. If you have a car, you might want to drive south on Hauptstrasse to explore these streets.

Kurfürstenstrasse forms the southern border between the Schöneberg and Tiergarten districts. Schöneberg was once an independent municipality—its origins date back to the 13th century—and it grew in importance over the years because it was on the major route between Berlin and Potsdam. More recently, it has been the administrative and political center of West Berlin.

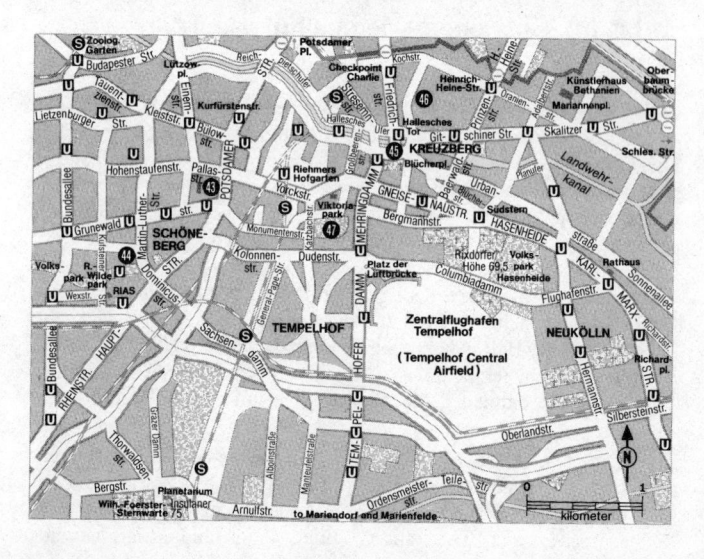

If you're taking public transportation, start your itinerary by taking the U-Bahn to the Kleistpark station. If you began at the Kurfürstenstrasse U-Bahn, walk down busy Potsdamer Strasse until you come to **Kleistpark** [43] on your right.

If you've followed any or all of the previous itineraries, you'll be acquainted with some of the historical figures and events that crop up again in this route. The park itself provides a cool, shady haven from the summer heat, but it isn't particularly distinctive. However, it was once rather important. From the late 17th century through the early 19th century, it served as the royal vegetable garden, and then became the city's first botanical gardens. The botanical gardens were moved from here to Dahlem (see Walk 9, page 80) in 1897. At that point the park was renamed Kleistpark after the great author Heinrich von Kleist (1777–1811) (see Walk 8, page 69). At the main entrance to the park stands the *Königskolonnaden* (King's Colonnade), designed in 1780 by Carl von Gontard; the colonnade originally stood on the Königsbrucke (at Alexanderplatz in today's East Berlin) and was moved here in 1910. Walk back through the park to the huge, dour, gray building behind it, the former *Kammergericht* (Supreme Court of Justice), built in 1913, which fronts on Elssholzstrasse. You're looking at a chilling piece of Berlin's past. This was the site of the monstrous Nazi "Volksgerichtshof," the so-called "People's Court" where show trials presided over by a judge named Roland Freisler resulted in literally hundreds of executions and deportations, including the death sentences of several people involved in the plot to kill Hitler (see Walk 3, page 47). Freisler's depravity extended to having secret movies made of his trials, in which he made a mockery of every imaginable rule of law. After the war, between 1945 and 1948, meetings of the Allied Control Council were held in this building (which then became known as the *Kontrollratsgebäude*), and in 1971 the Four Power Agreement was signed here. Eighteen years later, on December 11, 1989, the Allies met here again to discuss the quickly changing events in Berlin. The 540-room building is mostly empty today, although the Allied Air-Traffic Control Center is now headquartered on the ground floor.

If you're exploring this area on a weekend morning, be sure to check out the very popular, trendy atmosphere around the *Winterfeldplatz market.* To get there, walk one block to the north on Elssholzstrasse to Pallas-Strasse, where you turn left. One block farther on you'll see the action around Winterfeldplatz. It's not just the market that makes the place hum on Saturday and Sunday mornings. It's also the action in the surrounding cafés. So find a seat, order a coffee, and sit back to enjoy some good people-watching.

From the Kammergericht, if you're on foot or in a car, you can follow Elssholzstrasse back to Grunewald Strasse, where you turn right and continue for five blocks to Martin-Luther-Strasse.

Schöneberg City Hall

Turn left and follow the street a few blocks more to reach the *Rathaus Schöneberg*. It's also possible to hop into the U-Bahn at Kleistpark, take it two stops to *Bayerischer Platz*, and transfer there to the *Innsbrucker Platz* train: one more stop and you'll be at the political center of Berlin, the **Rathaus Schöneberg** [44].

The impressive Schöneberg City Hall was built between 1911 and 1914 to house the town's municipal administration. When Schöneberg was incorporated into Greater Berlin in 1920 along with several other autonomous towns, the Rathaus continued to function as headquarters for the district authorities. When Berlin was divided in 1948, the building became the seat of the West Berlin Parliament *(Abgeordnetenhaus)* and the Senate, as well as the official headquarters of West Berlin's governing mayor and the mayor of the district. Every day at noon the *Freedom Bell* (Freiheitsglocke) rings out from the 70-meter- (213-foot-) high bell tower. A postwar gift from the United States, the bell was presented to the Berliners by General Clay in 1950 and bears an inscription paraphrasing Abraham Lincoln's Gettysburg Address: "That this world, under God, shall have a new birth of freedom"—words prophetically well-suited to the re-unifying Germanys and to Berlin in particular. A bronze plaque to the left of the entrance commemorates President John F. Kennedy's stirring "Ich bin ein Berliner" speech, which he delivered to hundreds of thousands of Berliners on June 26, 1963, from the front of the Rathaus. The square in front of the Rathaus is named after Kennedy. The Silesian sandstone façade of the building, sandblasted for the city's 750th birthday celebration, now gleams as white as it did when new. If you're hungry or want to take a break, there's a good Ratskeller with an outdoor terrace on the left side of the building. The Ratskeller is a delightful institution you will find in many cities in the German-speaking part of Europe. Always located in a lower floor or cellar of a city hall, its official function is to serve as a place for the city fathers to hold receptions and other social events. In actual fact, however, it is always a restaurant featuring the region's typical foods and beverages.

Behind the Rathaus we find the expanse of Schöneberg's handsomest park, *Rudolph-Wilde-Park* (which becomes the *Volkspark* as it extends westward), with its statue of the *Goldener Hirsch* (Golden Stag), the animal used on

Schöneberg's coat of arms. On the park's southern edge, at Kufsteiner Strasse 69, *RIAS* (Radio in the American Sector—also a television station) has been broadcasting since 1946. Supported but not controlled by the U.S. government, it has served for many years as a source of all kinds of music as well as unbiased western-style news reporting, which once represented a lifeline to the truth for the eastern part of the city.

Stargazers may want to take a detour from here to visit Berlin's planetarium and observatory in Steglitz, but the detour is a rather complicated one unless you're in a car. Drivers take Hauptstrasse southbound and turn left down Saarstrasse. Just beyond Knausstrasse, the street becomes Thorwaldsenstrasse, which ends at the *Insulaner*, a 75-meter- (250-foot-) high hill made of war rubble, just beyond Prellerweg on Münsterdamm. You'll see the distinctive domes of the planetarium and observatory on your left, and there are parking facilities in front. This is too great a distance to walk comfortably, but you can catch the No. 87 bus at Innsbrucker Platz, and it will drop you directly in front of the planetarium on Münster Damm.

The **Wilhelm-Foerster-Sternwarte** (Observatory), on the summit of the Insulaner, is the largest public observatory in Germany. Lectures and viewings are offered daily at 8:00 P.M. (except Monday and Wednesday) and, from May through the summer, at 6:00 P.M. and 9:00 P.M. as well; on Sundays, on the hour from 3:00 to 6:00 P.M., and again at 8:00 P.M. At the foot of the Insulaner is the aluminum-domed *Zeiss-Planetarium,* named for the famous Zeiss projector which simulates the entire star-filled sky. There are also lectures on new sightings and developments in astronomy, and space films. *(Planetarium guided tours: Daily except Monday at 8:00 P.M., Tuesdays and Thursdays 6:00 P.M. and 8:00 P.M., Sundays 5:00 P.M. and 8:00 P.M. Admission fee for both. Call 79-00-93-0 for information.)*

Unless you're up for a very long walk, the simplest way to reach the next destination in this itinerary from Kleistpark is to catch the No. 4 bus going south on Dominicusstrasse. The bus turns up Hauptstrasse, makes a right on Kolonnenstrasse, and then continues down Dudenstrasse, which forms the boundary between the *Kreuzberg* district to the north, and *Tempelhof* to the south. Get off the bus at *Platz der Luftbrücke.*

Tempelhof

Although most visitors to Berlin associate Tempelhof with its famous airport, the history of this former farming village dates back to the 13th century, when it was founded by the Order of Knights Templar. Frederick William I created an area known as the *Tempelhofer Feld* (Tempelhof Field) in 1772 for use as a military training and parade ground. Tempelhof, along with Marienfelde, Mariendorf, and Lichtenrade to the south, was incorporated into Berlin in 1920 as the city's 13th district. From the late 19th century and up until 1975, when commercial flights were moved to a new airport at Tegel, the Tempelhof district with its famous airfield was at the very center of German aeronautical history.

The Allied airmen involved in the dramatic Berlin Air Lift are commemorated by the *Air Lift Memorial* located in the park known as the *Platz der Luftbrücke* (Air Lift Square). Designed by Eduard Ludwig and unveiled in 1951, the concrete sculpture curves upward to three extensions which symbolize the three Allied air corridors over East Germany that allowed the airlift to take place. Tempelhof Airport, in the American sector, was the center of the action during the Soviet Union's 1948–1949 blockade of the city. On "Operation Vittles," up to 1,300 planes—most of them four-engined DC 54 "raisin bombers"—landed here every day, bringing food and other basic provisions to the citizens of Berlin. Another, unofficial airlift, called "Operation Little Vittles" brought candy bars to the city's kids. The seventy Allied airmen killed during this monumental operation are remembered on the bronze plaque at the base of the memorial. One of the old "raisin bombers" is on display at *Gate 5* of the airfield.

To the east of Platz der Luftbrücke you find the buildings and airfield of the **Zentralflughafen Tempelhof.**

Frederick William I's imperial parade grounds were made into a base for the Kaiser's new air transportation unit in the late 19th century. The artist Arnold Böcklin, whose painting, *Island of the Dead,* now hangs in the National Gallery, was one of the many would-be pilots who made unsuccessful attempts at flight from Tempelhof. It wasn't until 1908, however, when pioneer American aviator Orville Wright staged an amazing 19-minute air show over the field, that "flying machines" became a part of Tempelhof's history. By 1920, even though the planes were taking off from and landing on a grass strip, Berlin-Tempelhof was considered the most modern airport in Europe. By 1938 it was serving more air traffic than Paris, Amsterdam, and London. *Deutsche Luft Hansa,* the forerunner of today's *Lufthansa* airlines, was founded at Tempelhof in 1926. The airfield terminal buildings that were constructed between 1934 and 1939 continued to serve the airport until 1975, when Berlin's air traffic was moved to new facilities at Tegel-Süd. At this time Tempelhof became primarily an American military airfield. But some indefinable remnant of the airport's old excitement and glamour lingers on even today. For years, the terminal buildings stood empty and the airport was kept on the alert in case of an emergency at Tegel. With the

CENTRAL BERLIN

Berlin's most famous landmark, the Emperor William Memorial Church, was built in the late 19th century.

The Bahnhof Zoo train station serves as the hub of Berlin's transportation.

Breitscheidplatz, off the Kurfürstendamm, is a gathering spot for impromptu concerts and celebrations of all kinds.

The Porcelain Cabinet in Schloss Charlottenburg.

The magnificent neoclassical Deutsche Staatsoper is home to one of the world's finest opera companies.

The Siegessäule, a Berlin landmark, was built in the late 19th century to commemorate Prussian victories.

With the dismantling of the Berlin Wall, East and West met freely as the city reunified.

At midnight on January 1, 1990, East and West Berliners rang in a new era atop the Berlin Wall in front of the Brandenburg Gate.

Berlin's famous Unter den Linden.

Berlin's massive High Renaissance-style Cathedral was built between 1894 and 1905.

sudden surge of new flights into Berlin since reunification, planes are again landing at Tempelhof.

*

Get back on the No. 4 bus at Platz der Luftbrücke or on Columbiadamm at Friesenstrasse or Golssenerstrasse to continue on to the district of **Neukölln**.

Neukölln, with upwards of 300,000 residents, is the most heavily populated district in Berlin. Called Rixdorf until 1912, it grew rapidly during the industrial boom in the 19th century, attracting hundreds of thousands of workers from the eastern provinces, most of whom lived in miserable "Hinterhof" tenements (dark apartment buildings with two or three inner courtyards, where even more people lived) that were quickly put up to house them. The history of Neukölln is associated with the Socialist Workers' Movement, which grew up here, and it remains basically a blue collar district today. Nearly all of Berlin's 200,000 Turks—the largest foreign population in the city—live in Neukölln and Kreuzberg to the north, and you'll see countless Turkish shops, restaurants, and residents on the streets here. (Berlin's first Muslim cemetery, in fact, is located on Columbiadamm.)

By the way, Turkish snack bars dot the entire area, featuring wonderful Near Eastern food at rock bottom prices. Try a Döner kebab (the Turkish equivalent of the better-known Greek gyros), or a refreshing salty yogurt and buttermilk beverage called *ayran*.

Get off the No. 4 bus at the *Rathaus Neukölln* (Neukölln Town Hall), built in 1908 and located on one of Neukölln's busiest shopping streets, Karl-Marx-Strasse. Walk south to Richardstrasse and turn left. Here, tucked away between Richardstrasse and Kirchgasse, is the wonderfully restored area known as **Böhmisches Dorf** (Bohemian Village), where Protestant refugees from Bohemia established a settlement in 1737. A plaque in *Richardplatz*, the former village square, features a Hussite chalice of the Bohemian brothers as one of its emblems. It is dedicated to Frederick William I, who granted the persecuted refugees asylum. The *Bethlehemskirche* (Bethlehem Church) dates back to the 17th century.

To continue the tour of Neukölln, walk back up Karl-Marx-Strasse to *Hermannplatz*, or, alternatively, catch the U-Bahn at the Neukölln station and take it three stops north to Hermannplatz. The district's three main streets—Sonnenallee, Karl-Marx-Strasse, and Hermannstrasse—converge here. In front of the Hermannplatz U-Bahn you'll see two bronze figures dancing atop a pillar. Designed by Joachim Schmettau, who also created the fountain in Breitscheidplatz (see Walk 1, page 29), the *"Tanzendes Paar"* (Dancing Couple) refer to the late-19th-century Rixdorf Polka, which was first performed at the Neue Welt (New World) dance hall in Rixdorf and went on to become world famous. The surrounding area was spruced up for Berlin's 750th birthday celebrations in 1987.

Cross over to enter the *Volkspark Hasenheide, which lies between Columbiadamm and Hasenheide. The pleasant tree-lined meadows of this park, once the Great Elector's hunting grounds, became the site of Germany's first sports gymnasium and public athletic field in 1811. The man responsible for this sports revolution, Friedrich Ludwig Jahn, is memorialized by a statue in the park. Bear in mind that in the early 19th century sports of any kind—except for hunting—were considered somewhat immoral. In 1848, Jahn, called the "Father of Sports," was thrown into Spandau Citadel for revolutionary political activities.

If you're up for a little wandering in the park, head west towards the elevated spot known as *Rixdorfer Höhe*, yet another Berlin hill built out of landscaped war rubble, and a particularly appropriate site for Katharina Singer's sculpture, *"Trümmerfrau,"* or "Rubble Woman." Not nearly enough attention has been paid to the hardworking group of women who literally cleared away the wreckage of the destroyed city.

For the quickest and most convenient way back to downtown Berlin from here, take the U-Bahn at Hermannplatz or Südstern at the northwestern corner of Volkspark Hasenheide.

WALK 11: *Kreuzberg

See map on page 82.

Kreuzberg is one of the most fascinating areas of Berlin today, a place most tourists never visit, but one that amply rewards the adventurous traveler with a number of surprises. This small Berlin district—the most densely populated in the city—is home to a volatile mixture of young artists and old-age pensioners, punks and yuppies, Turks, and free spirits of all shapes, sizes, and colors. Upwardly mobile Berliners have gentrified Kreuzberg 61 (a part of the district named after its postal zone), but Kreuzberg SO 36 (a different neighborhood) definitely retains some of its rough edges and "alternative" status. Add the largest number of Turkish workers in Berlin, with their special stores, markets, restaurants, cuisine, and customs, and you have an idea of the people-watching possibilities in Kreuzberg. This special walk will show you everything that makes Kreuzberg distinctive, from an 18th-century building housing the Berlin Museum to beautifully restored 19th-century apartment blocks and squares—even a Turkish market or two. And when you've finished, you'll truly be able to say you saw something of the "real" Berlin.

Start your tour of Kreuzberg at the *Kochstrasse U-Bahn station*. One block north of here was **Checkpoint Charlie,** one of the two crossing points into East Berlin for non-German visitors between 1961 and 1990. Now that the two Berlins and Germanys have reunited, "Charlie" has become yet another reminder of the city's recent past—the Allied blockhouse was removed in June, 1990, and the demise of its East German counterpart followed soon thereafter. It seems likely that some part of "Charlie" will be preserved as an historically relevant monument, but nothing is certain. In October, 1961, two months after the Berlin Wall was erected and at the height of cold war tensions, Soviet and U.S. tanks faced off at Checkpoint Charlie. On November 9, 1989, when the Wall opened, Charlie was one of the first crossing points East Berliners used to walk into the West, and the site of a joyous, spontaneous reunion between citizens on both sides.

If you're interested in the history of the Berlin Wall, cross over to the **Haus am Checkpoint Charlie** museum. It's full of fascinating exhibitions that show escape routes, specially constructed escape vehicles, the Berlin Wall in art, and changing documentary shows on the theme of freedom. There is an added poignance here now that the Wall has disappeared and people no longer have to resort to desperate measures to escape from a totalitarian regime. *(Hours daily 9:00 A.M.–10:00 P.M.; admission fee; cafeteria.)*

Walk west on Kochstrasse to Wilhelmstrasse, turn left, and you'll come almost immediately to Anhalter Strasse. Follow Anhalter Strasse to Stresemannstrasse. To your right you'll see the massive bulk of the **Martin-Gropius-Bau** (Martin Gropius Building), which has become one of Berlin's most interesting exhibition spaces. Until recently, this beautifully restored building was the home of the Kunstgewerbemuseum (Museum of Applied Arts), which has now moved to a modern building in the Kulturforum. The Martin-Gropius-Bau contains the *Berlinische Galerie* (Berlin Gallery), with a permanent show called "20th Century Art in Berlin." It also hosts changing exhibitions on all aspects of the city's art, artists, and art scene, the *Jewish section* of the Berlin Museum (featuring documents, pictures and art work pertaining to Berlin's Jewish population), and, on the second floor, the *Werkbund-Archiv* with its *Museum of Everyday Life in the 20th Century. (Hours Tuesday–Sunday 10:00 A.M.–10:00 P.M.; closed Monday; admission free.)*

The deserted, desolate area around the Martin-Gropius-Bau is haunted by Berlin's Nazi past. The immediate vicinity was headquarters for Hitler's dread SS and Gestapo. Nazi officials like Heinrich Himmler, SA leader Reinhard Heydrich (who headed the meetings of the "Wannsee Conference," which determined the "final solution" for European Jews), and Adolf Eichmann had their offices here. To one side of the Martin-Gropius-Bau, in the excavated kitchen building of the demolished Gestapo prison, there is a documentary exhibition called *Topographie des Terrors* which deals with this horrifying chapter of modern history. (Hours Tuesday–Sunday 10:00 A.M.–6:00 P.M.; closed Mondays; admission free.)

Walk south down Stresemannstrasse toward Anhalter Strasse; as you approach *Askanischer Platz* you'll see on your right what appears at first glance to be some ruin from ancient Rome transported to Berlin. This is all that remains of the *Anhalter Bahnhof*, Berlin's largest and busiest long-distance train station before the war. Built between 1875 and 1880, it was dynamited to extinction—except for this lonely portion—in 1952. Beside the ruins of the station the new *Kreuzberg City Hall* is currently under construction.

It's a few long and not particularly scenic blocks from here down Stresemannstrasse to our next destination, and you may want to hop on the No. 24 bus and take it to the stop nearest Hallesches Tor U-Bahn station. *Mehringplatz*, right behind the U-Bahn station, is notable for its collection of new and architecturally interesting buildings grouped in a circle around a pedestrian area and shopping arcades.

Turn left up Lindenstrasse just east of the station and follow it north for three long blocks to reach the ***Berlin Museum** [46]. Erected in 1735, the classical yellow and white façade of this beautifully proportioned building attests to its age and former function as the *Kammergericht* (Supreme Court) of Frederick William I. This is where the remarkable E. T. A. Hoffmann (1776-1822) once practiced law. Attorney, author, critic, essayist, composer, theater director—some of his short stories served as the basis of Jacques Offenbach's opera "The Tales of Hoffmann." If you're interested in the history of Berlin, step inside. There are portraits of Berliners, displays of local Berlin history, collections of furniture, views of the city, Berlin toys, and enough other bric-a-brac to provide a brief, intriguing visit. The *Alt-Berliner Weissbierstube*, attached to the museum, is an excellent place to sample that Berlin specialty, *Weissbier* (White Beer), a special top-fermented wheat beer. *(Hours Tuesday–Sunday 10:00 A.M.–10:00 P.M.; closed Monday; admission free.)*

To continue your exploration of Kreuzberg, you have to backtrack from here to the Hallesches Tor U-Bahn station. Cross over the *Landwehrkanal* to *Blücherplatz* where you'll find the **Amerika Gedenkbibliothek** [45]. Based on number of volumes lent, the American Commemorative Library is Germany's largest public library, and another indication of

American interest in Berlin since the end of the war. The library was financed by contributions from Americans from all walks of life to provide Berliners with the equivalent of an American free public library, open to everyone with books for every interest, in contrast to the largely specialized, academically oriented libraries the city had known before. The library has an immense Berlin section and an extensive record and tape collection. Construction of a new addition is slated to begin soon. *(Hours Tuesday–Saturday 11:00 A.M.–8:00 P.M.; Monday 4:00–8:00 P.M.; closed Sundays and holidays.)*

A marvelous architectural surprise awaits you as you head down Mehringdamm to Yorckstrasse, and then turn right. You might want to pause at the unusual little *Berlin-Kinomuseum* (Berlin Movie Museum) at Grossbeerenstrasse 54. It screens historical black-and-white movies from bygone days on Wednesdays, Fridays, and Saturdays at 8:30 P.M. and 10:30 P.M. There's also a small exhibit area that displays movie posters and photographs illustrating Germany's important film industry over the years.

On the opposite side of the street is one of the three entrances to **Riehmer's Hofgarten,** one of Kreuzberg's most successful restorations (the other two entrances are on Yorckstrasse and Hagelberger Strasse). Until fairly recently, Berlin's postwar city planning favored demolition over renovation, except in cases of particular historic significance—a trend that caused the destruction of countless old neighborhoods and salvageable buildings. The tide has shifted now to *"behutsame Stadterneuerung"* (careful urban renewal), and Riehmer's Hofgarten is one result. Enter through any of the portals to get a glimpse of this historic group of 24 apartment buildings clustered around a generous oasis of greenery. The complex was built by Wilhelm Riehmer between 1870 and 1871. The area is accentuated by several chic cafés, movie theaters, and a disco called *Golgotha* in the park across the street.

Cross over for an easy climb to the top of the hill which gave the district its name, *Kreuzberg* [47].

*Kreuzberg

The name Kreuzberg, which means "Mountain of the Cross," dates from 1821 when the architect Schinkel's *Monument to the Wars of Liberation* was erected on the hill's summit. The 20-meter- (66-foot-) high monument, which commemorates the 1813–1815 Wars of Liberation against Napoleon, is crowned by an enormous cast iron cross. You'll pass a rushing waterfall as you enter the surrounding *Viktoriapark* and ascend for a view of Kreuzberg.

Head east from here down Kreuzbergstrasse, crossing Mehringdamm, and continue down Bergmannstrasse to Nostitzstrasse and turn right. Make a left at the next corner to reach **Chamissoplatz,** another restored area. There's plenty of charm and authentic atmosphere galore in this late-19th-century neighborhood, so take your time strolling about the area.

Head back to Bergmannstrasse and continue along past restaurants, antique stores, and enticing little shops to Zossener Strasse and the lively **Marheineke Markt-Hall** (Marheineke Market Hall), another lucky 19th-century survivor of postwar demolition fever. This is a good example of a typical neighborhood shopping center in old Berlin.

Now continue down Bergmannstrasse to Baerwaldstrasse, where you're right on the quiet edge of four old *cemeteries* where the likes of writer E. T. A. Hoffmann (see Berlin Museum above), poet Adelbert Chamisso (1781–1838), and composer Felix Mendelssohn-Bartholdy (1809–1847) are buried. Walk up Baerwaldstrasse to Carl-Herz-Ufer, a canal-side promenade, and turn right. Along *Planufer* you'll see the elaborate façades of several restored apartment buildings. This is a prime residential area in today's Kreuzberg, but when most of these late 19th-century buildings were erected, they typically contained dingy *Hinterhofe* (rear courtyards) crammed with shops, factories and crowded, unsanitary apartments. By now, most of these courtyards have been removed. Across the Landwehrkanal you can see the vaulted roof of the modern *Ballerbau,* an urban renewal project undertaken by the Internationale Bauausstellung (International Building Exhibition) as part of its planning scheme for Kreuzberg.

Cross *Kottbusser Brücke* and take a right at Skalitzer Strasse. Turn left when you reach Mariannenstrasse and head up the street to reach *Mariannenplatz.* Now you're in the heart of **Kreuzberg SO 36,** with its distinctive mixture of old, new, and "alternative." There are shops and restaurants with Arabic names, small esoteric bookshops and markets catering to the district's varied subcultures, old beer parlors, corner Kneipen (taverns), as well as smart cafés and elegantly restored buildings. Punks, intellectuals, yuppies, and counterculturists of all persuasions live side-by-side with Berlin's densest concentration of Turkish families, who came to Berlin as "Gastarbeiter" (guest workers), and today comprise the city's largest foreign contingent. Although there's been a lot of friction among these groups over the years, the basic atmosphere is now one of integration—nowhere more evident than at **Mariannenplatz.** At the center of the square is the *"Fire Department" fountain* by Kurt Mühlenhaupt. Set back from it in a beautifully rebuilt mid-19th-century building is the well-known Kreuzberg arts center known as **Künstlerhaus Bethanien.** In addition to housing a Turkish public library and the Kreuzberg arts council, this former hospital provides space for artists' studios and exhibition rooms, theaters, and alternative printing presses. In the square you might find yourself in the midst of a block party, a rock concert, or a Turkish folk festival. At the end of the street is the largest church in West Berlin, the *Thomaskirche* (St. Thomas Church), with the diminishing remains of the Berlin Wall behind it.

Muskauer Strasse begins across from the main entrance of Bethanien. Take this wonderfully restored residential street two blocks to Pücklerstrasse, turn left, and you'll see the entrance of the brick-faced **Eisenbahn-Markthalle** (Railroad Market Hall) *(hours Monday–Friday 7:30 A.M.–6:00 P.M.; Saturday 8:00 A.M.–1:00 P.M.; closed Sunday).* There's no telling what you might find here. Everything from fresh flowers to kitschy knick-knacks are sold. So walk through and leave by the Eisenbahnstrasse exit, turning right to get back on Muskauer Strasse. At Zeughofstrasse you turn right again onto Skalitzer Strasse. Turn left. From here you can walk two blocks under the elevated U-Bahn tracks to the Schlesisches Tor station, where the westbound U1 line will take you back downtown.

WALK 12: Through the Wedding and Reinickendorf Districts

See map on page 95.

Our final West Berlin tour takes you through two very different districts, both of which formed the postwar French sector of the city. Don't expect to see French soldiers or Parisian bistros on this route, however. Wedding is a blue collar district with hardly a trace of those gentrified niceties you see in Kreuzberg. It's here, if anywhere, that you'll hear the real *Berlinerisch* dialect spoken. Reinickendorf, with its enormous Tegel Lake and peaceful green countryside extending to the northernmost borders of the city, offers more bucolic pleasures. In Tegel you'll be able to visit a charming 18th-century villa and, from there, head off to the farming village of Lübars. This is Berlin in all its amazing diversity. The itinerary, to which you should devote a day, covers a lot of ground, and provides directions for drivers as well as bus and subway routes. If you are particularly interested in seeing Humboldt-Schloss Tegel, keep in mind that it is only open on Sunday afternoons from 2:00–6:00 P.M.

This tour actually begins in *Charlottenburg-Nord*, where two important memorials serve to remind us of the countless victims of the Nazis, who used Berlin as their capital and headquarters. As you walk down the streets of Berlin today it's difficult to imagine the scenes of horror and repression that once filled the city: the burning of the synagogues in 1938; the rounding-up of Jews and political dissidents at Wannsee station, where they were shipped off to extermination camps, and the executions and street hangings. All the more reason, then, to pause for a few minutes at these memorials and reflect on that history lesson we can never afford to forget.

Begin this portion of the tour at *Jakob-Kaiser-Platz U-Bahn station*. From the station, walk north on Tegelerweg to Heckerdamm, where you turn right. About a block down, on your left, you'll come to *Maria Regina Martyrum*. Drivers take Otto-Suhr-Allee from *Ernst-Reuter-Platz*, turn right at Luisenplatz and continue up Tegelerweg, around Jakob-Kaiser-Platz to Heckerdamm. Turn right and continue for about a block to reach **Maria Regina Martyrum** [48].

Built in 1962, the church of Mary Queen of Martyrs is a religious memorial dedicated to the

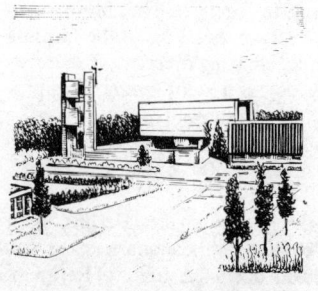

St. Mary Queen of Martyrs

"Martyrs for the Freedom of Belief and Conscience 1933–1945." The church was designed by two architects from Würzburg, Hans Schadel and Friedrich Ebert, and built with funds from Germany's Roman Catholic community. Adjacent to the church are the parish house and the large *ceremonial courtyard*, with its symbolic reference to prison and concentration camp courtyards. A powerful bronze block, its pedestal encircled by a crown of thorns, forms an open-air altar. Otto Herbert Hajek created both the altar and the abstract *Stations of the Cross* on the right wall of the church. The *Lower Church* contains a symbolic grave for all the Nazi victims denied a proper burial or whose burial places are unknown.

By foot or car, continue down Heckerdamm to Friedrich-Olbricht-Damm and turn right, then left almost immediately on Hüttigpfad and the **Gedenkstätte Plötzensee**. The memorial here honors "The Victims of the Hitler Dictatorship 1933–1945" and was put up in 1952 by the Berlin Senate in the courtyard of the former *Zuchthaus Plötzensee* (Plötzensee Prison), which is now a juvenile detention home. At least 2,500 men, women, and adolescents—most of them resistance fighters and political opponents of the regime— met their deaths in a small red brick building behind the Plötzensee prison. This execution building has been restored and

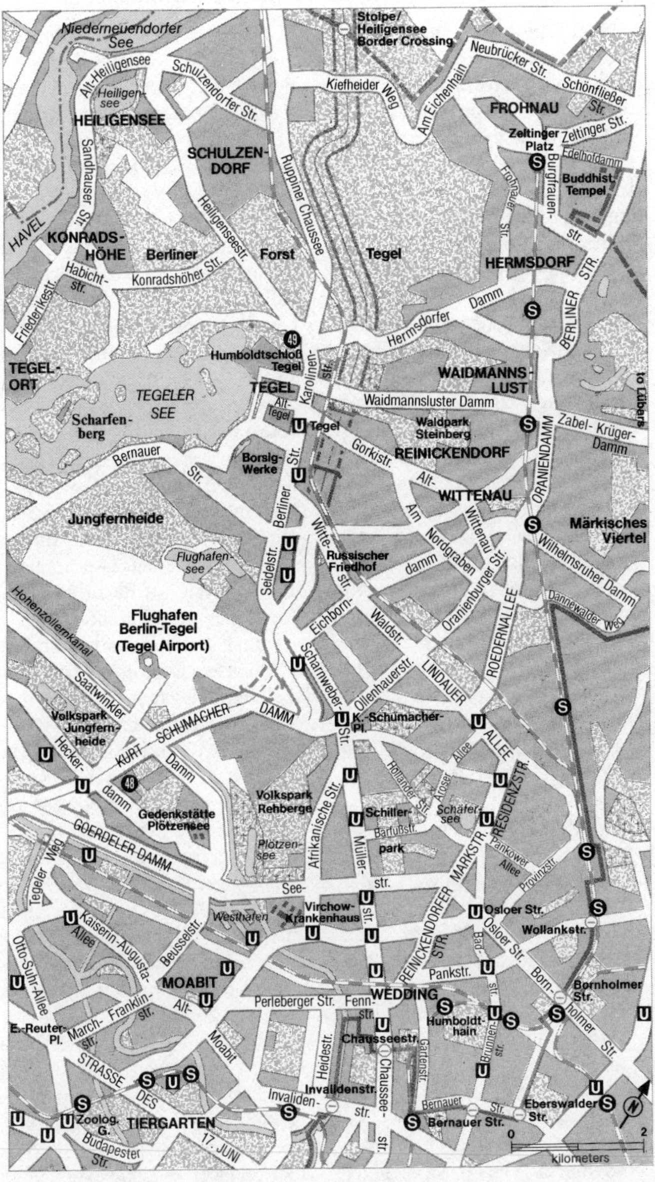

Niederneuendorfer See
Stolpe/ Heiligensee Border Crossing
Alt-Heiligensee
Heiligensee
HEILIGENSEE
Schulzendorfer Str.
SCHULZENDORF
Kiefheider Weg
Neubrücker Str.
Schönfließer Str.
Am Eichenhain
FROHNAU
Zeltinger Platz
Zeltinger Str.
Edelhofdamm
Buddhist. Tempel
Burgfrauen-str.
Frohnauer Str.
Sandhauser Str.
Ruppiner Chaussee
Heiligenseestr.
HAVEL
KONRADSHÖHE
Berliner
Forst
Tegel
HERMSDORF
BERLINER STR.
Habicht-str.
Konradshöher Str.
Friederikestr.
Hermsdorfer Damm
Humboldtschloß Tegel
49
Karolinen-str.
TEGEL-ORT
TEGEL
WAIDMANNSLUST
to Lübars
TEGELER SEE
Scharfenberg
Alt-Tegel
Tegel
Waidmannsluster Damm
Zabel-Krüger-Damm
Waldpark Steinberg
REINICKENDORF
Gorkistr.
Bernauer Str.
Borsig-Werke
Berliner Str.
Alt-Wittenau
WITTENAU
ORANIENDAMM
Jungfernheide
Märkisches Viertel
Am Nordgraben
Wittenau
Wilhelmsruher Damm
Witte-str.
Russischer Friedhof
Seidelstr.
Flughafensee
damm
Oranienburger Str.
ROEDERNALLEE
Dannewalder Weg
Hohenzollernkanal
Flughafen Berlin-Tegel (Tegel Airport)
Eichborn-
Waldstr.
Scharnweber-Str.
Ollenhauerstr.
LINDAUER
Saatwinkler
Volkspark Jungfernheide
KURT SCHUMACHER DAMM
K.-Schumacher-Pl.
ALLEE
Hecker-damm
Damm
48
Allee
Holländer Str.
Aroser
RESIDENZSTR.
Afrikanische Str.
Volkspark Rehberge
Gedenkstätte Plötzensee
Schiller-park
Schäfersee
Barfußstr.
GOERDELER DAMM
Plötzensee
Müller-str.
MARKSTR.
Pankower Allee
Provinzstr.
Tegeler Weg
See-str.
Virchow-Krankenhaus
Westhafen
Osloer Str.
Kaiserin-Augusta-Allee
Beusselstr.
REINICKENDORFER STR.
Bad-str.
Wollankstr.
Otto-Suhr-Allee
MOABIT
Pankstr.
Born-holmer Str.
Bornholmer Str.
Alt-Moabit
Perleberger Str.
Fenn-str.
WEDDING
Franklin-str.
E.-Reuter-Pl.
March-str.
Humboldt-hain
Chausseestr.
Heidestr.
Gartenstr.
Brunnen-str.
STRASSE DES 17. JUNI
Invalidenstr.
Invaliden-str.
Chaussee-str.
Bernauer Str.
Eberswalder Str.
Zoolog. G.
TIERGARTEN
Budapester Str.
0
2
kilometers

forms the most poignant section of the memorial. The executions, which took the form of mass hangings (360 men in one day in 1943), beheadings with an axe and, later, a guillotine, continued up to the very end of the war, despite heavy damage to the building by Allied bombs. An urn to one side of the memorial wall contains earth from Nazi concentration camps. A scroll buried beneath the foundation stone of the memorial reads, "During the years of the Hitler dictatorship, from 1933–1945, hundreds of human beings were put to death by judicial murder on this spot. They died because they chose to fight against the dictatorship for human rights and political freedom. They included people from every walk of life and nearly every country. With this Memorial Berlin honors those millions of victims of the Third Reich who, because of their political convictions, their religious beliefs or racial origins, were vilified, abused, deprived of their freedom or murdered."

Follow Hüttigpfad to Seestrasse. If you're driving, take a left on Seestrasse and follow it to Müllerstrasse, where you turn left again. Follow this road, which becomes Scharnweberstrasse, Seidelstrasse, Berlinerstrasse, and finally Karolinenstrasse to *Tegel*. Pedestrians catch the No. 65 bus going east on Seestrasse through the **Wedding** district as far as the Seestrasse U-Bahn station, and transfer there to the U6 subway going north. The last stop, Tegel, is where you get out. From here you walk a short distance to the north on Karolinenstrasse to Adelheidallee and the grounds of ***Humboldt-Schloss Tegel** [49]. *(House and grounds open on Sunday only, 2:00–6:00 P.M.)*

The "Humboldtschlösschen" ("Little Humboldt Castle"), as its architect Karl Friedrich Schinkel called it, actually started life as a country chalet during the reign of Joachim II (ca. 1550). Between 1821 and 1824 Schinkel completely transformed it into a residence for the Humboldt brothers. Wilhelm von Humboldt was a distinguished member of the Prussian Interior Ministry who also served as the Prussian Ambassador to Rome and later founded the University of Berlin in 1810. Alexander von Humboldt was a scientist, explorer, and naturalist. The house and property belong to the Humboldt family to this day. Built in Renaissance style, the two-story central portion of the building is flanked by four three-storied towers decorated with reliefs by Christian Daniel Rauch, depicting the gods of the eight winds (based on the "Tower of the Winds" in Athens). The design of this beautifully proportioned and classically simple building became a model of its kind. Dozens of other Berlin villas copied it. The interior is full of memorabilia of the two brothers and exudes a true breath of early- to mid-18th-century patrician taste. Furniture, ancient sculptures (many originals replaced by copies) collected by Wilhelm in Rome, and family portraits fill the rooms. If you have the time, you might wander around the beautiful *Castle Gardens*. An avenue of old linden trees passes by the 400-year-old *Humboldt Oak* to the **Humboldt Family Tomb*, designed by Schinkel in 1830 and graced by a copy of Thorwaldsen's statue of "Hope." Both Humboldt brothers are buried here.

You now have a number of different options for seeing more of Reinickendorf. If you're driving, you can see several of the following places. If you're traveling by bus you'll have to limit yourself to one of them. The district is called the "green north" because forests cover nearly a quarter of its surface.

For a pleasant lakeside hike from Humboldt-Schloss Tegel, turn right before crossing the canal and follow the canalside path to *Greenwichpromenade*, an esplanade that runs along the northeastern shore of **Tegeler See** (Tegel Lake). This is the starting point for the excursion steamers that ply the lake. You can see what appears to be the façade of a castle across the lake. This is the *Villa Borsig*, built in 1911 for the grandson of locomotive and industrial magnate Ernst Borsig and now used as a conference center. When you're ready to head back or move on, return to the Tegel U-Bahn station via Alt-Tegel, a pedestrian street that connects the promenade with Tegel's shopping area.

If you'd like to visit **Heiligensee,** a small fishing village with farmsteads clustered around the village square, drive northwest from Humboldt-Schloss Tegel on Karolinenstrasse, which becomes Heiligenseestrasse as it turns west and crosses the *Berliner Forst* (Berlin Forest). After a stop in the village you can continue on via Heiligenseestrasse, which turns south around the lake and becomes Sandhauserstrasse. Turn left onto Habichtstrasse and follow it back to Heiligenseestrasse, where a right turn takes you back to Tegel. If you're on foot and want to visit Heiligensee, catch the No. 14 bus at the Tegel U-Bahn station and take it all the way to the village green at Alt-Heiligensee. Hannah Hoch (1890–1978), the artist credited with creating the collage technique and the only woman artist to join the Dada group, is buried in the churchyard next to the 16th-century village church. Hoch was one of the many artists branded as "degenerate" by the Nazis, and was consequently unable to show her work for years. To return to Tegel U-Bahn from Alt-Heiligensee, catch the No. 13 bus, which departs from the village green.

Another excursion possibility combines Hermsdorf and Frohnau. **Hermsdorf,** originally founded in the 13th century, is now filled with lavish country homes. **Frohnau,** which also has its share of expensive country houses, was designed between 1908 and 1911 as *Gartenstadt*

Frohnau, a "garden city," where the air was so highly esteemed that it was recommended as especially beneficial to opera singers. Berlin's only polo field is located in this fancy suburb, as is one of Europe's few *Buddhist Temples.* Located in a hilltop park at Edelhofdamm 54, the temple was constructed in East Asian style between 1922 and 1924 for the physician and philologist Paul Dahlke. Since 1963 the temple has been owned by the "Buddhist Society of Sri Lanka," which sends monks here to serve the 300-member congregation. *Directions:* By bus: the No. 15 from Tegel U-Bahn station makes stops at both Hermsdorf and Frohnau. At Frohnau you can catch the S-Bahn back to the city. By car: Karolinenstrasse to Waidmannsluster Damm, turn right, and then left on Hermsdorferdamm, which will take you all the way to Hermsdorf. To continue on to Frohnau, turn left on Falkentaler Steig and right on Frohnauer Strasse to the village.

If you are of Russian ancestry, you might want to visit the generally overlooked **Russian Cemetery** at Wittestrasse 37 in Reinickendorf. The Brotherhood of St. Vladimir bought the property in 1890. In 1893, the cemetery was opened, landscaped with Russian trees planted in 40 tons of Russian soil sent here by Czar Alexander III. The beautifully restored *Chapel of Saints Constantine and Helena* was constructed in 1894. Under the Cyrillic lettering of their gravestones, many refugees from Czarist Russia were buried in the traditional Russian-Orthodox manner—with their heads pointing east. The handsomest memorial here is dedicated to the Russian court conductor and renowned composer Mikhail Glinka (1804–1857), who died in Berlin but was buried in his homeland. *Directions:* By car or foot: South on Berliner Strasse, left on Wittestrasse; the cemetery is on the other side of Holzhauserstrasse, overlooking the autobahn.

The place we recommend most is the old farming village of ***Lübars,** which has managed to retain its rural character despite encroachments from all sides. The fields may stretch right up to the walls of new high-rises, but Lübars still remains the only village in West Berlin where farmers grow grain and maintain dairy herds. A little church built in 1793 stands on the village square, as does the old tavern *Zum lustigen Finken* ("The Cheerful Finch"). The village is surrounded by the fields and meadows of the *Tegeler Fliess River* and there is a pleasant nearby beach. *Directions:* By car: Karolinenstrasse to Waidmannsluster Damm, turn right. Once past the S-Bahn tracks, the street becomes Zabel-Kruger-Damm and will take you to Lübars. By bus: the No. 20 from the Tegel U-Bahn station. Return with the same bus, but you can get out at the Waidmannslust stop to catch the S-Bahn back into the city.

WALK 13: *Brandenburger Tor–**Unter den Linden–Dom

See map on page 100.

This walk down Berlin's famous Unter den Linden provides an excellent introduction to East Berlin, and can easily be done in about three hours. You may want to combine it with Walk 14, which takes you to the beautifully restored Platz der Akademie a few blocks south of Unter den Linden. The walk begins at the Brandenburg Gate and continues down Unter den Linden, passing several buildings of great historical importance from the 18th and 19th centuries, and ends at the immense Berlin Cathedral. Now that the two Berlins are reunified, East Berlin is changing from day to day—a fact that should add even more interest to your visit.

Before Germany was officially reunified, it became possible for foreign visitors to cross into East Berlin directly at the Brandenburg Gate in June, 1990. The S-Bahn and U-Bahn stations (lines 6 and 8) that had been closed because of the Wall have now been reopened, creating several additional entrances to the eastern part of the city. However, for nearly thirty years the only way to enter the former capital of the GDR was at the Friedrichstrasse S-Bahn station or by taking the U-Bahn to Kochstrasse and crossing over there at *Checkpoint Charlie* (see Walk 11, page 89). We still recommend beginning this tour at one of these two centrally located historic points.

From Friedrichstrasse Bahnhof walk south on Friedrichstrasse to Unter den Linden and turn right. From Checkpoint Charlie walk north on Friedrichstrasse and turn left on Unter den Linden. If you're starting at Checkpoint Charlie, you may find it convenient to begin your tour with Walk 14, which winds through the beautifully restored Platz der Akademie. From there you continue on to Unter den Linden and turn left to reach the ***Brandenburger Tor** [50]. (For a description, see Walk 3, page 43.) From 1961 to November, 1989, a view of the gate from the East Berlin side terminated with the sight of the Wall directly be-

Brandenburg Gate

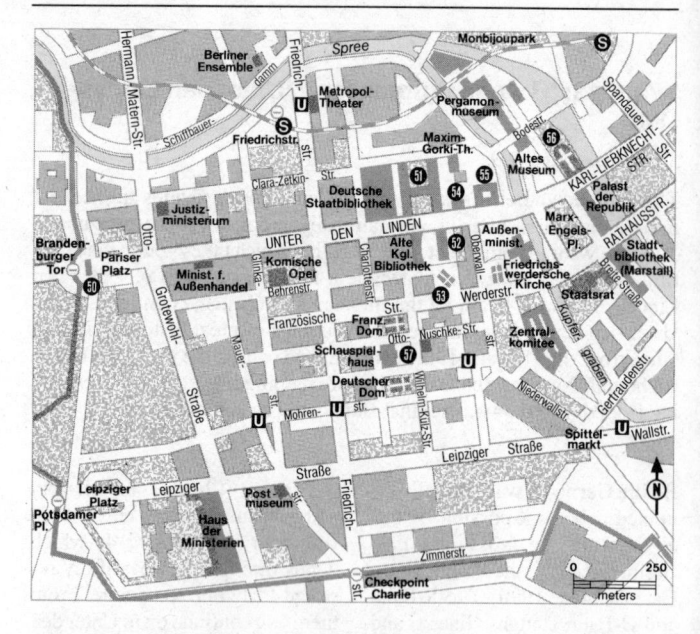

hind it. Today, the only wall you'll see is made up of vending stands, selling "Western" refreshments, military souvenirs, GDR memorabilia, and pieces of the Wall.

Pariser Platz, a large open square where souvenir stands and wurst-sellers now cater to tourists, marks the beginning of Unter den Linden. All the buildings on this square—originally constructed on commission from Frederick William I—were destroyed in World War II. These included the French and American Embassies, the legendary Adlon Hotel, and the home of painter Max Liebermann, who, after looking out his window at the torchlight parade celebrating the Nazi party's election victory on January 30, 1933, closed the curtains on the Linden side of his house and never reopened them.

Cross Otto-Grotewohl-Strasse and you are on ****Unter den Linden,** one of Berlin's most famous and historically significant streets. This grand boulevard, which extends more than a kilometer (about three-quarters of a mile) from the Brandenburg Gate to Marx-Engels-Platz, was originally laid out in 1647 on orders from Frederick William, the Great Elector. He used it as a path from the Berlin Palace (the site of today's *Palast der Republik*) to his hunting grounds in the Tiergarten. Six rows of walnut and linden trees—1,000 trees per row—were planted at that time. Over the next 100 years, rows of houses were erected on both sides of the avenue, but they were torn down by Frederick the Great in 1770 as part of his grandiose architectural scheme for Berlin and then gradually replaced by enormous villas. From the middle of the 18th century into the early 19th century, a series of impressive buildings turned the avenue into a Prussian showplace.

Until the end of the Second World War, Unter den Linden (Under the Linden Trees) was the social and historical heart of Berlin. It was the city's greatest shopping and café street—a much-loved promenade where Berliners came to see and be seen. Traffic passed through the Brandenburg Gate and moved on to what was then Charlottenburger Chaussee (today's Strasse des 17. Juni in West Berlin). But the buildings and the street itself were reduced to charred rubble during the war, and without funds from the Marshall Plan (which helped West Berlin rebuild) reconstruction moved slowly. When the Wall went up in 1961, the street was closed off just beyond the Brandenburg Gate. Its axis changed from west to east, towards *Marx-Engels-Platz* and, beyond it, *Alexanderplatz*. The first new buildings to go up—the Russian and Polish embassies—gave a kind of drab, featureless shape to further development of the avenue, and the pre-war glamor of Unter den Linden became a distant memory. Now that the two Berlins are one again, there will inevitably be a spate of new building, preservation, and reconstruction to consolidate the work that has already been done and to resurrect something of the boulevard's old excitement. Luxury stores have already sprung up.

This newer portion of "the Linden" around Pariser Platz was home to a number of important embassies and ministries of the GDR, all of them dismantled now that the country has become reunified. At the corner of Otto-Grotewohl-Strasse, on your right, was the *Institute for Applied Economic Research,* where Socialist economics were given an ironic twist when Yamaha opened a big showroom on the ground floor in 1990, and the *Ministry for Public Education.* Beyond it lies the huge complex of the *Russian Embassy,* constructed between 1950 and 1952 and decorated with hammers and sickles. Across the street are the *Polish* and *Hungarian embassies* and the *Foreign Trade Ministry.* Other embassies on "The Linden" are the *British Embassy* at No. 30/34 and the *Italian* and *French embassies* at No. 40.

By turning right on Glinkastrasse and walking one block to Behrenstrasse, you come to the famous *Komische Oper,* a relatively new building from the 1950s regarded by many as housing the best opera company in the German-speaking world. After the war, Austrian opera director Walter Felsenstein headed the company for thirty years. He forged a new honest dramatic style for music-theater and trained some of the world's best stage directors. (See page 156 for ticket information.)

Back on Unter den Linden, continue on to Friedrichstrasse, which runs north-south. It was once one of Berlin's liveliest (and, in the 1920s, naughtiest) strips, brimming with clubs, cafés, revues, theaters, and hotels. A long-range planning scheme for revitalizing the street was in effect before reunification and will now be stepped up. The new *Grand Hotel*, opened in 1987, was a luxurious foretaste of things to come in East Berlin, and the *Café Bauer* inside offers the kind of elegance for which the Linden was once noted. The other buildings in the immediate vicinity mostly have that drab utilitarian look that characterizes so much of postwar Soviet-inspired East Berlin—many face-lifts are in the offing.

You can see some of the newer buildings—not all of them architectural gems, by any means—and acquaint yourself with several theaters by taking a detour north on Friedrichstrasse from Unter den Linden. The new *Metropol Hotel* is on your left and across the street from it stands the *Internationales Handelszentrum* (International Trade Center), another Japanese venture. Just beyond the S-Bahn tracks you'll come to the *Admiralspalast*, home of the musical and operetta house called the *Metropol Theater* and the well-known satirical cabaret *"Die Distel"* ("The Thistle;" see page 156 for ticket information). Cross the Spree on the *Weidendammer Brücke* (Weidendammer Bridge) with its fin-de-siècle balustrades and ornate cast-iron lamps, pass the *Spree Terrassen* (Spree Terraces) on your right, and at Ziegelstrasse you'll come to the *Friedrichstadtpalast*, a restored music hall that now features some of the most extravagant and glitzy revues outside Las Vegas (see page 156 for ticket information). Theater lovers, even if they don't know German, should definitely see a performance at the *Berliner Ensemble*, one block west of Friedrichstrasse on Schiffbauerdamm. This was Bertolt Brecht's theater after the war and remains dedicated to his works and theatrical ideas (see page 156 for ticket information). A statue of Brecht is located in the small park in front of the theater.

From Friedrichstrasse continue east on Unter den Linden for one block. The massive building on your left, some parts of it restored with lighter-colored stone, is the **Staatsbibliothek** (German State Library), completed in 1914. Free tours are given on the first Sunday of every month. There's also a good, reasonably priced café/restaurant here, where you can mingle with students and staff.

Pink chestnuts flank **Humboldt-Universität** [51], the next building on your left. The main building of Humboldt University, with its entrance on Unter den Linden, was constructed between 1748 and 1766 by Johann Boumann as a palace for Prince

Henry, the brother of Frederick II. In 1810, on the initiative of the renowned philologist and diplomat Wilhelm von Humboldt (see Walk 12, page 96), the palace was turned into an institute for higher learning. A statue of Humboldt sits in front of the gates. It was called Frederick William University until 1949, when it was renamed Humboldt University. Over the years many eminent scholars and 27 Nobel Laureates served on the faculty here, including the philosopher Hegel, philologists Wilhelm and Jacob Grimm (of *Grimm's Fairy Tales* fame), physicists Max Planck and Albert Einstein, chemist Otto Hahn, and bacteriologist Robert Koch, who first discovered the cholera agent and identified the tuberculosis bacilli. Ideological and political pressures placed on students and faculty after the war resulted in the founding of the Free University in West Berlin in 1948–1949. It remains to be seen how students trained under the Marxist-Leninist ideology will respond to the more open intellectual atmosphere of a united country. The courtyard and front sidewalk are now the scene of an open-air book market during the week.

In front of the university, C. D. Rauch's **Equestrian Statue of Friedrich II** (1851) has recently been returned to its prominent place in the middle of Unter den Linden. For years, the East German government refused to display the statue because it represented Prussian militarism. It had been removed to the palace of Sanssouci in Potsdam. The base of the monument commemorates Frederick II's "inner circle" of poets, philosophers, military officers, and politicians.

Across the street, the *Women's Federation Building* of 1891 stands beside a new building with a Baroque façade that dates from 1721. It was taken from the former **Gouverneurshaus** (Governor's House) that once stood on Rathaus Strasse. Emperor William I lived in the building known as the **Altes Palais** (Old Palace), which adjoins Bebelplatz. C. F. Langhans designed this palatial residence between 1834 and 1837.

Facing Bebelplatz is the curving, ornate façade of the **Alte Bibliothek** (Old Library), built from 1774 to 1780. You may not see the resemblance, but Berliners call the building the *Kommode,* or "chest of drawers." The library has been used as a reading room by students from Humboldt University since 1969. Across from it, fronting on Unter den Linden, is the magnificent neoclassical **Deutsche Staatsoper** [52].

The German State Opera was the first opera house to occupy its own building, unattached to a palace or castle. It was built as the Royal Opera under Frederick the Great between 1741 and 1743 to designs by G. W. von Knobelsdorff. That the building exists at all is something of a miracle, because it has been completely destroyed twice—first by a fire in 1843, then by bombs in World War II. After a historically authentic reconstruction—only the auditorium seating was partially redesigned—the theater was reopened in 1955, and restored again in 1968. Today it is home to one of the finest opera companies in the world. The acoustics in the wood-paneled auditorium are spectacular. The subtlest pianissimo carries easily to the top balcony, a quality that will doubtless make for many sterling performances in years to come. (See page 156 for ticket information.)

Directly behind the Staatsoper is the compact dome of **St.-Hedwigs-Kathedrale** [53]. The Roman Pantheon served as the model for St. Hedwig's Cathedral, which was begun in 1747 on the orders of Frederick the Great and completed by Boumann in 1773. Bernhard Lichtenberg, provost of the cathedral in 1941, was one of the few church officials to speak out against the euthanasia policies of the Third Reich. He was arrested and died in 1943 on his way to the concentration camp in Dachau. His remains were brought back to St. Hedwig's in 1965. Reconstructed after the war, St. Hedwig's reopened in 1963 and is now the cathedral church of the Roman Catholic Bishop of Berlin. It's well worth a visit for its massive interior dome and abstract stained-glass windows. (Organ recitals on Wednesday at 3:30 P.M.)

These buildings around Bebelplatz—the Staatsoper, the Old Library, St. Hedwig's, the Old Palace, and the Humboldt University building—formed what was known as the **Forum Fridiricianum**. They offer visitors a good impression of what Unter den Linden looked like in the late 18th century. *Bebelplatz*, originally called *Opernplatz*, was the scene of a mass book burning by the Nazis on May 10, 1933—the chilling culmination of Josef Goebbels's propaganda campaign against "immoral and dangerous books and writings" (in most cases simply books written by Jews). Included in the 20,000 volumes tossed into the flames were works by Heinrich Heine, Karl Marx, Heinrich and Thomas Mann, Stefan and Arnold Zweig, Erich Kästner, Leon Feuchtwanger, Carl von Ossietzky, Kurt Tucholsky, Erich-Maria Remarque, Albert Einstein, and Sigmund Freud.

To the left of the opera house lies a park with statues of the Prussian generals Blücher, Yorck, Gneisenau, and Scharnhorst, as well as the *Operncafé* (Opera Café), housed in what was formerly the **Prinzessinnenpalais** (Princess's Palace). The Princess's Palace, completed in 1734, is connected to the **Kronprinzenpalais** (Crown Prince's Palace), built just a year earlier and now called the *Palais Unter den Linden*.

Cross the street to have a closer look at the ***Neue Wache** [54], which is today a *Memorial to the*

Victims of Fascism and Militarism. Karl Friedrich Schinkel based his design for this, his first neoclassical building, on a Roman fort. It was completed in 1818 and served as headquarters for the King's Guard. In the cool, temple-like interior, an eternal flame burns in a prismatic block of crystal above the *Tomb of the Unknown Soldier* and the *Tomb of the Unknown Resistance Fighter.* Gone, however, are the soldiers of the Volksarmee (People's Army), who once guarded the memorial.

Behind the Neue Wache, in a small park lined with chestnut trees, are two more buildings from the same era. The patrician palace once known as *Am Festungsgraben,* today the *Zentrales Haus der Deutsch-Sowjetischen Freundschaft* (Central House of German-Soviet Friendship), and the beautiful **Maxim Gorki Theater,** built by Ottmer in neoclassical style and completed in 1827 for use as the Academy of Singing.

As you continue down Unter den Linden, the next building on your left is the ***Zeughaus** [55]. The Armory is Berlin's largest Baroque building and one of the most beautiful in Germany. Construction began on it in 1695 and was completed in 1706, making it the first major building to be put up on the new Unter den Linden boulevard. Andreas Schlüter was the primary architect, and he was also responsible for most of the sculptures and the 22 famous ***Masks of Dying Warriors* in the interior courtyard. Four female figures at the entrance allegorically represent the "arts" of arithmetic, geometry, fireworks, and mechanics. Note, too, the sculpted military helmets that decorate every exterior ground floor window. The entire edifice is a manifestation of the growing military and economic power of the Brandenburg-Prussian state after the Thirty Years War, and during its construction (1701) the Prince Elector of Brandenburg had himself crowned as Frederick I, King of Prussia. Since 1952, the Armory has been the home of the **Museum für Deutsche Geschichte* (Museum of German History). The exhibits once presented history from an ideological Marxist-Leninist viewpoint before reunification took place in 1990. This bias was completely overturned when the museum mounted a major new show, featuring banners, signs, segments of the Wall, and other material used in or relevant to the "gentle revolution" of November, 1989. Some of this material will remain on permanent exhibition. *(Hours Monday–Thursday 9:00 A.M.– 6:00 P.M.; Saturday and Sunday 10:00 A.M.– 5:00 P.M.; admission fee.)*

The *Foreign Ministry*—with darkened windows and an abandoned air that bespeak its uncertain future—was built in 1967 on the former site of the Command Post, and stands beside the colonnaded terrace of Palais Unter den Linden. The monument to the diplomat Baron von Stein has been restored to its former place in front of the building. Behind the ministry, at *Werderscher Markt,* there is another Schinkel building, the neogothic **Friedrich-Werdersche Church**, which dates from 1828. Schinkel, responsible for a multitude of neoclassical buildings in Berlin, wanted this church to have a more "English" character. The restored interior is now, appropriately enough, the *Schinkel Museum* and features an exhibition of the works of this eminent and prolific architect. In the near future, the church will house the collection of 19th-century sculpture. *(Hours Wednesday–Sunday 10:00 A.M.–6:00 P.M.; admission fee.)*

Cross over the Spree canal called *Kupfergraben* via the *Marx-Engels-Brücke* (Marx-Engels Bridge) beside the Armory. The bridge, called *Schlossbrücke* (Palace Bridge) when it was completed in 1824, is yet another Schinkel creation. Schinkel was also responsible for the restored statues—including the *Goddess of Victory*—which once again adorn the bridge.

Once you have crossed the bridge you are on **Marx-Engels-Platz**. This area, set up as a palace kitchen garden in 1573, became the pleasure grounds of the old Berlin Palace, which was demolished in 1951, despite great protest. The palace had been the residence of the Hohenzollerns from 1451 to 1918, and it was one of the most important Baroque architectural monuments in Germany. Schlüter had worked on it from 1698 to 1706, followed by Eosander von Göthe. The *Eosander Portal,* all that remains of the old palace, was incorporated into the main façade of the *Staatsratsgebäude* (State Council Building) at the far right of the square. The actual site of the palace is now occupied by a very unworthy successor, the **Palast der Republik** (Palace of the Republic), bitterly referred to as the "Ballast der Republik" by disgusted Berliners on both sides of the wall. This nondescript white elephant, with its coppery reflective glass windows, opened in 1976. It contains restaurants, a large concert hall, a gallery, and a theater. It is currently undergoing major repairs owing to the dangerous presence of asbestos in the air.

Set far back to the left of the square stands the *Altes Museum,* part of the complex of museums that make up the *Museumsinsel* (Museum Island) described in Walk 15.

The last stop on this walking tour is the gigantic **Berliner Dom** [56]. A typical product of the Wilhelmian era (the Reichstag is another example), the Berlin Cathedral was designed by Julius Raschdorff between 1894 and 1905 in a version of High Renaissance style. Badly damaged in the war, the renovation of its exterior was completed in 1984 and cost about 40 million marks, most of it provided by the West German Protestant Church. Interior renovation is not yet complete, although services will again be celebrated and the cupola reopened by the end of 1991. Until then, you can visit the restored *"Imperial Staircase,"* with its polished marble columns and gilded decorations, for a glimpse of the cathedral's former glory. The *Hohenzollern Crypt* beneath the church, now a museum, contains the remains of The Great Elector, King Frederick I, and Frederick William II.

(Hours Monday–Saturday 10:00 A.M.– noon, 1:00–5:00 P.M.; Sunday noon–5:00 P.M.; admission fee.)

The quickest way to return to West Berlin from the cathedral is via the S-Bahn at Marx-Engels-Platz (take Karl-Liebknecht-Strasse to Spandauer Strasse and turn left).

WALK 14: Checkpoint Charlie–**Platz der Akademie–**Unter den Linden

See map on page 100.

The restored Platz der Akademie is East Berlin's most beautiful square, one that is often overlooked by visitors. This 18th- and early 19th-century urban architectural ensemble is unlike anything you'll see in the western portion of the city, and brings vividly to mind what parts of the city looked like before the devastation of the last world war. By way of contrast, the walk begins in an area of new construction. The entire route can be covered in an hour, so you may want to combine it with the previous itinerary, which starts at the Brandenburg Gate on Unter den Linden (see Walk 13), or the following one, which takes you to the great museums on Museum Island (see Walk 15).

Although borders no longer exist in Berlin, you can take the historic crossing to East Berlin from the Kochstrasse U-Bahn station via the former *Checkpoint Charlie* (see Walk 11, page 89), and head north on Friedrichstrasse. Turn left at Leipziger Strasse for a brief detour. In one block you'll come to the *Postmuseum,* located in the former Royal Postal Ministry building. The oldest of its kind, this museum traces the development of postal and telegraphic services (hours Tuesday–Saturday 10:00 A.M.–6:00 P.M.; closed Sunday and Monday). If you want to see an example of Nazi era architecture, continue on Leipziger Strasse another block. At the corner of Leipziger Strasse and Otto-Grotewohl-Strasse stands the former *Aviation Ministry,* built by E. Sagebiel between 1934 and 1936. Up until the outbreak of the Second World War, Otto-Grotewohl-Strasse was Berlin's Government Quarter and the location of the British Embassy, the Presidential Palace, the Foreign Office, the Chancellory, and a number of ministries.

Now go back to Friedrichstrasse. The buildings all around you are a veritable beehive of new construction activity, part of an enormous revitalization scheme that will eventually transform the entire area. Cross Leipziger Strasse and look down the street at the high-rise apartment buildings to the east. Over the past few years, the postwar wasteland of Leipziger Strasse was developed into a Socialist showcase residential street, with new apartments, shops, and cafés. This modern stretch is a vast improvement over the shabby structures that cover so much of postwar East Berlin.

Continue north on Friedrichstrasse. The entire area looks like one huge construction site. Turn right at Mohrenstrasse. You'll see the dome of the German Cathedral and the new *Domhotel* to your left. At Charlottenstrasse turn left, and then right on Johannes-Dieckmann-Strasse, which takes you past the German Cathedral into ****Platz der Akademie** [57].

Entering this square—the most beautiful in Berlin—it's hard to imagine the amount of damage it suffered in the last war. By the end of the war the entire square had been reduced to a pile of smoldering rubble, and it remained in ruins until reconstruction began in 1977. In the 17th century it was the marketplace for a new area laid out by King Friedrich I, called *Friedrichstadt*. Elector Friedrich Wilhelm had Johann Arnold Nering draw up new plans for the area in 1688, after an influx of French Huguenot refugees settled here. The Huguenots—French Protestants—had been forced to flee from France after the Tolerance Edict of Nantes was repealed in 1685. About 20,000 of them came to Brandenburg-Prussia where they were offered asylum under Friedrich Wilhelm's Edict of Potsdam. Until 1950, the square was called the *Gendarmenmarkt* (Gendarme Market) after the "Gens d'Armes" regiment, which had its guardhouse and stables here from 1738 to 1782. The present name, Platz der Akademie, dates from 1950, when the 250th anniversary of the Academy of Sciences was celebrated. The Academy occupies the buildings that form the eastern side of the square. The **Schiller Monument** by Begas, dating from 1868, stands in the center of the square.

The ***Französischer Dom** (French Cathedral) on the north side of the square was the first public building to be erected here, and it still remains the church of the Huguenot congregation. Its cornerstone was laid in 1701, and the sanctuary was dedicated in 1705. Louis Cayart and Abraham Quesnay were responsible for the design and construction.

The French Cathedral reopened in 1984 following its postwar refurbishment. It now houses the small but interesting *Hugenottenmuseum* (Huguenot Museum) which traces the history of the Huguenots in France and Berlin-Brandenburg (hours Tuesday, Wednesday, Saturday 10:00 A.M.–5:00 P.M.; Thursday 10:00 A.M.–6:00 P.M.; Sunday 11:30 A.M.–5:00 P.M.; admission fee). It's a strenuous climb up to the elegant *Turmstuben* (Tower Restaurant and Wine Bar), but well worth the effort (hours daily 10:00 A.M.–midnight). Even higher up is the *Balustrade*, where you're rewarded by a fabulous 360 degree view of the entire city. From here you can see the Reichstag, the Kongresshalle, and all of Berlin's major sights (hours daily 10:00 A.M.–6:00 P.M.; admission free). The entrance to the beautifully restored church, where services are held, is around to the left of the square (hours Tuesday–Saturday 10:00 A.M.–5:00 P.M.; Sunday 1:00–5:00 P.M.; organ recitals first Thursday of every month at 7:30 P.M.).

Standing like a mirror image on the south side of the square, and built at about the same time, you can see the ***Deutscher Dom** (German Cathedral). When they were new, neither church had the magnificent domes that characterize them today. These were added between 1780 and 1785 by Carl von Gontard. Reconstruction work continues on the German cathedral but should be completed soon.

The two cathedrals flank Karl Friedrich Schinkel's first large-scale building, the beautiful neoclassical ***Schauspielhaus** (Playhouse), constructed between 1818 and 1821. This building, once a famous dramatic theater, was built on the foundations of the National Theater designed by Carl Gotthard Langhans in the first years of the 19th century and destroyed by fire in 1817. Previously, the site had been occupied by the French Theater, constructed on orders from Frederick the Great in the last quarter of the 18th century. When the National Theater opened, German-language plays supplanted the French drama that had been standard features of court culture under Frederick the Great. The German tradition continued in the Schauspielhaus, where the first production was Goethe's *Iphigenie auf Tauris* in 1821, followed by the premiere of Carl Maria von Weber's opera *Der Freischütz*. In 1984 the Schauspielhaus reopened as Berlin's most magnificent concert hall. The Berlin Philharmonic and other formerly "West German" musical groups now play here as part of a new cultural exchange program. The ticket office is under the massive stairway.

Take a final look at the lovely cobblestone French-style square, planted with trees in front of the French cathedral. Turn left on Französische Strasse for one block. At Friedrichstrasse turn right for two blocks, passing the *Grand Hotel* (see Walk 13, page 102), to reach ****Unter den Linden*. From here you can begin Walk 13, which covers all the major sights on this famous boulevard, or continue on with Walk 15, which takes you to the museums on *Museumsinsel* (Museum Island).

WALK 15: **Museumsinsel

See map opposite.

Museum Island is an appropriate name for the section of Berlin covered in this walk. Five major museums, filled with treasures from around the globe, are located here on the northern tip of an island formed by the Spree and one of its canals. If your time is limited, head straight for the Pergamon Museum, with its spectacular display of an ancient temple. The richly varied collections in the other museums—the Old Museum, the Bode-Museum, the National Gallery, and the New Museum (currently being restored and closed to the public)—provide the less hurried visitor with a feast of additional masterpieces.

Since the war and the division of the city, politics have played a major role in determining the museum holdings of both West and East Berlin. During the course of the war many works were destroyed. Afterwards, priceless art treasures that had once formed a unified and spectacularly rich collection were divided. A host of new museums was built in West Berlin (in Dahlem and the Kulturforum) to house works that had formerly been shown in the old museum complex here on Museum Island. In East Berlin, even the terminology used to date works of art was secularized. Instead of using B.C., for example, the East Berliners preferred the more neutral v.u.Z. (before our time). The collections are now in the process of being consolidated.

Please note that in 1991, the archaeological collections now housed in the Charlottenburg museums will be moved to the Pergamon Museum and the Altes Museum here on Museum Island.

Museum Island is one of the most important museum complexes in the world. The museum center dates back to the early 19th century, when Friedrich William III issued a decree stipulating that the privately owned art works of the royal family should be made accessible to the general public—for which purpose a public museum was to be created, similar to the ones already in existence in Paris (the Louvre) and London (the British Museum).

Accordingly, Schinkel was commissioned to design the *Altes Museum* (Old Museum), which opened in 1830 at the northern end of the pleasure garden of the Berlin Palace. This magnificent neoclassical building is the second-oldest (after Munich's Glypothek) museum in Germany. The *Neues Museum* (New Museum), designed by Stüler, followed in 1847, and Strack's *Nationalgalerie* opened its doors in 1876. Ernst von Ihne was the architect for the domed *Bode-Museum* (called the Kaiser-Friedrich-Museum until 1956), built between 1897 and 1904 and meant to be the "keystone" of Museum Island. Last to be completed was the *Pergamon-Museum*, today the best known and most frequently visited of all the museums. Work began in 1909 but was interrupted by the First World War. The museum was finally completed in 1930. All of the museums suffered major war damage and have been reconstructed—with the exception of the Neues Museum, which has not yet reopened.

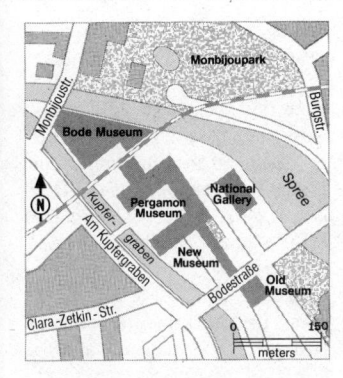

There are several easy ways to reach the museum complex. From Bahnhof Friedrichstrasse you can walk south to **Unter den Linden*, turn left, and follow "The Linden" all the way to *Marx-Engels-Platz*. The *Altes Museum* is to your left, next to the Berlin Cathedral (see Walk 13, page 106). From Checkpoint Charlie, walk north on Friedrichstrasse to Unter den Linden and turn right to reach the Altes Museum. Faster still, take the S-Bahn to Marx-Engels-Platz and walk to the *Friedrichsbrücke* (Friedrich Bridge) via Burgstrasse. As you cross the bridge, the *Nationalgalerie* is to your right and the Altes Museum to your left.

*Altes Museum

(Altes Museum hours: Wednesday–Sunday 10:00 A.M.–6:00 P.M.; closed Monday and Tuesday.)

Schinkel's superb neoclassical 1830 building with its arcade of Ionic columns was the first museum to be constructed in the complex. An enormous granite bowl measuring 7 meters (23 feet) in diameter and weighing 80 metric tons stands in front of it on a pedestal. The museum was reopened in 1960 and contains three important collections. In the *Kunst der DDR der Nationalgalerie* (Art of the DDR from the National Gallery) section on the upper floor (soon to be moved), you'll find representative 20th-century work by East German artists, including sculpture by Eugen Hoffmann, Fritz Cremer, and Werner Stotzer, and paintings by Wilhelm Lachnit, Otto Niemeyer-Holstein, Harald Metzkes, Willi Sitte, Wolfgang Mattheuer, and Werner Tübke; and in the *Sammlung Ludwig Aachen*, contemporary works by Warhol, Hockney, Tinguely, Roy Lichtenstein, and others. The *Kupferstichkabinett* features a wide-ranging collection of prints, engravings, and lithography that covers all of Europe from the 15th century up to the present day (open Monday–Friday only, from 10:00 A.M.–4:00 P.M.; entrance to the right of the museum).

Walk to the left of the Altes Museum along the canal and you'll come to the **Neues Museum,** currently under reconstruction and not open to the public. It will eventually house the Egyptian Museum and the Prehistoric and Early Historical Collection. Behind it, to your right, is the National Gallery, with an entrance on Bodestrasse.

*Nationalgalerie

(Nationalgalerie hours: Wednesday–Sunday 10:00 A.M.–6:00 P.M.; closed Monday and Tuesday.)

The National Gallery, housed in a building designed to look like a Corinthian temple, was built between 1867 and 1876. Over the years, the museum has suffered grievous losses from war damage and the removal of whole collections to West Berlin, although this situation will be rectified in the near future, when the Galerie der Romantik, currently in Charlottenburg Palace, is moved here. Its modern art collection was also a target for the Nazi destruction of "immoral, degenerate and un-German" art in the 1930s. Despite this, however, the museum still provides an excellent overview of the development of painting and sculpture in Germany from the end of the 18th century to the present day. The *19th Century Section* is especially strong, and will introduce you to the work of several important German artists from this period, some of whose work you can see elsewhere in Berlin. Included are Christian Daniel Rauch's marble *bust of the Danish sculptor Bertel Thorvaldsen* (1816) and Reinhold Begas's bronze *Bather* (1867). There's also a piece by Auguste Rodin dating from the turn of the century. Among the German paintings you'll find Friedrich Georg Weitsch's 1806 *Portrait of Alexander von Humboldt,* Karl Begas the Elder's romantic portrait of his wife, *Frau Wilhelmine Begas* (1828), Adolph Menzel's **Iron Rolling Mill* from 1875, Arnold Böcklin's *Hochzeitreise* (Honeymoon) (1878), and important works by *Max Liebermann, Max Slevogt, and Lovis Corinth. Other countries are brilliantly represented by Goya's world-famous **Maypole* and works by Dégas and Cézanne. The **20th Century Section* features paintings and sculptures from the Expressionists, the Bauhaus, and the "Brücke" and "Blue Rider" movements. Of special interest: paintings by Max Pechstein, Ernst Ludwig Kirchner, Karl Schmidt-Rotluff, Oskar Kokoschka, Alexei von Jawlensky, and Otto Dix; sculptures by Ernst Barlach, Rudolf Belling, Wilhelm Lehmbruck, and Joachim Karsch; and photomontages by John Heartfield.

Walk back down Bodestrasse past the New Museum, cross the bridge over the canal, and turn right. The next bridge takes you into the courtyard of the Pergamon, East Berlin's most popular museum.

***Pergamon-Museum

(Pergamon Museum hours: Wednesday–Sunday 10:00 A.M.–6:00 P.M.; on Mondays and Tuesdays only the architectural halls of the Near Eastern Museum and the Collection of Antiquities, including the Pergamon Altar, are open from 10:00 A.M.–6:00 P.M.; free English-language cassette tours are available explaining the historical context of the works.)

The enormous, three-winged Pergamon Museum, completed in 1930, contains the **Antikensammlung* (Antiquity Collection) with the world-famous ***Pergamon Altar, the **Vorderasiatisches Museum* (Near Eastern Museum), the *Islamisches Museum* (Islamic Museum), the *Ostasiatische Sammlung* (Far Eastern Collection), and the *Museum für Völkskunde* (Ethnological Museum). Obviously you'll have to pick and choose what most appeals to your tastes and interests. All the archæological collections from West Berlin are slated to be moved to the Pergamon and Altes museums in the near future.

**Antikensammlung.

The history of the Antiquity Collection goes back to the time of the Great Elector, but it was not until the reign of Frederick the Great that

Pergamon Altar

the collection really became important. For reasons that become obvious the first moment you see it, pride of place goes to the fabulous ***Pergamon Altar,** considered one of the Seven Wonders of the ancient world. Its entire western side was reconstructed here in its own hall. Part of the huge Temple of Zeus and Athena, dating from 180–160 B.C., it was discovered by German archaeologists in Pergamon (a center of Late Hellenistic culture in Western Turkey) in 1876. Sections of the 120-meter (395-foot) frieze that surrounded the altar—depicting a battle between the gods and the giants—have been incorporated into the altar itself. The remaining sections hang on the walls surrounding it. Above the monumental staircase lies a room containing the *Small Pergamon Frieze* (also known as the *Telephos Frieze*). In the center of the room is a *Floor Mosaic from the Palace of Attalos II* (160–150 B.C.).

Another showpiece is located in the *Saal der Römischen Baukunst* (Hall of Roman Architecture). This is the ornate, two-storied ****Market Gate of Miletus,** a Roman building façade dating from the time of Emperor Marcus Aurelius (ca. A.D. 165). The beautiful *Orpheus Mosaic* set in the floor of this room dates from the 2nd century A.D. and comes from the dining room of a private villa in Milet.

Included among the many superb works of early Greek and Roman sculpture in the Antiquities Collection are the **Goddess with a Pomegranate* (ca. 575 B.C.)—the so-called "Berlin Goddess"—with remarkably preserved colors and a suitably mysterious smile, the equally enigmatic *Enthroned Goddess of Tarento* (ca. 470 B.C.), the *Wounded Amazon,* a 5th century B.C. Roman copy of a Greek original in bronze, the charming **Dice Player,* another Roman copy in marble, the stern marble **Bust of the Emperor Caracalla* from A.D. 212, and the **Slave Boy,* a Hellenistic work from Tarento.

Vorderasiatisches Museum. The Near Eastern Museum, with a vast collection comparable only to the one in the British Museum in London, offers a comprehensive overview of 4,000 years of Near Eastern history, art, and culture. The museum is particularly distinguished by its extensive collection of ancient architectural monuments, of which the *****Processional Road from Babylon, decorated with yellow lions on a blue tile background, and Nebuchadnezzar II's ***Ishtar Gate** (both ca. 580 B.C.) are the best known. Across from the Ishtar Gate stands an impressive reconstruction of the **Façade of the Parthian Palace from Assur.* Massive winged beasts—part lion, part bird, part human—guard the entry into another room filled with Assyrian artifacts. Also worth seeing are the *Fortress Gate of Senjirli* (10th–8th century B.C.), the *Victory Stele of King Asarhaddon* (Assyrian, 680–699 B.C.), and the *Giant Bird of Tell Halaf,* dating from ca. 900 B.C.

Islamisches Museum. Established in 1904, the Islamic Museum offers an expansive collection that ranges from the very beginnings of Islamic art to the present day. Of particular importance is the **Façade of the Desert Castle of Mschutta,* dating from the 8th century A.D. It was a gift from the Turkish Sultan Abdulhamid to Emperor Wilhelm II. Two intricately decorated *prayer niches* from 13th century mosques form another part of the collection, as does the 17th-century *Aleppo Room,* taken from the home of a Christian merchant. Outstanding examples of 16th- and 17th-century rugs from Turkey, Anatolia, and Egypt, ancient ceramics, and shadow-puppets represent the applied arts. The collection of *Persian and Indian Miniatures* is also highly recommended.

Ostasiatische Sammlung.

Countless pieces in the museum's Far Eastern collection, first established in 1907, were destroyed in the last war. The collection will eventually be moved to the Dahlem museum complex. Today the museum is noted for its collection of *Chinese Art,* particularly ceramics, with pieces ranging from the Neolithic period to the present day. Vases and bowls of blue-white porcelain from the 18th-century Qianlong period and the 15th-century Ming Dynasty are shown with other treasures such as jade carvings, 18th-century candle holders, and sculptures from the Tang Dynasty (618–907). Connoisseurs of Japanese woodcuts will find a brilliant example from the series "Eight Views of Ryukyu Island" by Hokusai (1760–1849).

Museum für Völkskunde.

The Ethnological Museum, which will soon be relocated, lost fully 80 percent of its collection in the war, and has been slowly built up since then. Here you'll find various examples of German textiles, including traditional costumes, ceramics, furniture, and toys that were used in everyday life. The finest piece in the collection is a 17th-century tiled stove from Winterthur in Switzerland.

Cross the bridge from the Pergamon Museum and turn right. The next bridge—*Monbijou Brücke*—leads to the Bode-Museum.

*Bode-Museum

(Bode-Museum hours: Wednesday–Sunday 10:00 A.M.–6:00 P.M.; closed Monday and Tuesday; admission fee.)

This domed neobaroque building dates from the turn of the century (1897–1904) and was originally called the Kaiser-Friedrich-Museum. It was renamed in 1956 for its founder, Wilhelm von Bode (1845–1929), who was the General Director of the Berlin Museums for many years. At presstime, six major collections were housed in the Bode: Egyptian, Early Christian and Byzantine, Sculpture, Painting, Pre- and Early History, and Coins. With the reshuffling of holdings among the different museums, however, the Bode will eventually take on an entirely different character and become the new home of the varied collections of applied arts.

The museum has a remarkably beautiful interior with marble walls and two curving staircases. There's a pleasant café on the terrace of the second floor. An equestrian statue of Frederick the Great, dating from 1703, guards the domed vestibule.

*Ägyptisches Museum.

The entire scope of Egyptian culture, from the Prehistoric and Early Historical period (5000 to 2778 B.C.) to the Greco-Roman era, is presented in the Egyptian Museum. When reconstruction work is completed on the Neues Museum, the Egyptian collections from East and West Berlin will be moved there. Until that time, an amazing amount of material, particularly large-scale sculptures, remains on display at the Bode. The collection includes objects of international significance.

The most important treasures include *King Narmer's Alabaster Baboon* (ca. 3000 B.C.), the *Reliefs from King Ne-user-Re's Temple to the Sun* (ca. 2400 B.C.), with their graceful depictions of desert animals, the wooden *Statue of Per-her-nofret* (ca. 2450–2290 B.C.), the curious *Cubed Hassock of Sen-en-Mut*, the bronze casket-sculpture of a *Sacred Cat* (ca. 550 B.C.), and the seated statue of the official *Chertihotep* (ca. 1870 B.C.), carved from brown sandstone. Particularly fascinating are four sculpted heads of Egyptian royalty found at Amarna, all dating from ca. 1350 B.C.: the *Head of a Princess*, the *Head of a Queen*, the stucco *Head of Ikhnaton*, and the unfinished but nonetheless haunting *Statue of Nefertiti*, whose painted limestone bust, currently in Charlottenburg (see page 54), will soon be brought to Museum Island. The strikingly painted depictions of *Ahmes-Nofretete* and *Amenophis I* as protective deities of the city of the dead date from about 1200 B.C. and come from Deir el-Medinah. Added to this is a rich collection of mummy cases and mummy portraits, in particular the vivid *Mummy Portrait of a Bearded Man*, which dates from ca. A.D. 200 and shows Roman influence, and the *Mummy Portrait of Aline, Daughter of Herod* (ca. A.D. 25). The spectacular *Golden Treasury* from the pyramid of a Meroitic queen has been on display since 1989.

In our mechanized and computerized age of junk mail and instant telefaxed messages, it's easy to forget how precious handwritten communications were to the ancients—so do have a look at the museum's enormous *Papyrus Collection*, which includes papyri, parchments, wax and wooden tablets, and pieces of stone covered with hieroglyphics and messages in ancient Greek, Latin, and Coptic scripts. These documents and letters date from ca. 1800 B.C. to the 2nd century A.D.

Frühchristlich-byzantinische Sammlung.

The Early Christian-Byzantine Collection is composed primarily of Mediterranean art from the 3rd to the 18th century. There is an excellent display of Coptic (Egyptian Christian) art, which includes grave reliefs and painted wooden tablets, carved reliefs from Rome and Constantinople, and a 6th-century Early Byzantine masterpiece, the *Apse Mosaic from the Church of San Michele in Africisco in Ravenna*. Considerable space has been devoted to a collection of Late Byzantine *icons* from Eastern Europe and the Mediterranean.

*Skulpturensammlung. Although over half of its previous contents is now in Dahlem (see page 78) awaiting consolidation with its eastern counterpart, the Sculpture Collection still houses several outstanding works, including pieces from Germany (13th to 16th century) and the Italian Renaissance. German, Austrian, and Flemish sculpture are represented by the wonderfully expressive 13th-century **Trier Prophets* and **Naumburg Crucifix*, a *Head of Mary* (1400) from Salzburg, the *Group of Lamenters* dating from 1420, Tilman Riemenschneider's **Adoration of the Christ Child* from the early 16th century, and Anton Pilgram's late-15th-century *Pulpit Figure*. The **Passion Altar* from Antwerp and Jan Borman's **Prophet* from Brussels, two works dating from the early 16th century, are both excellent. Significant works from the Italian Renaissance include the **Portrait Bust of a Princess from Urbino* (ca. 1475), the powerful **Portrait Bust of Lorenzo de Medici* (after 1530), which tells you everything you need to know about this brutal Florentine, an early-15th-century **Madonna* by Donatello, Benedetto da Maiano's **Enthroned Madonna* (ca. 1480), and Alessandro Algardi's marble **Portrait of the Cardinal from Montalto*.

Gemäldegalerie. Half of the works that once comprised the Painting Gallery are now on view in Dahlem (see page 77) and will eventually be consolidated, but an important and worthwhile collection covering Germany, Italy, and the Netherlands from the 15th to the 18th centuries still remains here and is well worth a look. The particular strength of the collection lies in works of 17th-century *Dutch and Flemish masters* such as Jan Brueghel the Elder, Jordaens, Ruysdael, Bol, and Terborch, and Italian paintings by Filippo Lippi, Guido Reni, Canaletto, and Tiepolo. Nicolas Poussin's **Self-portrait* is a highlight of the French school, and Thomas Gainsborough's **Portrait of the Painter's Wife* of the English school. Look for Lucas Cranach the Elder's **Portrait of Katharina Bora* in the *Collection of Miniatures*.

Museum für Ur- und Frühgeschichte. The Museum of Prehistory and Early History, once the largest and most important of its kind in Europe, will eventually be moved to the Neues Museum along with the Egyptian Museum. Although much of the collection is now housed in Charlottenburg (see page 53), the finds displayed here still present a fascinating picture of the earliest epochs of European history. Included are parts of self-taught 19th-century archaeologist Heinrich Schliemann's collection of **Trojan antiquities* (his discovery proved to a doubting world that Troy was not simply a legend), Paleolithic implements from the Old Stone Age (ca. 200,000 B.C.),

Bronze Age vessels from Turkey, pieces of bronze jewelry from ca. 1500 B.C. and 800–500 B.C., exquisite examples of glass from the Roman era (3rd–4th century A.D.) and the 7th century, and a wooden cult figure from Friesia dating from the 6th century A.D.

Münzkabinett. The Coin Cabinet, with its half-million exhibits, adds a certain undeniable veracity to the old saying "money makes the world go around." Housed in the oldest part of the museum, it boasts one of the largest collections of its kind in the world, and the pieces on display represent only a fraction of the museum's holdings (the rest can only be viewed by appointment). Gold and silver Greek and Roman coins, dating from the 7th century B.C. to about A.D. 300, are stamped with representations of Athena, owls (symbol of ancient Athens), Poseidon, Homer, athletes, and Roman emperors. Bishops, kings, and emperors appear on gold and silver solidi, denari, groschen, and double royal d'ors from the Merovingian and Carolingian dynasties and the Middle Ages. There are Oriental coins from the 3rd to the 10th centuries A.D., and 15th to 18th century silver coins from Germany, Austria, Russia, Spain, and France. In addition, there is a collection of Renaissance medallions, seal stamps from the 14th and 15th centuries, and bank notes from 17th-century Sweden and 19th-century Prussia and Austria.

WALK 16: Alexanderplatz–Marienkirche–Rathaus– *Nikolaiviertel (–Markisches Museum)

See map opposite.

Our last walk in Berlin takes in the huge square known as Alexanderplatz, nearby St. Mary's Church, and the Old Berlin City Hall before continuing on to the historic heart of the city, the Nicholas Quarter. Two to three hours will be sufficient to see these sights, but you may want to round out the tour by going on to visit the Mark Brandenburg Museum, which shows the historical development of Berlin from its earliest beginnings to the present day.

Begin the tour by taking the S-Bahn or No. 100 bus from Bahnhof Zoo to **Alexanderplatz.** The name of Berlin's old Wool Market and Parade Ground was changed to Alexanderplatz in honor of a visit by the Russian Czar Alexander I in 1805. Right up to the Second World War "the Alex" was one of the busiest places in the capital—the representative piece of the old Berlin Alfred Döblin used as the setting for his novel *Berlin Alexanderplatz* (later made into a German television mini-series by Rainer

Werner Fassbinder). Before the war, nine streets from the city's northern districts converged at "the Alex," making it a busy traffic hub. After the war, which reduced the entire area to little more than rubble, East Berlin city planners eschewed historical reconstruction in favor of "new planning free of nostalgia." Although this wasn't necessarily a bad idea, the execution of it was unimaginative. As a result, Alexanderplatz seems somewhat austere, with the glum-looking buildings that often characterize ideological architecture. The square was not designed for a casual stroll but rather as a grand public square for political rallies. Indeed, it was here that huge crowds gathered to cheer leaders of the GDR, just as previous generations had hailed Hitler and his henchmen and the various kings and emperors who preceded them.

As public sentiment has a way of turning and the winds of perestroika made their way to Berlin, this square became one of many gathering points in East Germany for thousands of people demanding a change in government in 1989. Now that change has been effected, today's Alexanderplatz is a huge flea market, dotted with booths and stands selling all sorts of merchandise, including GDR military uniforms, insignia, and other mementos from the former regime.

The new 39-story Interhotel *"Stadt Berlin"* rises behind the S-Bahn station and, to one side of it, East Berlin's largest department store, *Centrum*. Now that former

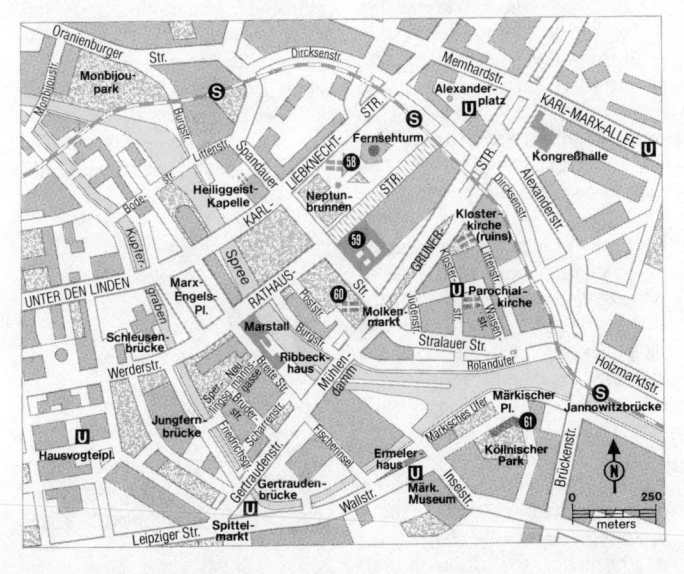

East German consumers can "buy West," stores like Centrum, once filled with generally shabby Eastern Bloc merchandise, have been completely overhauled and restocked with western goods. On the other side of the hotel is the *Reisebüro-Hochhaus* (Travel Bureau Skyscraper), where you can obtain theater tickets and private lodging or hotel rooms in this part of the city, as well as the eastern states of Brandenburg, Sachsen, Thüringen, and Mecklenburg/Vorpommern (hours Monday–Wednesday, Friday 10:00 A.M.–6:00 P.M.; Thursday 10:00 A.M.–7:00 P.M.; Saturday 9:00 A.M.–noon). Close to the S-Bahn is the *World Chronometer,* an international clock that is a popular meeting place and the *Brunnen der Völkerfreundschaft* (Fountain of Friendship among the Nations).

In front of you, dominating the square—and seemingly the entire city—is the 365-meter- (1,200-foot-) high **Fernsehturm** (Television Tower), completed in 1969 and known to Berliners as the "Telespargel" (Telesparagus). At the base of the tower is a complex of triangular buildings, one of which contains the **Informationszentrum,** where you can pick up general information on the city and arrange to rent rooms. (*Hours Tuesday–Friday 8:00 A.M.–7:00 P.M.; Saturday and Sunday 10:00 A.M.–6:00 P.M.; Monday 1:00– 7:00 P.M.*) If it's a clear day, you might want to shoot up to the *observation platform* for a 200-meter- (660-foot-) high

*view of Berlin and its surrounding areas, or eat in the slowly revolving *Telecafé* (hours daily 8:00 A.M.– 11:00 P.M.). The entrance is in the first building.

Head now towards the church located to one side of the square behind the television tower. This is the **Marienkirche** [58]. The Church of St. Mary—the second oldest in Berlin after St. Nicholas (see description below)—was built here in the 15th century above the remains of an earlier structure. The 18th-century architect C. G. Langhans designed the present Gothic-like steeple in 1790. St. Mary's restored *interior offers a pleasant respite from city noise. In the hall of the tower you'll find the faint traces of a 22-meter- (72-foot-) long medieval fresco called *The Dance of Death,* painted by an unknown master after the devastating plague of 1484. The ornate Baroque *pulpit* by Andreas Schlüter dates from 1703, and the bronze *baptismal font* in the choir from the 15th century. You'll also want to see the magnifi-

St. Mary's Church

cent *organ* built in 1719–1721 by J. Wagner; if you're lucky you'll hear it being played. *(Hours Monday–Thursday 9:00 A.M.– noon and 1:00–4:00 P.M.; Saturday noon–4:00 P.M.; organ recitals every Sunday at 4:00 P.M. from May through October.)*

From the church head toward the nearby **Neptunbrunnen** (Neptune Fountain), a late-19th-century creation by Reinhold Begas. The city of Berlin presented the bronze fountain to the Kaiser in 1901. Four fin-de-siècle beauties representing what were once four great German rivers— the Rhine, the Elbe, the Oder, and the "Weichsel"—sit below Neptune on the fountain's rim. (The Weichsel is again called the Vystula and runs right through downtown Warsaw.)

Across Rathaus Strasse you'll see the impressive **Rathaus** [59]. Old Berlin's City Hall stood at this location as early as the end of the 13th century. The present building—called *Rotes Rathaus* (Red City Hall) because of its red brick façade—is the fifth to stand on the site. Built in a neo-Renaissance style between 1861 and 1870 to plans by H. F. Waesemann, its 74-meter- (243-foot-) high tower quickly became a city landmark. A stone frieze relating the history of Berlin runs around the second floor of the building. Badly damaged in the war, the City Hall was reconstructed in 1955. (Across the street you'll find two sculptures by Fritz Cremer that commemorate the postwar clean-up and rebuilding of Berlin:

the *Reconstruction Helper* and the *Rubble Woman*.) If you're looking for a place to eat, there's a well-known, handsome *Ratskeller* in the building.

Cross Spandauer Strasse and take one of the paths through the park known as **Marx-Engels-Forum**. In the center of the park you'll see the massive figures of *Karl Marx* and *Frederick Engels*, authors of the historical theory that was heavily reconstructed into a number of political ideologies. Cross *Marx-Engels-Forum* when you come to the Spree and continue along the riverside promenade known as Spreeufer. You'll see an enormous grey building across the river. The part closest to the *Rathaus-Brücke* (City Hall Bridge) is the **Alter Marstall**, the old Military Stable built between 1665 and 1670 to serve the Berlin Palace. The building is attached to the **Ribbeckhaus** (Ribbeck House), which fronts on Breite Strasse. The only intact Renaissance town house in Berlin—it dates from 1624—the Ribbeck mansion adjoins the late-19th-century *Neuer Marstall* (New Military Stable), now the home of the city library and archives.

Continue on Spreeufer to *Kirchplatz*, where you'll see Kiss's 1849 bronze statue of St. George (called *The Dragon Slayer*), flanked by new town house construction. The scale and shape of the poured concrete buildings suggests an earlier historical style in keeping with the surrounding buildings of the **Nikolaiviertel* (St. Nicholas Quarter), which was restored for the 1987 celebrations of Berlin's 750th birthday. There's a café on either side of St. George, should you wish to stop for a bit.

Looking up Propststrasse you can see the beautiful twin-towered church that gives this quarter its name, the **Nikolaikirche** [60]. Built around 1230, the Church of St. Nicholas is the oldest in Berlin. A three-naved cathedral dedicated to the patron saint of sea-going merchants, this Gothic church serves as a reminder of Berlin's past as an important river trade route. Much altered over the years, especially after the Reformation, St. Nicholas was given a major restoration between 1876 and 1878—and was then destroyed by fire towards the end of the Second World War. Rebuilding began in 1982, with the church acting as a centerpiece for the major historical reconstruction scheme that has transformed the entire St. Nicholas quarter. Since 1987, St. Nicholas has been used as an annex to the *Markisches Museum* to house various exhibits ranging from historical weapons and armor to gold jewelry. It's worth a quick stroll, and gives you a chance to admire the beautifully restored interior of the church itself. *(Hours Tuesday–Friday 9:00 A.M.–5:00 P.M.; Saturday 9:00 A.M.–6:00 P.M.; Sunday 10:00 A.M.–6:00 P.M.)*

*Nikolaiviertel

This area near the *Mühlendammbrücke* (Mühlendamm Bridge) is the historical heart of the ancient settlement of Berlin-Cölln. The central square of old Berlin was located on *Molkenmarkt* (Dairy Market), and a ford crossed over the Spree to Cölln's *Fischerinsel* (Fisherman's Island) and the *Cöllner Fischmarkt* (Cölln Fish Market) on the other side. Destroyed in the war, the area became the focus of a major historical reconstruction scheme in 1982, and work was completed in time for Berlin's 750th birthday celebrations five years later. Nearly 800 apartments, 22 restaurants, and 30 shops were built—historically significant buildings from other parts of the city were moved and reconstructed here, and new buildings went up in a style reminiscent of a medieval town center. All in all, the project has been a great success.

Stroll all around the church and its surrounding cobblestone streets and courtyards to take in the flavor of the quarter. The seals of Berlin's ancient guilds are inlaid in the trough of the *Handwerkbrunnen* (Craftsmen's Fountain) in front of the church, and a relief of the oldest seal of the city is engraved on its monument stone. To one side of the fountain stands a reconstruction of the ancient inn *Zum Nussbaum* (At the Sign of the Nut Tree), where the artist Heinrich Zille—whose earthy drawings of Berlin's blue collar population in the 1920s are still popular—was a regular (hours daily 10:00 A.M.–midnight). On the opposite side of the fountain is the *Knoblauchhaus* (Garlic House), with its "Historical Wine Rooms" on the ground floor—you can sip a glass between 5:00 P.M. and 2:00 A.M.

Walk down Poststrasse to Mühlendamm and turn left. At No. 4 Mühlendamm is the *Berliner Handwerksmuseum*, with an exhibition on Berlin's trade guilds from the Middle Ages to the 19th century (hours Monday 10:00 A.M.– 5:00 P.M.; Tuesday and Wednesday 9:00 A.M.– 5:00 P.M.; Saturday and Sunday 10:00 A.M.–6:00 P.M.). On the opposite corner you'll see the Baroque façade of the **Ephraim-Palais** (Ephraim Palace), considered the most beautiful town house in the city during the 18th and 19th centuries. Temporary exhibits from the Märkisches Museum are displayed inside, and there's a restaurant *(hours Monday 10:00 A.M.– 4:00 P.M.; Tuesday and Sunday 10:00 A.M.– 5:00 P.M.; Wednesday and Saturday 10:00 A.M.– 6:00 P.M.).*

*

From the Nikolaiviertel you can wend your way back to the S-Bahn at Alexanderplatz in a few minutes. If you're in a museum mood, you can extend this walk by crossing the Mühlendammbrücke over the Spree and continuing down Mühlendamm to *Fischerinsel*, where you turn left. Take this street to Märkisches Ufer on the other side of the Spree canal and turn left again. This is a lovely riverside street lined with restored mansions. The neoclassical *Ermeler Haus* is a restaurant offering riverside dining in good weather. Next to it is a restored 1740 town house. The **Otto-Nagel-Haus** (Otto Nagel House) at No. 16–18 features a collection of revolutionary and anti-fascist art and other exhibitions *(hours Sunday– Thursday 10:00 A.M.–6:00 P.M.; Wednesday 10:00 A.M.–8:00 P.M.; closed Friday and Saturday; admission free).*

Turn right at the next street, Inselstrasse, and then left at the first corner. Wallstrasse will lead you to the *Köllnischer Park*, where a statue of Heinrich Zille and part of a 17th-century fortification tower are located. The enormous **Märkisches Museum** building is located in this park.

If you're interested in Old Berlin history and artifacts, this museum won't disappoint you. The Mark Brandenburg Museum was founded in 1874 and moved into this fortresslike structure in 1908. The exhibitions in its 38 rooms span the entire history of Berlin. Especially noteworthy is the *collection of Berlin porcelain and faïence* from the Berlin-Brandenburg region and the section on *Berlin Theater History*, both located on the second floor. The third floor features rooms devoted to Berlin painting and applied arts and a delightful *collection of mechanical musical instruments.* There is a charming walled terrace garden tucked away to one side of the museum. *(Hours*

Wednesday–Sunday 10:00 A.M.–6:00 P.M.; closed Monday and Tuesday.)

The fastest way back to Alexanderplatz from here is by U-Bahn, which you can catch at the Märkisches Museum station just down the street.

Other Sights to See in East Berlin

Although not included in the previous walks around the eastern portion of Berlin, you might want to explore the following places, even though (or because) they are off the beaten tourist path.

*Museum für Naturkunde (Museum of Natural History)

(Invaliden Strasse 43. S-Bahn and U-Bahn to Friedrichstrasse, then Bus 57 or 59 north to museum. Hours Tuesday–Sunday 9:30 A.M.–5:00 P.M.; closed Monday.)

If you're interested in natural history and would like to view the largest fully-restored dinosaur skeleton in the world, drop in for a visit at this museum. One of the leading natural history museums in the world, it houses the mineral, zoological, and paleontological collections of Humboldt University. Prehistoric skeletons—from an archaeopteryx to a 12-meter- (40-foot-) high Brachosaurus—are the main points of interest here.

*Kunstgewerbemuseum im Schloss Köpenick (Handcrafts Museum in Kopenick Castle)

(Schlossinsel [Palace Island], Köpenick. S-Bahn to Spindlersfeld, walk down Oberspree Strasse to the palace. Hours Wednesday to Sunday 10:00 A.M.–6:00 P.M.)

Housed in a Baroque palace built by Dutch architect Rutger von Langerfelt between 1680 and 1690 for Crown Prince Friedrich III, it features exhibits dating from the Late Middle Ages to the present day, including historical furniture, porcelain, glass, and leather articles. Highlights of the various collections: the 10th-century *jewels of Princess Gisela* and King Frederick I's *Silver Buffet*, made between 1695 and 1698. The palace rooms are beautifully restored and an appropriate setting for the treasures in them.

Sowjetisches Ehrenmal (Soviet Memorial)

(Treptower Park. S-Bahn to Treptower Park.)

Located at the far end of the 195-acre Treptow Park, which was laid out in 1885, the colossal Soviet

Memorial commemorates the city's liberation by the Russian army in 1945. A grey stone statue of a mourning Russian mother stands in the forecourt of a field of honor where some 4,800 Russian soldiers who died in the 1945 Battle of Berlin lay buried. The memorial ends at a Hill of Honor, in which an additional 200 Russian soldiers are buried in a 33-meter (108-foot) pyramidal mausoleum crowned by an enormous bronze statue of a Red Army soldier carrying a rescued child in his arms, his sword lowered on a broken swastika. Most of the building material comes from the ruins of Hitler's *Reichskanzlei* (Chancellory).

Müggelsee

(S-Bahn to Friedrichshagen, then walk south on Bolsche Strasse to the shores of the lake.)

A favorite excursion spot—as popular in its own way as the Wannsee in West Berlin—the 1,865-acre Müggel Lake in the Köpenick district has a *beach* at its northern end (not recommended for swimming, however). Across the lake, the gentle slopes of the *Müggelberge* (Müggelberg Mountains) rise, with the *Müggelturm* (Müggel Tower) atop the *Kleine* (Small) *Müggelberg*. Built in 1961 with a restaurant inside, the tower provides a splendid *panoramic view across the lake to the surrounding countryside. From here, hiking trails lead off to Müggelheim, Rahnsdorf, and Friedrichshagen.

Synagoge Oranienburger Strasse

(Oranienburger Strasse 30. S-Bahn to Oranienburger Strasse, then walk down the street of the same name to reach the synagogue.)

The synagogue on Oranienburger Strasse was designed by the architect Eduard Knoblauch and built in Moorish-Byzantine style between 1859 and 1866. As Jews became increasingly threatened by the rise of National Socialism in the 1930s, the synagogue's traditional function as a gathering place and cultural center increased in importance. It was often used as a concert hall for Jewish artists who were banned from performing in other places. On November 9, 1938—"Kristallnacht"—members of the Nazi SA-police troop severely damaged the building, and further destruction occurred when a bomb struck the synagogue in February, 1943. The ruins of the main façade were left as a memorial after the war. Newly reconstructed, the building will serve as the "New Synagogue-Centrum Judaicum."

Tierpark Berlin in Friedrichsfelde (Zoo)

(U-Bahn to Tierpark, hours daily from 7:00 A.M.; in winter from 8:00 A.M.)

The 400-acre Berlin Zoo was created in 1955 on the grounds of the Schlosspark (Palace Park) Friedrichsfelde. Nearly 8,000 animals of over 900 different species roam about the open enclosures and in special sections. Deer, elephants, kangaroos, bison, and pelicans are some of the animals you can find here. The *polar bear enclosure* is noteworthy, as are the *terrarium* and the *Alfred-Brehm-Haus* for lions and tigers. **Schloss Friedrichsfelde** (Friedrichsfelde Palace), built between 1690 and 1719, is also in the park and offers tours of its historic rooms at 11:00 A.M., 1:00, and 3:00 P.M. Concerts and lectures are often held here as well.

Cemeteries

*Dorotheenstädtischer Friedhof (Dorotheenstadt Cemetery). *(Chaussee Strasse. S-Bahn to Friedrichstrasse, then No. 57 or 59 bus north to Tieckstrasse. Hours daily 9:00 A.M.–4:00 P.M.)*

Dorotheenstadt is East Berlin's most important historical cemetery. Here lie the philosophers *Fichte* (1762–1814) and *Hegel* (1770–1831), the architect *Schinkel* (1781–1841), the novelist *Heinrich Mann* (1871–1950), and, beside his wife, actress *Helene Weigel* (1900–1971), the playwright *Bertolt Brecht* (1898–1956).

Friedhof Weissensee (Weissensee Cemetery). *(Herbert-Baum-Strasse 45. S-Bahn to Ernst-Thälmann-Park, then No. 24, 28, or 58 streetcar to Antonplatz, walk about a block to Herbert-Baum-Strasse and turn right to reach the cemetery.)*

One of the largest Jewish cemeteries in Europe, Weissensee contains the graves of *Lesser Ury, Samuel Fischer, Theodor Wolff,* the Resistance fighters *Herbert Baum* and *Richard* and *Charlotte Holzer,* and other prominent figures from Berlin's Jewish past.

Friedhof Schönhauser Allee (Schönhauser Allee Cemetery). *(Schönhauser Allee 23–25. U-Bahn to Senefelderplatz, then walk north on Schönhauser Allee to the cemetery.)*

The Old Jewish Cemetery contains the graves of the composer *Giacomo Meyerbeer* (1791–1864) and the painter *Max Liebermann* (1847–1935), among other prominent Jewish Berliners.

SPECIAL EXCURSION: *Potsdam–***Schloss Sanssouci

Frederick the Great's Sanssouci Palace in Potsdam is to Berlin what Louis XIV's Versailles is to Paris: Each stands as a visual signature of the dominant personality in the city's history. One of the greatest and most beautiful examples of European Rococo, the palace itself is surrounded by a magnificent park filled with an abundance of remarkable buildings. This tour guides you through the historic city of Potsdam and takes in all

Special Excursion: Potsdam—Sanssouci

the major sights at Sanssouci. Allow one full day for this excursion. It takes about an hour to reach Potsdam from Bahnhof Zoo.

To reach Potsdam by car: Take the Avus highway south to Ernst-Thälmann-Strasse, which cuts through the Babelsberg district and leads to Friedrich-Engels-Strasse. Take Frederich-Engels-Strasse to Heinrich-Mann-Allee, turn right, cross the bridges, and continue on Friedrich-Ebert-Strasse to the *Nikolaikirche* and the start of the walking tour.

To get to Potsdam using public transportation: the simplest way is to take the S-Bahn to Wannsee. Signs there will guide you to the Potsdam S-Bahn trains. Take the S-Bahn from Wannsee to Potsdam West; from there, you catch the No. 1, 4, or 6 tram to Platz der Einheit. Alternatively, across the street from the Wannsee station you can catch the No. 99 bus, which goes all the way to the Nikolaikirche (Bassinplatz stop) and the start of this tour. The bus trip takes about 35 minutes, depending on traffic. You can also take the S-Bahn to Wannsee and, from there, the No. 6 bus to its last stop, Glienicker Brücke (see Walk 8, page 73). On the other side of the bridge you can hop on the No. 3 or 7 streetcar, which will take you to Platz der Einheit, close to the Nikolaikirche.

*Potsdam

This former garrison town on the Havel River is one of Germany's most historically and artistically important sites, although you might not think so from the dilapidated air of many of its outlying and inner city streets. Potsdam, like so much of Berlin, was severely damaged in the air-raid attacks of World War II, and rebuilding has been a slow and at times arduous proposition. Postwar neglect, lack of funds, and pollution all took their toll. The pace of reconstruction has moved into the fast track, however, now that Potsdam has been declared the capital of the March Brandenburg and is nearing its thousandth anniversary in 1993. Whole sections of the city are being spruced up and given the kind of face-lift Berlin received in 1987 when it celebrated its 750th birthday. Potsdam's new city government—the first freely elected government in years—and cooperation between east and west has substantially accelerated the city's overhaul. Even before reunification, the two countries merged the administration of the important palaces in the area to improve restoration and maintenance efforts in these historically significant buildings.

Potsdam received its town charter in the 13th or 14th century. Devastated by the effects of the Thirty Years' War (1618–1648), it did not gain importance until the "Great Elector" Friedrich William, enchanted by the lovely countryside, chose the area to be his second seat of residence (outside Berlin). The *Edict of Pots-*

dam, issued here by Friedrich William in 1685, granted settlement rights to the persecuted French Protestants (Huguenots) (see Walk 14, page 108), many of whom then came to Potsdam and went to work as skilled craftsmen in the great palaces at Sanssouci. Successive Prussian kings—especially Frederick II (Frederick the Great) and Frederick William IV—left their mark on the town. To escape from Berlin and the rigors of court life, Frederick II built a "small" country palace in Potsdam where he could retire "sans souci" ("without a care") and indulge his passions for music, poetry, and philosophy. The philosopher Voltaire and the composer Johann Sebastian Bach were among the king's visitors at Sanssouci. Potsdam retained its "royal connection" with the Hohenzollerns through the 19th century and up to the revolution of 1918.

It was from Potsdam that Hitler laid out the foundation for the Third Reich's expansionist policies in 1933—and witnessed their result twelve years later when the city was laid waste in an Allied bombing on the night of April 14, 1945. When the war ended, the victorious Allies gathered in Potsdam's *Cecilienhof Palace* (now a hotel) to decide Germany's fate—a conference that culminated in the signing of the *Potsdam Agreement* on August 2, 1945.

The tour begins in Potsdam's *Alter Markt*. The *Potsdam Information Office*, on the ground floor of a new building, is a good place to pick up a city map and information on the cultural events taking place in the city or to reserve a room if you're staying over night (hours daily 9:00 A.M.–6:00 P.M.).

The restored **Nikolaikirche** (Church of St. Nicholas), rebuilt in the middle of the 19th century to original plans by Karl Friedrich Schinkel, dominates the market place. The **Altes Rathaus** (Old City Hall) stands on the south side of the square. Built in 1753 and impressively restored, it now houses the *Kulturhaus "Hans Marschwitza,"* a cultural center with changing exhibitions. A gilded mid-18th-century statue of Atlas crowns the building. Directly beside it is the **Knobelsdorffbau**, a city palace dating from 1750. An obelisk in the center of the square commemorates the city's most important architects. The new construction impinging on one side of the Alter Markt will eventually yield a new theater. Controversy already swirls around its escalating price tag.

Head back to Friedrich-Ebert-Strasse and cross it to get to the **Marstall** (Stables). This building served as an orangerie when it was built in 1685. Von Knobelsdorff extended the structure in 1746. Today it acts as a *film museum* and contains a restaurant and a gallery (*hours 10:00 A.M.–5:30 P.M.; closed Mondays*).

Take Friedrich-Ebert-Strasse down past the *Platz der Einheit*, a park on your right, to Brandenburger Strasse. Turn right to reach Am Bassin and a lively local market that's often set up in front of the

Special Excursion: Potsdam—Sanssouci

Catholic *Church of Saints Peter and Paul*. To your right is the main bus station with its modern blue roof. To your left is the **Holländisches Viertel** (Dutch Quarter), a residential area whose gabled, two-story red-brick houses were constructed by Dutch builders between 1734 and 1742.

Head up Brandenburger Strasse, Potsdam's major restored shopping street, lined with shops, outdoor stalls, restaurants and cafés. To your right, on Friedrich-Ebert-Strasse, you'll see the neo-Gothic ochre-colored **Nauener Tor** (Nauen Gate), dating from 1755. Four green buildings form the cornerstones of Dortus Strasse. Continue straight on to the **Brandenburger Tor** (Brandenburg Gate) in front of the *Platz der Nationen*. Unger and Gotthard redesigned the gate in its present form in 1770. There is a charming little fountain to your right and restaurants on either side of the square.

Cut across the Platz der Nationen to your right and head up the Allee Nach Sanssouci, at the end of which is an entrance to the grounds of Sanssouci.

***Sanssouci

The most important artists of their day contributed to the design of the buildings and the 741-acre landscaped park of Sanssouci. Frederick the Great created the original design for the grounds, and his planning is still evident in the restored vineyard terraces and the area immediately surrounding the palace. Von Knobelsdorff laid out the eastern section of the palace gardens in the form of French parterres. The western part was created by Büring and Manger in Anglo-Chinese style at the time of construction of the *New Palace*. During the second round of building under Frederick William IV, the renowned landscape architect Peter Joseph Lenné, who landscaped the Pfaueninsel and the Klein-Glienicke Palace (see Walk 8, page 73) laid out the beautiful *Marlygarten* and the *Sicilian Garden*.

A chestnut avenue with Italianate pavilions leads from the park's entrance to a right turn, where you have your first glimpse of the palace of Sanssouci perched at the top of a series of beautifully scaled terraces. Continue down another chestnut-lined promenade with a moat on either side, cross the bridge, and you'll come to the beautiful **Great Fountain,** with its water jet splashing in a pool surrounded by classically inspired statuary. It's a view Frederick never enjoyed himself because the pumps built in the 18th century to supply the palace fountains turned out to be inadequate for the job at hand. Two long avenues lead off from here, one towards the *New Palace* (see description below), the other towards the *Obeliskportal* (Obelisk Portal) and the 18th-century obelisk beyond it (this is another main entrance to Sanssouci).

Climb up the six *terraced vineyards* planned by Frederick the Great and dedicated to Bacchus,

130 Special Excursion: Potsdam–Sanssouci

Sanssouci Palace with terraced vineyards

the Greek god of wine. There are 840 niches for grape vines, each one ingeniously protected by a glass door that can be opened in summer and closed in winter. At the top you face the impressive south façade of Schloss Sanssouci.

***Schloss Sanssouci.

The palace was built between 1745 and 1747 by Georg Wenzeslaus von Knobelsdorff, one of the 18th century's most important architects, as a summer residence for Frederick II. French was spoken at the Prussian court in those days, and German used only for confidential matters or addressing soldiers or servants.

The southern, or garden front, of the 12-room, one-story palace is some 97-meters (318-feet) long and has a protruding semi-circle in the center topped by a small cupola. Caryatids sculpted by Friedrich Christian Glume frame the rounded windows. Two separate buildings flank the palace. The *Picture Gallery* (now closed), to your right (east) side as you face the palace, was built between 1755 and 1763 by Büring to house a collection of Flemish and Italian paintings, making it one of Germany's oldest museums. It is balanced on the western side by the *Neue Kammern* (New Chambers), built to house Frederick the Great's guests (tours daily except Friday; admission fee).

Follow the palace façade around to your right, through the exquisite wrought-iron *Gitterpavillon*, an open-air pavilion with gilded capitals, and then turn left to reach the true "front" of the palace.

The north façade of Sanssouci presents an entirely different aspect. A colonnade embraces a court of honor and frames a view of the *Ruinenberg* in the distance. If it looks like a bit of ancient Rome, it's because the 18th-century designers had exactly that picturesque effect in mind. This is the entrance to Sanssouci, where you'll find the ticket office (Kasse). If you want to see the rooms, you must be part of a guided tour (admission fee). It's wise to get here as early as possible: only 1,800 visitors are allowed in per day, in strictly regulated groups of 40. You will be assigned a tour time, which may be at a much later hour than you had hoped. Tours are given in German only, but you'll be able to appreciate the rooms even if you don't understand the language.

The *interior is decorated in magnificent Rococo and contains an abundance of treasures from the time of Frederick the Great. Until his death in 1786, Frederick spent his summers at Sanssouci, here in the palace he loved most. (In fact, sometime in 1991 his body will be returned here for burial.) The palace was then irregularly lived in—mostly by foreign princes—until 1840, when Frederick William IV and his wife Queen Luise became seasonal occupants. The state seized Sanssouci after the 1918 revolution and opened it to the public in 1926. Much of the castle and surrounding area was heavily damaged in World War II, and restoration did not begin in earnest until 1963. It is now nearly complete, and displays all the magnificent Rococo splendor of Frederick's "carefree palace." Sanssouci was recently placed on UNESCO's list of cultural treasures, which will likely spur on restoration of the other buildings on the grounds.

You can spend an entire day exploring the rest of the grounds and buildings that comprise Sanssouci. A 2.5 km. (1.5 mile) avenue leads from the Great Fountain west to the New Palace. Follow this beautiful French-style allee past the *Glocken Fontane* and two statuary groves. A pathway to your left leads to the splendid ***Chinese Tea House,** an 18th-century gem of Rococo chinoiserie designed by Büring and completed in 1756. Gilded statues of Chinese tea drinkers flank the front entrance of what is now a museum with an exhibition of Asian and European porcelain, and a fanciful figure under a parasol sits atop the cupola. Back on the main allee, a path to your right leads to the twin-towered, Italian Renaissance-inspired **Orangerie,** constructed by two of Schinkel's protegés, Stüler and Hesse, in the mid-19th century. It's a bit of a climb to reach the building, which was once occupied by Empress Charlotte of Russia and her husband Czar Nicholas I and is currently in need of extensive restoration. Farther on to your right stands the **Drachenhaus** (Dragon House), another "picturesque" 18th-century building. Originally the house of the royal winegrower, it is now a café.

At the end of the long, leafy promenade is the late-Baroque Neues Palais.

Neues Palais. Constructed between 1763 and 1769 (immediately after the Seven Years War), the 200-room New Palace, with its pale pink façade, was built partially to flaunt the undiminished wealth of the Prussian treasury. It was used as a royal guest house and as another summer house for the Hohenzollern royalty. Büring—who built the Picture Gallery and the Chinese Tea House—was in charge of construction until 1764, after which Carl von Gontard took over. The *interior (tours only; admission fee) is divided into single apartments accessible by four staircases. Especially notable is Gontard's *Grotto Hall,* with its colored inlaid marble floor and walls decorated with shells, minerals, corals, and glass stalagmites, and the beautifully restored 18th-century *Theater.* Behind the palace is another Gontard contribution: the **Communs,** where the employees and lower members of the court once lived. The original purpose of this structure, which resembles two small palaces connected by a colonnade and triumphal arch, was to hide the offensive swampland behind it from Frederick the Great's eyes. Today it's used as a teacher-training college and is being restored.

If you cut southeast from the New Palace through the *Park Charlottenhof* (the park is to your left as you face the New Palace), you can see two additional buildings. The grounds here are not broken into formal gardens, but have the look of an English parkland dotted here and there with garden deities. The beautiful classically inspired **Charlottenhof Palace,** designed by Schinkel and surrounded by a 716-acre garden laid out by Lenné, dates from 1825–1829. A path leads north to an Italianate villa that was built about the same time. It is known as the **Römanische Bäder** (Roman Baths). It originally housed the Sanssouci gardeners.

Continue on the path until you come to a bridge where you turn right and pass through a building. Don't leave by the gate here, but follow the path across the stream and turn right. An asphalt path leads back behind the Chinese Tea House and the main path to Sanssouci. At the Great Fountain, head down the path to the Obelisk Portal, which exits to Schopenhauer Strasse. Turn right and follow the street to the Platz der Nationen. From here you can retrace your steps down Brandenburger Strasse to the main bus terminal, where the No. 99 bus will take you back to the Wannsee S-Bahn station.

Practical Information

This chapter is divided into sections designed to help you plan and research your trip. It offers tips on transportation to and around Berlin, customs regulations, hotels, restaurants, nightlife, museums, theaters, sources of further information, and other items of interest. (See listing in *Contents* for the full range of subjects covered.)

Choosing When to Go. Since the collapse of the Berlin Wall in late 1989 and the subsequent reunification of East and West Germany, Berlin's charged political, economic, and social climate has captured world attention. As the two cultures of East and West Berlin mix for the first time since the 1960s, great changes have already begun to affect both sides of the city.

Berlin's lively schedule of events draws visitors the whole year round. The beautiful weather from May through October enhances the pleasure of exploring this vibrant city during the peak travel season. Among the city's special events during this time are the German-American Folk Festival and the Franco-German Folk Festival, which take place from June through August, and the International Berlin Marathon, a 42 km. (25 mile) run through Berlin.

Berliners and tourists alike enjoy the city's many cultural activities. Berlin's Philharmonic Orchestra opens its winter concert series in November. The Berlin Jazz Festival and the city's famous antiques fair also take place in November. Rows of outdoor tents at the annual Christmas market entice visitors with their antiques, beautifully crafted gift items, and atmosphere of *Gemütlichkeit* (good cheer). Professional cyclists take to the road in January to compete in the exciting Six-Day Race. The International Green Week Agricultural Fair also draws crowds to the city during January. Berlin's important film festival, the "Berlinale," takes place in February, and ranks in international stature with those held in Cannes and Venice.

National Holidays. Listed below are the holidays celebrated in Germany. Specific dates for some holidays vary from year to year.

New Year's Day (January 1)
Good Friday
Pentecost Monday
German Unity Day
All Saints Day (November 1)

Day of Prayer and National Repentance (November 22)
Christmas (December 25)
Boxing Day (December 26)

134 Practical Information

Average Monthly Temperatures in Berlin. The mildest, most pleasant weather coincides with the peak tourist season, from May through October. In winter, temperatures generally hover around the freezing point in Berlin.

Below is a listing of average daily temperatures by month in centigrade and Fahrenheit:

Average Monthly Temperatures

Jan. F° C°	Feb. F° C°	Mar. F° C°	Apr. F° C°	May F° C°	June F° C°
29 -2	31 -1	41 5	50 10	59 15	65 18

July F° C°	Aug. F° C°	Sept. F° C°	Oct. F° C°	Nov. F° C°	Dec. F° C°
69 21	67 19	61 16	50 10	40 4	33 1

Weight, Measure, and Temperature Equivalents. Throughout the text, metric weights and measures are followed by U.S. equivalents in parentheses; likewise, centigrade degrees are translated into Fahrenheit temperatures. The following table is a quick reference for U.S. and metric equivalents.

Metric Unit	U.S. Equivalent	U.S. Unit	Metric Equivalent
Length		**Length**	
1 kilometer	0.6 miles	1 mile	1.6 kilometers
1 meter	1.09 yards	1 yard	0.9 meters
1 decimeter	0.3 feet	1 foot	3.04 decimeters
1 centimeter	0.39 inches	1 inch	2.5 centimeters
Weight		**Weight**	
1 kilogram	2.2 pounds	1 pound	0.45 kilograms
1 gram	0.03 ounces	1 ounce	28.3 grams
Liquid Capacity		**Liquid Capacity**	
1 dekaliter	2.38 gallons	1 gallon	0.37 dekaliters
1 liter	1.05 quarts	1 quart	0.9 liters
1 liter	2.1 pints	1 pint	0.47 liters

(*Note: there are 5 British Imperial gallons to 6 U.S. gallons.*)

Dry Measure		**Dry Measure**	
1 liter	0.9 quarts	1 quart	1.1 liters
1 liter	1.8 pints	1 pint	0.55 liters

To convert centigrade (C°) to Fahrenheit (F°):
$C° \times 9 \div 5 + 32 = F°$.

To convert Fahrenheit to centigrade:
$F° - 32 \times 5 \div 9 = C°$.

Time Zones. Germany is on Central European Time (CET); that is, one hour ahead of Greenwich Mean Time (GMT) and six hours ahead of Eastern Standard Time (EST). Therefore, if it is noon in New York and Toronto, it is 6:00 P.M. in Berlin; and when it is noon in London, it is 1:00 P.M. in Berlin. There is a nine-hour time difference between Sydney, Australia and Berlin. Therefore, noon in Sydney translates into 3:00 A.M. in Berlin.

Berlin observes Daylight Savings Time (CET plus one hour) from early April until late September. Remember that the Germans employ a 24-hour clock to differentiate between the morning and evening hours. Midnight is expressed as 2400 hours; 1:00 A.M. as 0100 hours; noon as 1200 hours; 1:00 P.M. as 1300 hours, etc.

Passport and Visa Requirements. American, British, and Canadian visitors to Berlin must carry a valid passport in order to enter the country. Australian citizens must have a visa. Americans who plan to stay for longer than three months must also have a visa. British visitors can enter with an EC ID card.

Customs Entering Germany. Personal items used for professional or private purposes (i.e., jewelry, cameras, watches, radios, portable typewriters, etc.) do not have to be declared upon arrival in Germany. There is no limit on the amount of national currency and foreign bank notes that can be brought into the country.

Non-European citizens visiting Germany may also enter with the following duty-free goods: 400 cigarettes, 100 cigars, or 500 grams of tobacco; 1 liter of alcohol more than 22 percent proof or 2 liters of alcohol less than 22 percent proof; 2 liters of wine; 50 grams of perfume and ¼ liter of toilet water; as well as goods that total DM 115.

Residents of the EC may enter Germany with the following duty-free goods: 200 cigarettes, 75 cigars, or 400 grams of tobacco; 1 liter of alcohol more than 22 percent proof or 3 liters of alcohol less than 22 percent proof; 5 liters of wine; 75 grams of perfume and ⅓ liter of toilet water; as well as goods that total DM 780.

Customs Returning Home. To simplify passage through customs, travelers who have nothing to declare should follow the green signs. Travelers making a declaration of goods must follow the red signs.

If you travel with items from home that were manufactured abroad (i.e., cameras), carry all receipts with you to ensure that you will not pay duty.

U.S. residents may return to the States with $400 worth of foreign goods duty-free. A ten percent duty is levied on the retail value of the next $1,000 worth of merchandise. Beyond $1,400 worth of merchandise, the rate of duty is decided by the customs officer. (Specific arrangements can be made to combine individual exports.) Citizens over 21 may also return with 200 cigarettes, 100 non-Cuban cigars, one liter of alcohol, and one bottle of perfume.

Another option is to send home packages under $50 duty-free, as long as they're not mailed to your own address. You can send only one package marked UNSOLICITED GIFT—VALUE UNDER $50 to each address during a 24-hour period. The U.S. has established the Generalized System of Preferences (GSP), which allow a U.S. citizen to export particular items that exceed the $400 limit duty-free. You can receive a list of these articles at a customs office.

Many items are prohibited in the U.S. (e.g., certain species of plants, goods manufactured from tortoise shell, products made from endangered species, etc.). If you attempt to import such articles, they will be confiscated at customs. Prohibited products are detailed in a pamphlet called "Know Before You Go," published by the U.S. Customs Service. You can write to the following address to receive a copy: U.S. Customs Service, 6 World Trade Center, Customs Info., Room 201, New York, N.Y. 10048; or dial (212) 466-5550.

Duty-free allowances for British subjects for goods purchased outside the EEC or within the EEC in duty-free shops include the following: 200 cigarettes, 100 cigarillos, or 50 cigars (any equivalent of 250 grams of tobacco), one liter of alcohol over 22 percent proof, two liters under 22 percent proof, or two liters of wine, 50 grams of perfume, nine ounces of toilet water, and up to £32 worth of other goods.

British subjects may import the following goods which have been purchased within the EEC (but not in duty-free shops): 300 cigarettes, 150 cigarillos, 75 cigars or 400 grams of tobacco, one and a half liters of alcohol over 22 percent proof, three liters of alcohol under 22 percent proof, four liters of wine, 75 grams of perfume, 13 ounces of toilet water, and up to £250 worth of other goods.

Canadians may return with duty-free purchases of $100, or $300 if you've been away seven days or more. This includes 200 cigarettes, 50 cigars, two pounds of tobacco, and 40 ounces of liquor. Packages marked UNSOLICITED GIFT—VALUE UNDER $40 may be mailed to Canada duty-free (one package during a 24-hour period to any address except your own).

Australian residents may bring back $400 worth of duty-free purchases, 250 grams of tobacco, and one liter of alcohol.

Embassies and Consulates. General information and assistance can be obtained at the following offices:

American Consulate
Clayallee 170
D-1000 Berlin 33
tel. 030 823 4087

American Embassy
Neustädtische Kirchstrasse 4–5
1080 Berlin
tel. 220 27 41

British Consulate
Uhlandstrasse 7/8
D-1000 Berlin 19
tel. 030 309 5292

British Embassy
Unter den Linden 32/34
1080 Berlin
tel. 220 24 31

Canadian Consulate General
Europa-Center
D-1000 Berlin 30
tel. 011 49 30 261 1161

The British Embassy also handles the affairs of Canadian tourists.

German Embassies and Consulates. Listed below are a few offices of the German Embassy or Consulate:

In the U.S.:
German Embassy
4645 Reservoir Rd. NW
Washington, D.C. 20007–1998
tel. 202 298 4000

German Consulate
460 Park Avenue
New York, N.Y. 10022
tel. 212 308 8700

In the U.K.:
German Embassy
23 Belgrave Square
London SW1X 8PZ
tel. 235 50 33

In Canada:
German Consulate
3455 Rue de la Montagne
Montreal PQH3G 2A3
tel. 286 18 20

In Australia:
German Consulate
13 Trelawny Street
Sydney NSW 2025
tel. 328 77 33

Getting to Berlin by Air. Since reunification, the number of flights to Berlin has almost doubled. Although other airlines are now scrambling to obtain gates in Berlin, Lufthansa and its subsidiary, Euro-Berlin, currently offer the most flights to Berlin from other international cities. International and domestic flights land either at Berlin Tegel Airport or Schönefeld Airport, from which you can easily get ground transportation into the city. From Tegel, the No. 9 bus will take you to the heart of downtown Berlin (the Kurfürstendamm). There is S-Bahn service to and from Berlin Schönefeld, as well as a special bus that goes to Bahnhof Zoo. Please note that as the airports gear up for more air traffic, carriers other than those listed below will soon be offering direct flights to Berlin.

From the U.S.: The major air carriers that fly direct from New York to Berlin include Lufthansa and Trans World Airlines.

From the U.K.: Lufthansa and British Airways fly direct from London to Berlin.

From Canada: You can fly direct to Berlin via British Airways, which first makes a stopover in London. Other airlines departing from Canada may soon offer direct flights to Berlin.

From Australia: While no airlines fly non-stop from Australia to Berlin, indirect flights are available from Lufthansa and Qantas Airlines.

Hotels and Other Accommodations. Accommodations vary depending upon which side of the city you're visiting. Western-style tourist accommodations in formerly communist East Berlin are extremely limited, although that situation will certainly change over the next few years as this part of the city gears up for tourism. Most hotels there are part of the Mitropa chain, and cater to Western visitors. Keep in mind, however, that hotels in former East German territories are generally not computerized: it is wise to make reservations through an agency in America or one in Germany before you travel. West Berlin, on the other hand, offers a wide range of comfortable lodgings: international hotels that provide royal treatment; informal hotel pensions, whose quiet atmosphere provide immediate relief from the hectic city streets; or bed-and-breakfast establishments, whose conveniences frequently include bargain prices.

Free information concerning accommodations can be obtained before leaving home from any German National Tourist Office, or from any tourist information office (Verkehrsamt) in Germany. Local chapters will book rooms in hotels and pensions for a small fee, as well as provide general travel information, brochures on tours, and schedules for buses and trains.

The Mitwohnzentrale agencies provide excellent information about accommodations. They have comprehensive listings of lodgings for a variety of interests and can provide details on accommodations that range from an overnight stay in a room in a private home to a week in a bed and breakfast to a month in an upscale apartment. Mitwohnzentrale will also accept reservations over the phone. Contact Mitwohnzentrale at the following offices for information and reservations: Ku'damm Eck, 3rd Floor, Kurfürstendamm 227–8, tel. 882 66 94; Holsteinischerstrasse 55, tel. 861 82 22; Kreuzberg, Mehringdamm 72, tel. 786 60 02.

Now, more than ever, it is advisable to reserve rooms in advance. We also suggest that you ask if there will be a conference or trade show scheduled during your vacation time, which can result in tremendous crowds and inflated hotel prices.

Remember that a room in a more modestly priced establishment often does not include a private bath, so if this is important to you, be certain to request one when making your reservation. Many hotels offer a complimentary continental breakfast of sausages, cold meats, breads, and tea or coffee, but inquire in advance just to be sure.

The German National Tourist Office rates hotels according to five categories: Luxury, First Class, Second Class, Third Class, and Fourth Class. Our rating system is based on the German categories as follows:

- 🏨🏨🏨 Luxury and First Class hotels
- 🏨🏨 Second and Third Class hotels
- 🏨 Fourth Class hotels

Luxury and First Class designators indicate the highest quality of service, accommodations, and amenities offered, with prices rising accordingly.

Hotelpensions are usually smaller, quieter versions of hotels which are designed to give you hotel-quality service in a less formal atmosphere. Pensions range in type from large, comfortable homes to modest, small hotels. Pensions are appreciably lower in cost than hotels.

Hotelpensions are rated as follows:

- 🏨🏨🏨 Excellent and Very Good
- 🏨🏨 Good
- 🏨 Less Expensive

Bed and breakfast accommodations are also popular, as they provide a pleasant, cozy refuge in a home-style setting and offer an opportunity to meet people over the breakfast table. Tourism offices and Mitwohnzentrale organizations can help you choose one for your stay.

Hotels in West Berlin: 🏨🏨🏨 *(Luxury)* Bristol Hotel Kempinski Berlin, Kurfürstendamm 27, Berlin 15, tel. 8 84 34-0; Grand Hotel Esplanade, Lützowufer 15, Berlin 30, tel. 26 10 11; Inter-Continental Berlin, Budapester Strasse 2, Berlin 30, tel. 2 60 20; Mondial, Kurfürstendamm 47, Berlin 15, tel. 8 84 11-0; Palace in Europa-Center, Budapester Strasse, Berlin 30, tel. 25 49 70; Schweizerhof Berlin, Budapester Strasse 21–31, Berlin 30, tel. 2 69 60; Steigenberger Berlin, Los-Angeles-Platz 1, Berlin 30, tel. 2 10 80; Savoy-Hotel, Fasanenstrasse 9–10, Berlin 12, tel. 3 11 03-0.

🏨🏨🏨 Berlin Excelsior, Hardenbergstrasse 14, Berlin 12, tel. 31 991/3; Berlin Penta, Nürnberger Strasse 65, Berlin 30, tel. 21 00 70; Am Zoo, Kurfürstendamm 25, Berlin 15, tel. 88 43 70; Hotel Berlin, Kurfürstenstrasse 62, Berlin 30, tel. 26 05 0; Hotel Hamburg, Landgrafenstrasse 4, Berlin 31, tel. 26 91 61; President, An der Urania 16–18, Berlin 30, tel. 21 90 30; Residenz Berlin, Meinekestrasse 9, Berlin 15, tel. 88 28 91; Hotel Seehof, Lietzensee-Ufer 11, Berlin 19, tel. 32 00 20; Steglitz International, Albrechtstrasse 2, Berlin 41, tel. 79 005-0; Sylter Hof, Kurfürstenstrasse 116, Berlin 30, tel. 21 20-0; Queen's Berlin, Güntzelstrasse 14, Berlin 31, tel. 87 02 41; Schlosshotel Gehrus, Brahmsstrasse 4–10, Berlin 33, tel. 8 26 20 81.

🏨 Berlin Plaza, Knesebeckstrasse 63, Berlin 15, tel. 8 84 13-0; Econotel Berlin, Sommerlingerstrasse 24, Berlin 10, tel. 34 40 01; Agon, Xantener Strasse 4, Berlin 15, tel. 3 12 40 67; Astoria, Fasanenstrasse 2, Berlin 12, tel. 3 12 40 67; Atlanta am Kurfürstendamm, Fasanenstrasse 74, Berlin 15, tel. 8 81 80 49; Hotel Basel, Kurfürstendamm 125a, Berlin 31, tel. 8 91 30 81; Hotel Bogota, Schlüterstrasse 45, Berlin 15, tel. 8 81 50 01; Börse, Kurfürstendamm 34, Berlin 15, tel. 8 81 30 21; Frühling am Zoo, Kurfürstendamm 17, Berlin 15, tel. 8 81 80 83; Hecker's Deele, Grolmanstrasse 35, Berlin 12, tel. 88 90-1; Meineke, Meinekestrasse 10, Berlin 15, tel. 8 82 81 11; Savigny, Brandenburgische Strasse 21, Berlin 31, tel. 8 81 30 01; Ibis-Hotel Berlin, Messedamm 10, Berlin 19, tel. 30 39 30.

🏨 Budget-Hotel, Alt-Moabit 89, Berlin 21, tel. 3 91 41 79; Astrid Garni, Bleibtreustrasse 20, Berlin 12, tel. 8 81 59 59; Norddeutscher Hof, Geisbergstrasse 30, Berlin 30, tel. 24 80 65; Regina Garni, Kurfürstendamm 37, Berlin 15, tel. 8 81 50 31.

Hotelpensions in West Berlin: 🏨 *(Excellent)* Dittberner, Wielandstrasse 26, Berlin 15, tel. 8 82 64 85; Rheingold, Xantener Strasse 9, Berlin 15, tel. 8 83 10 49.

🏨 Arco, Kurfürstendamm 30, Berlin 15, tel. 8 82 63 88; Austriana, Pariser Strasse 39/40, Berlin 15, tel. 8 82 75 88; Elba, Bleibtreustrasse 26, Berlin 15, tel. 8 81 75 04; Schöneberg, Hauptstrasse 135, Berlin 62, tel. 7 81 88 30; Wittelsbach, Wittelsbacher Strasse 22, Berlin 31, tel. 8 61 43 71.

🏨 Bregenz, Bregenzer Strasse 5, Berlin 15, tel. 8 81 43 07; Castell, Wielandstrasse 24, Berlin 15, tel. 8 82 71 81; Central, Kurfürstendamm 185, Berlin 15, tel. 8 81 63 43; Columbus, Meinekestrasse 5, Berlin 15, tel. 8 81 50 61; Elfert, Knesebeckstrasse 13/14, Berlin 12, tel. 3 12 12 36; Fasanenhaus, Fasanenstrasse 73, Berlin 15, tel. 8 81 67 13; Ingeborg, Wielandstrasse 33, Berlin 12, tel. 8 83 13 43; Kleistpark, Belziger Strasse 1, Berlin 62, tel. 7 81 11 89; Krebs, Heerstrasse 2, Berlin 19, tel. 3 02 26 60; Radloff-Rumland, Kurfürstendamm 226, Berlin 15, tel. 8 81 33 31; Wien, Martin-Luther-Strasse 45, Berlin 30, tel. 2 11 42 82.

🏨 Cortina, Kantstrasse 140, Berlin 12, tel. 3 13 90 59; München, Güntzelstrasse 62, Berlin 31, tel. 8 54 22 26; Splendid, Konstanzer Strasse 1, Berlin 15, tel. 8 81 69 46; Pension Am Viktoria-Luise-Platz, Viktoria-Luise-Platz 12a, Berlin 30, tel. 2 11 40 95.

Hotels in East Berlin: 🏨 *(Luxury)* Grand Hotel, Friedrichstrasse 158–164, tel. 02 20 920; Metropol, Freidrichstrasse 150–153, tel. 02 22 040; Palast, Karl Liebknecht-Strasse 5, tel. 02 24 10.

🏨 Berolina, Karl-Marx-Allee 31, tel. 02 210 9541; Stadt Berlin, Alexanderplatz, tel. 02 21 90; Unter den Linden, Unter den Linden 14, tel. 02 220 0311.

⌘ Adria, Friedrichstrasse 134, tel. 02 282 5451; Newa, Invalidenstrasse 115, tel. 02 282 5461.

⌂ Hospiz am Bahnhof Friedrichstrasse, Albrechtstrasse 8, tel. 02 282 5396; Hospiz Augustrasse, Augustrasse 82, tel. 02 282 5321.

Currency Regulations. Currency is based on the Deutschmark (DM) and the pfennig (pf). Coins of 50, 20, 10, 5, and 2 pfennigs are in circulation, as well as Deutschmark coins, which are available in denominations of 5, 2, and 1. The government issues bank notes for 1,000, 500, 100, 50, 20, and 10 Deutschmarks.

There are no limits on the amount of currency that can be brought into or taken out of Germany. To receive the best rate of exchange, first track currency fluctuations in the newspaper before leaving home, and then change your money at a bank. Currency exchange facilities are located in most banks, at the airport, and at commercial exchange shops (Wechselstuben), which also process traveler's checks. You can exchange currency and traveler's checks at the entrance to the Zoo station, which is open Monday through Saturday, 8:00 A.M.–9:00 P.M., and on Sunday and public holidays from 10:00 A.M.–6:00 P.M. If you must, you can exchange currency at hotels or restaurants but their rates are less favorable and there is often a surcharge.

Business Hours and Closings. Banks are usually open 8:00 or 9:00 A.M.–3:00 or 4:00 P.M., Monday through Friday, with an hour lunch break beginning around noon. Some banks open later but extend their hours to 5:00 or 6:00 P.M.

Government offices and buildings generally open around 9:00 or 10:00 A.M. and close at 6:00 or 7:00 P.M. Hours may vary, however, from business to business.

Department stores and larger shops open their doors Monday through Friday, 9:00 A.M.–6:00 P.M., and on Saturday from 9:00 A.M.–2:00 P.M. Shopping hours are extended to 6:00 P.M. on the first Saturday of each month and every Saturday in December because of the Christmas season. Many stores in the Kurfürstendamm area remain open until 8:30 P.M. on Thursday. Larger shopping complexes are open Monday through Friday until 9:00 or 10:00 P.M.

Museums are generally open Tuesday through Sunday 10:00 A.M.–6:00 P.M. Most museums are closed on Mondays. Be aware that smaller museums may close around lunchtime.

Postage. Post offices are open Monday through Friday, 8:00 A.M.–6:00 P.M. Main branches open 8:00 A.M.– 12:00 noon on Saturday. On weekdays, smaller branches close for lunch between 12:30 and 2:30 P.M. There is a desk at the Zoo station that remains open 24 hours a day; there are also postal facilities available at Tegel airport that operate between

142 Practical Information

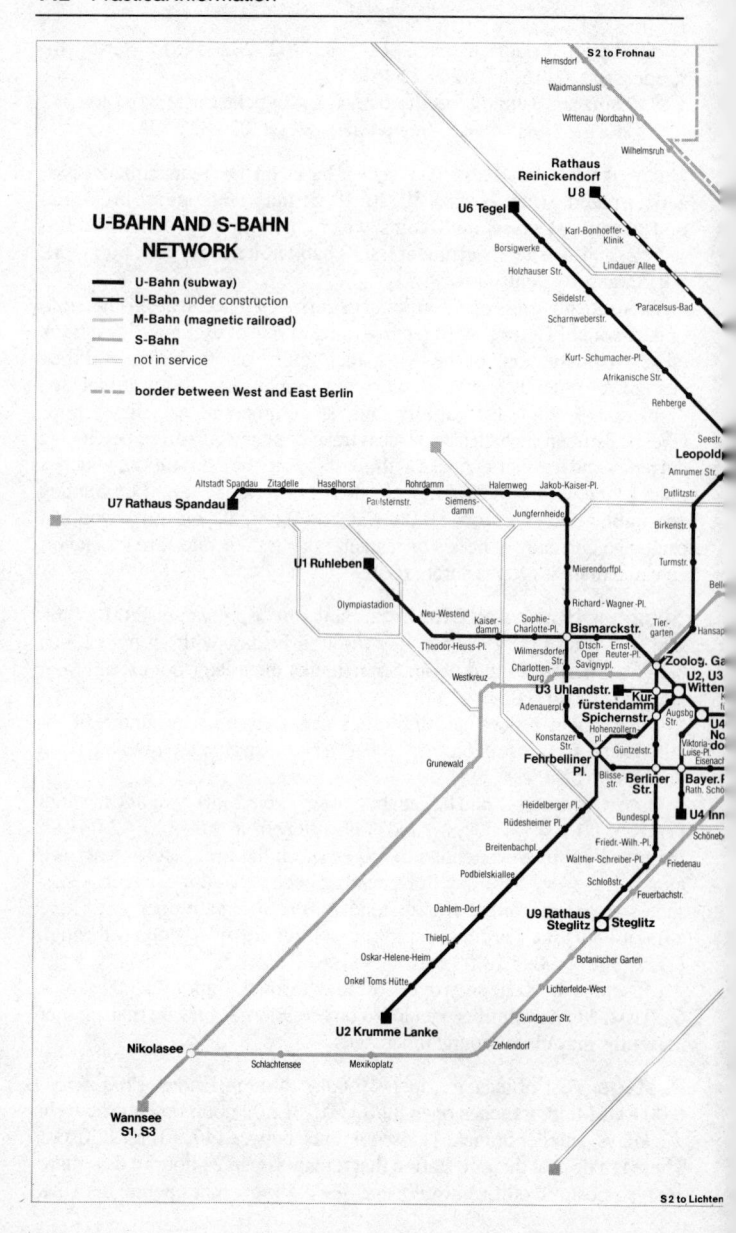

U-BAHN AND S-BAHN NETWORK

- U-Bahn (subway)
- U-Bahn under construction
- M-Bahn (magnetic railroad)
- S-Bahn
- not in service

- - - border between West and East Berlin

S2 to Frohnau

Hermsdorf
Waidmannslust
Wittenau (Nordbahn)
Wilhelmsruh

Rathaus Reinickendorf U8
U6 Tegel
Karl-Bonhoeffer-Klinik
Borsigwerke
Lindauer Allee
Holzhauser Str.
Seidelstr.
Paracelsus-Bad
Scharnweberstr.
Kurt-Schumacher-Pl.
Afrikanische Str.
Rehberge
Seestr
Leopold
Amrumer Str.
Altstadt Spandau Zitadelle Haselhorst Rohrdamm Halemweg Jakob-Kaiser-Pl.
Putlitzstr.
U7 Rathaus Spandau Paulsternstr. Siemensdamm Jungfernheide
Birkenstr.
Mierendorffpl.
Turmstr.
U1 Ruhleben
Richard-Wagner-Pl.
Bell
Olympiastadion Neu-Westend Kaiserdamm Sophie-Charlotte-Pl. **Bismarckstr.** Tiergarten Hansa
Theodor-Heuss-Pl. Wilmersdorfer Str. Dtsch. Oper Ernst-Reuter-Pl. **Zoolog. Ga**
Charlottenburg Savignypl. **U2, U3**
Westkreuz **U3 Uhlandstr.** **Kurfürstendamm** **Witten**
Adenauerpl. **Spichernstr.** Augsbg. Str. **U4**
Hohenzollernpl. **No**
Konstanzer Str. Viktoria-Luise-Pl. **do**
Fehrbelliner Pl. Güntzelstr. Eisenach
Grunewald Blissestr. **Berliner Str.** **Bayer. P**
Heidelberger Pl. Bundespl. Rath. Scho
Rüdesheimer Pl. **U4 Inn**
Breitenbachpl. Friedr.-Wilh.-Pl. Schöneb
Podbielskiallee Walther-Schreiber-Pl. Friedenau
Dahlem-Dorf Schloßstr. Feuerbachstr.
Thielpl. **U9 Rathaus Steglitz** **Steglitz**
Oskar-Helene-Heim Botanischer Garten
Onkel Toms Hütte Lichterfelde-West
Sundgauer Str.
Nikolasee **U2 Krumme Lanke** Zehlendorf
Schlachtensee Mexikoplatz

Wannsee S1, S3

S2 to Lichten

Practical Information 143

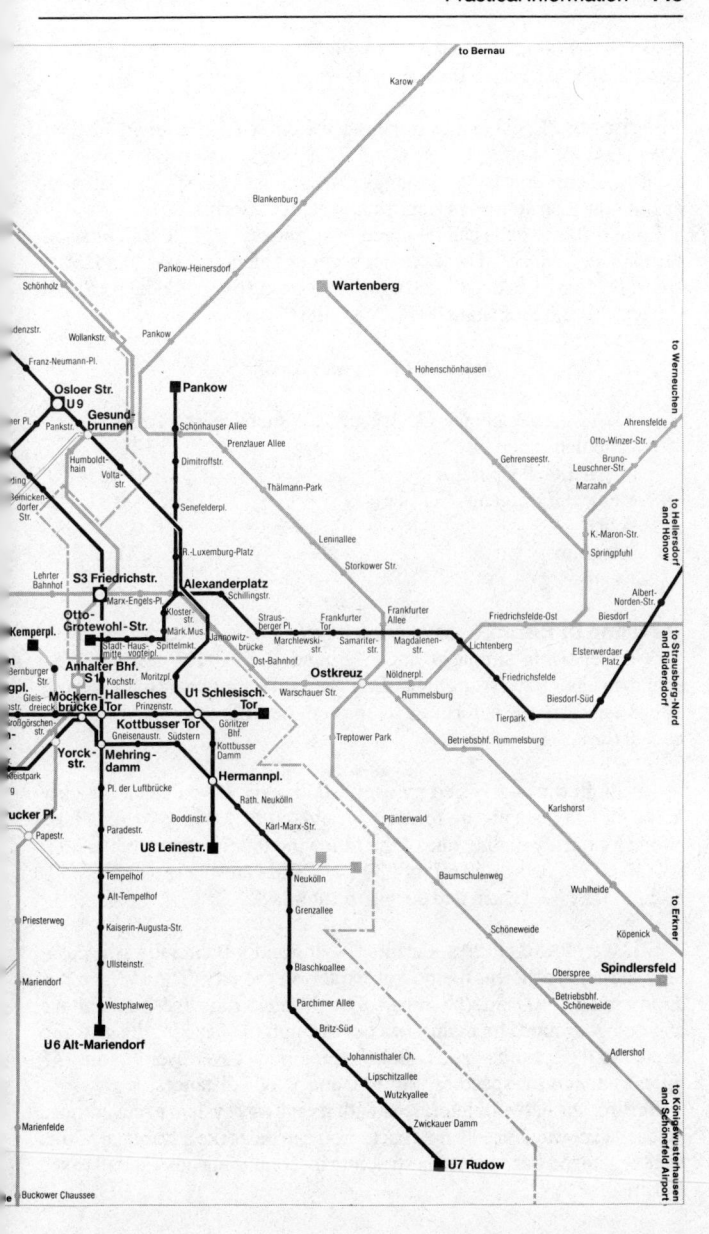

6:30 A.M.–9:00 P.M., Monday through Friday, and at the International Congress Center from 9:00 A.M.–4:00 P.M.

Telephones. Local calls can be made from telephones marked *"National."* Public phones accept 10 and 50 pfennigs, as well as DM 1 coins; local calls cost at least 23 pfennigs. Most phones come equipped with operational instructions in English as well as in German.

Long distance calls can be made from phones marked *"Inlands und Auslandsgespräche."* These phones accept 10 pfennigs, DM 1 and DM 5 coins. If you wish to dial direct, use the following dialing codes: U.S. and Canada 001; Great Britain 0044; Australia 0061.

Help and Emergency Numbers

ADAC (Allgemeiner Deutscher Automobileclub)	1 92 11
Ambulance and Fire	112
International Operator	0 01 18
Medical Emergency Service	31 00 31
Police	110
Telegrams	11 31
Weather	11 64

Traveling in Berlin. Whether you travel by subway, ferry, or drive a car, it's relatively simple to move around Berlin. The Berliner Verkehrsbetriebe (BVG) runs the U-Bahn and S-Bahn subway lines, as well as bus and ferry lines, forming a thorough network that reaches all corners of the city.

Taxis. Berlin is serviced by over 5,000 taxis. If you cannot readily find a cab, taxi stands are located throughout the city, or you can telephone for one by dialing one of the following four numbers: 030 69 02, 030 26 10 26, 030 21 60 60, or 030 24 02 02. Fares increase after midnight, on the weekends, and during the holidays.

Subways and Buses. Berlin's U-Bahn and S-Bahn subway is probably the most efficient method of exploring the city. The U-Bahn has approximately 109 km. (68 miles) of track and its nine lines travel above and below ground. Its main lines cut through the heart of the city and stretch to the suburbs. The S-Bahn's three lines cover over 71 km. (45 miles), and it is the speediest way to manage long distances.

Berlin's bus network interfaces with its subway system to cover those areas the subway lines do not reach. You can best take advantage of this well-organized transportation structure by combining bus and rail to see Berlin.

A single ticket *(Einzelfahrschein Normaltarif)* is valid for the entire subway and bus system, and permits you to make as many transfers between trains and buses as you like in a two-hour period. A multiple ticket *(Einzelfahrschein Kurzstreckentarif)* is used mostly for short trips since it permits you to travel to three subway destinations on any single subway line or any combination of lines or six bus stops on any combination of buses. The *Berlin Ticket* provides unlimited travel on trains and buses for 24 hours—an excellent value for those who plan a busy day of sightseeing. A combined day ticket *(Schmetterlingslinien)* offers access to Berlin's beautiful lakes and parks. For longer stays, the *Umweltkarte,* good for a month of unlimited travel on U-Bahn, S-Bahn, or bus, is a bargain. Other special tickets that are good for a week are also available.

The U-Bahn and S-Bahn are run on an honor system, and if you are caught traveling without a ticket, you can be fined DM60. Unless you have a special week- or month-long pass, be sure to punch your ticket in one of the red validation machines.

Both single and multiple tickets may be purchased from vending machines at U-Bahn and S-Bahn stations. Combined day tickets and the Berlin Ticket are available at the BVG offices at the Bahnhof Zoo station or at the Kleistpark U-Bahn station. Consult a BVG office for further information and to receive schedules by phoning 030 21 65 08.

Driving in Germany. Germany's road network, which extends over 3,000 km. (1,800 miles), is considered superlative by European standards.

Documentation. All drivers must carry an international driver's license or their own national driver's license (check with a German embassy, consulate, or tourism office to find out if you need an international license). You can apply for an international license at your local Automobile Association of America (AAA) or the equivalent organization in Great Britain, Canada, or Australia.

You must purchase temporary insurance in case of a car accident; an International Insurance Certificate (called a green card) can be used if it is validated for Germany (this can be processed via your local automobile association).

Car Rentals. Allaround, Avis International, Europa Service Car Rentals Arnim, European Car Rental, First and Second Hand Rent, Guse Car Rental, Hertz Car Rental, and Inter Rent are among the agencies that lease cars.

Driving Regulations. In Germany, driving is on the right-hand side of the road. The general rule at an intersection is that the car to your right has the right of way.

The law requires all front-seat passengers to have their seat belts fastened in the car. Children under 12 years of age must ride in the back seat.

You must carry a first aid kit in the car, as well as a warning triangle to signal that you need assistance in case of an accident.

Speed Limits. Traveling on an Autobahn (highway) can be harrowing for even the most experienced drivers; there are no speed limits, and some drivers can make you feel as if you've suddenly entered the Indianapolis 500. A suggested speed range of 100–130 km. (about 62–78 miles) per hour serves as a guideline for driving on the Autobahn—but always remember to drive defensively. Speed limits for other major roads range from 80–100 km. (about 48–62 miles) per hour and drop down to 50 km. (30 miles) per hour in cities and congested areas.

Gas. Berlin is liberally peppered with service stations, many of which are open around the clock. If you travel outside the city, rest areas and filling stations dot the roadways at regular intervals. Gas is available in high or low octane, and major credit cards are welcomed. There are fewer gas stations in the eastern portion of the city.

Assistance and towing services are well organized in Berlin. You can call the following automobile associations which are available for assistance 24 hours a day:

ADAC City Breakdown Service, tel. 1 92 11
ACE City Breakdown Service, tel. 2 11 22 55
AVD City Breakdown Service, tel. 4 62 20 70

Restaurants and Cafés. Before reunification West Berlin could boast more than 6,000 restaurants, bars, cafés, pastry shops, and taverns, as well as delightful country restaurants on the outskirts of town. East Berlin, by comparison, had about 800 such establishments.

The staple of Berlin social life, the *Kneipe* (tavern) is where Berliners gather for convivial chatter and a bite to eat. Similar to a pub, Kneipen are great places to relax with a glass of beer and a light snack. If you want a more substantial meal in a publike atmosphere, visit a Gaststätte.

If you crave an afternoon snack, go to a café for some *Kaffee und Kuchen* (coffee and cakes). This time-honored tradition, like British high tea, is very popular among Berliners. The cafés offer an array of cakes, pastries, and chocolates to nibble as you sip your coffee.

Berlin's native culinary art may not be as celebrated as French cuisine, but the food is solid and substantial. There is a huge selection of first class restaurants that also offer international cuisine, and there are many ethnic establishments. You can dine on specialties ranging from Indian curry to Yugoslavian chicken paprika to Polish piroges.

Traditional Berlin dishes include pig knuckles with sauerkraut, liver with onions and apples, eel in dill sauce, and curry-wurst, which is a sausage fried with or without its skin.

Great quantities of "Berliner Weisse," a wheat beer into which a dab of raspberry syrup has been poured, are consumed here. Aside from the well-known rye and pumpernickel, you can sample many varieties of breads, including Brötchen, Mohnbrötchen, and Milchbrötchen. Some breads contain delicious fillings.

As Berlin has no mandatory closing times for restaurants, one can dine relatively late. As in most of Europe, Berliners do not traditionally sit down to dinner until about 8:00 P.M.

Restaurants in Berlin are rated according to our own system, as follows:

**** Superb
*** Very Good
** Good
* Standard

Restaurants in West Berlin: *Traditional/Nouvelle German cuisine:* ****Bamberger Reiter, Regensburgerstrasse 7, tel. 030 24 482; Rockendorfs, Dusterhauptstrasse 1, tel. 030 402 30 99. *** Alt Luxembourg, Pestalozzistrasse 70, tel. 030 323 87 30; Conti Fischstuben, Bayreuthstrasse 42, tel. 030 219 020. ** Hecker's Deele, Grolmanstrasse 35, tel. 030 88 901; Mundart Restaurant, Muskauerstrasse 33–34, tel. 030 612 20 61. * Alt-Berliner Wiesbierstube, Lindenstrasse 14, tel. 030 251 01 21; Hardtke, Meinekestrasse 27, tel. 030 881 98 27; Ratskeller Schöneberg, John F. Kennedy Plaza, tel. 030 783 21 27.

Italian cuisine: *** La Cascina, Delbruckstrasse 28; Ponte Vecchio, Spielhagenstrasse 3, tel. 030 342 19 99.

French cuisine: *** Café Einstein, Kurfürstenstrasse 58; Chapeau Klack, Pfalzburgerstrasse 55.

Greek cuisine: ** Akropolis, Wielandstrasse 28; Dionysos, Schöneberger Ufer 47.

Restaurants in East Berlin: *Traditional German cuisine:* **** Ermelerhaus, Märkisches Ufer 10–12, tel. 02 279 4036; Ganymed, Schiffbauerdamm 5, tel. 02 282 9540. *** Schwalbennest, Rathauss Strasse at Marx-Engels-Forum, tel. 02 212 4569; Zur Goldenen Gans, Friedrichstrasse 158–162 (in Grand Hotel), tel. 02 20920. ** Berlin Esprit, Alexanderplatz in Hotel Stadt Berlin, tel. 02 2190; Ratskeller, Rathaus Strasse 14, tel. 02 212 44 64. * Alex Grill, Alexanderplatz in Hotel Berlin, tel. 02 21 90; Alt-Cöllner Schankstuben, Friedrichsgracht 50, tel. 02 212 59 72; Arkade, Französische Strasse 25, tel. 02 208 02 73; Neubrandenburger Hof, Wilhelm-Pieck-Strasse/Borsigstrasse; Raabe Diele, Märkisches Ufer 10–12 in Ermelerhaus, tel. 02 279 40 36; Zur Letzen Instanz, Waisenstrasse 14–16, tel. 02 212 55 28.

Cafés in West Berlin: Am Neuen See, Lichtensteinallee; Bristol, Kurfürstendamm 35; Café Einstein, Kurfürstenstrasse 58; Café Hardenberg, Hardenbergstrasse 10; Café M, Goltzstrasse 34; Huthmacher,

Hardenbergstrasse 39; Kempinski, Kurfürstendamm 27; Kranzler, Kurfürstendamm 18/19; Krumme, Joachimstaler Strasse 41; Leysieffer, Kurfürstendamm 218; Möhring, Kurfürstendamm, corner Uhlandstrasse; Mövenpick, Europa-Center; Wintergarten, Fasanenstrasse 23.

Cafés in East Berlin: Am Marstall, Rathaus Strasse, am Nikolai-Viertel; Berliner Kaffeehaus, Alexanderplatz; Café 130 Radke, Chausseestrasse 130; Café Arkade, Französische; Café im Palais, Poststrasse 16; Operncafé, Unter den Linden; Pressecafé, Karl-Liebknecht-Strasse 29; Raabediele, Märkisches Ufer 10–12; Sophieneck, Grosse Hamburgerstrasse/Sophienstrasse; Telecafé, Television Tower.

Bars and Nightlife. Berlin has long been noted for its bars and nightclubs, which run the gamut from sedate neighborhood Kneipen to enormous glitzy discos. Something can be found for every taste and preference in this city, and part of the fun of visiting is sampling the city's after dark attractions. You can stop in a bar at almost any hour and be served, but the action in more sophisticated places doesn't pick up until after 11:00 P.M.

Bars and Nightclubs in West Berlin: Abraxas, Kantstrasse 134; Annabell's, Fasanenstrasse 64; Basement, Mehringdamm 107; Big Apple, Bundesallee 13/14; Big Eden, Kurfürstendamm 202; Blue Note, Courbierestrasse 13; Chez Alex, Kurfürstendamm 160; Dorett, Fasanenstrasse 74; Dschungel, Nürnberger Strasse 53; First, Joachimstaler Strasse 15; I-Punkt, Europa-Center; Irish Pub, Europa-Center; Kudorf, Joachimstaler Strasse 15; La vie en rose, Europa-Center; Metropol, Nollendorfplatz 5; New Eden, Kurfürstendamm 71; Schatulle, Fasanenstrasse 39.

Gay bars and nightclubs in West Berlin: Andreas' Kneipe, Ansbacher Strasse 29; Begine, Potsdamer Strasse 139; Blue Bay Bar, Eisenacher Strasse 3; Chez nous, Marburger Strasse 14; Dollywood, Kurfürstenstrasse 114–116; Flip-Flop, Kulmerstrasse 20; Kleine Philharmonie, Schaperstrasse 14; Paramount, Hauptstrasse 120; Tom's Bar, Motzstrasse.

Bars and Nightclubs in East Berlin: Alibi, Saarbrückerstrasse 14; Café Nord, Schönhauser Allee; Nachtbar Pinguin, Rosa-Luxemburg-Strasse 39; Schoppenstuben, Schönhauser Allee.

Gay bars and nightclubs in East Berlin: These can be found in the Mehrzweckgebäude, Buschallee 87.

General Sources of Information. Branches of the Berlin Tourist Office (Verkehrsamt) can assist with inquiries and provide background information on the city. These offices supply you with city and regional maps, hotel listings, and literature on special sights, as well as tour packages.

Verkehrsamt Berlin
(Tourist Office)
Europa-Center
Entrance on Budapester Strasse
tel. 2 62 60 31

Verkehrsamt
Tegel Airport
tel. 41 01 31 45

Verkehrsamt Bahnhof Zoo Station
Zoologischer Garten
tel. 3 13 90 636

Informationszentrum Berlin
Hardenbergstrasse 20
tel. 3 10 04 0

Kulturinformation
Budapester Strasse 48
tel. 25 48 90

Any German National Tourist Office will be knowledgeable about the rapid changes in Berlin. They have brochures detailing accommodations, as well as pamphlets on day trips and nightlife.

In the U.S.:
747 Third Avenue
New York, N.Y. 10017
tel. 212 308-3300

In the U.K.:
Nightingale House
65 Curzon Street
London W1Y 7PE
tel. 01 495 3990

In Canada:
Box 417, 2 Funday
Place Bonaventure
Montreal H5A 1B8

In Australia:
Lufthansa House, 12th Floor
143 Macquarie Street
Sydney 2000
tel. 02 221 1008

The Berlin-Information center on Panoramastrasse in the eastern section provides maps for walking tours and educational brochures. Its hours are 1:00 P.M.–6:00 P.M. on Monday, Tuesday to Friday 8:00 A.M.–6:00 P.M., and 10:00 A.M.–6:00 P.M. on Saturday and Sunday.

The former East Berlin travel agency, located at Reisebüro-Hochhaus, Alexanderplatz 5, provides information; tel. 215 44 02. Hours are 8:00 A.M.–8:00 P.M., Monday through Friday, and on Saturday and Sunday 9:00 A.M.–6:00 P.M.; tel. 02 221 1008.

Cultural Information. Two bi-monthly magazine publications, *Tip* and *Zitty,* provide comprehensive, in-depth information on cultural events in Berlin, including theater listings, rock concerts, film exhibitions, and flea market locations. *Berlin-Programm,* issued monthly, contains listings for opera, theater, and classical and popular music concerts.

150 Practical Information

Shopping. Berlin is a fertile source for tempting goods to take home with you. Begin at the KaDeWe, Germany's largest (seven story) department store, which offers everything from designer gowns to imported caviar.

Berlin's major shopping thoroughfare, the Kurfürstendamm and its extension, Tauentzienstrasse, is lined with chic boutiques, department stores, and tasteful shops. The Europa Center also boasts scores of shops that sell finely crafted jewelry, designer clothing, and lots of souvenirs. There are dozens of flea markets with tons of bric-a-brac and antiques, as well as shops in the Kurfürstendamm that offer collectibles in a less hectic setting. Porcelain is still produced at the Staatliche Porzellan Manufactur (formerly the Royal Prussian Porcelain Factory). Reproductions of great works of art found in Berlin's Egyptian Museum and other city museums can be purchased in the Gipsformerei der Staatlichen Museen Preussicher Kulturbesitz.

Clothing Sizes. Listed below are the standard clothing-size equivalents for the United States, Great Britain, and Europe.

		U.S.	U.K.	Europe
Chest	*Small*	34	34	87
	Medium	36	36	91
		38	38	97
	Large	40	40	102
		42	42	107
	Extra Large	44	44	112
		46	46	117
Collar		14	14	36
		14½	14½	37
		15	15	38
		15½	15½	39
		16	16	41
		16½	16½	42
		17	17	43
Waist		24	24	61
		26	26	66
		28	28	71
		30	30	76
		32	32	80
		34	34	87
		36	36	91
		38	38	97
Men's Suits		34	34	44
		35	35	46
		36	36	48

	U.S.	U.K.	Europe
	37	37	49½
	38	38	51
	39	39	52½
	40	40	54
	41	41	55½
	42	42	57
Men's Shoes	7	6	39½
	8	7	41
	9	8	42
	10	9	43
	11	10	44½
	12	11	46
	13	12	47
Men's Hats	6¾	6⅝	54
	6⅞	6¾	55
	7	6⅞	56
	7⅛	7	57
	7¼	7⅛	58
	7½	7⅜	60
Women's Dresses	6	8	36
	8	10	38
	10	12	40
	12	14	42
	14	16	44
	16	18	46
	18	20	48
Women's Blouses and Sweaters	8	10	38
	10	12	40
	12	14	42
	14	16	44
	16	18	46
	18	20	48
Women's Shoes	4½	3	35½
	5	3½	36
	5½	4	36½
	6	4½	37
	6½	5	37½
	7	5½	38
	7½	6	38½
	8	6½	39
	8½	7	39½
	9	7½	40

152 Practical Information

	U.S.	U.K.	Europe
Children's Clothing	2	16	92
(*One size larger for knitwear*)	3	18	98
	4	20	104
	5	22	110
	6	24	116
	6X	26	122
Children's Shoes	8	7	24
	9	8	25
	10	9	27
	11	10	28
	12	11	29
	13	12	30
	1	13	32
	2	1	33
Children's Shoes	3	2	34
	4½	3	36
	5½	4	37
	6½	5½	38½

Museums. The following is a list of museums in Berlin. Although we have provided hours and admission fees for some museums in the text, we recommend that you call to verify that the museum is open at the time you wish to visit and that the particular exhibit you wish to see will be available. Most museums are open Tuesday–Sunday 10:00 A.M.–6:00 P.M., and closed on Mondays. Many small museums also close during lunchtime.

Museums in West Berlin

Abgussammlung antiker Plastik des Instituts für Archäologie der FU Berlin
Schloss-Strasse 69b
tel. 3 42 40 54/8 38 37 12/4

Ägyptisches Museum
Schloss-Strasse 70
tel. 32 09 11

Antikenmuseum
Schloss-Strasse 1
tel. 32 09 11

Anti-Kriegs-Museum
Genter Strasse 9
tel. 4 61 78 37

Bauhaus-Archiv
Klingelhöferstrasse 13–14
tel. 25 40 02 0

Berlinische Galerie-Gropiusbau
Stresemannstrasse 110
tel. 25 48 63 02

Berliner Post- und Fernmeldemuseum
An der Urania
tel. 2 12 82 01

Berlin-Museum
Lindenstrasse 14
tel. 25 86 0

Berlin-Pavillon
Strasse des 17. Juni
tel. 3 91 79 51

Botanischer Museum
Königin-Luise-Strasse 6–8
tel. 83 00 60

Bröhan-Museum
Schloss-Strasse 1a
tel. 3 21 40 29

Brücke-Museum
Bussardsteig 9
tel. 8 31 20 29

Deutschlandhaus
Stresemannstrasse 90
tel. 2 61 10 46

Geheimes Staatsarchiv Preussischer Kulturbesitz
Archivstrasse 12
tel. 83 20 31

Gemäldegalerie
Arnimallee 23
tel. 8 30 11

Georg-Kolbe-Museum
Sensburger Allee 25
tel. 3 04 21 44

Jüdische Abteilung des Berlin-Museums in Martin-Gropius-Bau
Stresemannstrasse 110
tel. 25 48 65 15

Käthe-Kollwitz-Museum
Fasanenstrasse 24
tel. 8 82 52 10

Kunstbibliothek
Jebenstrasse 2
tel. 31 01 16

Kunstgewerbemuseum
Tiergartenstrasse 6
tel. 2 66 29 11

Kupferstichkabinett
Arnimallee 23/27
tel. 8 30 11

Kongresshalle/Haus der Kulturen der Welt
John-Foster-Dulles-Allee 10
tel. 3 94 12 11

Landesarchiv
Kalckreuthstrasse 1– 2
tel. 21 23 1

Landesbildstelle Berlin (Bildarchiv)
Wikingerufer 7
tel. 3 90 92 1

Lapidarium
Hallesches Ufer 78
tel. 25 86 0

Mauermuseum
Haus am Checkpoint Charlie
Friedrichstrasse 44
tel. 2 51 10 31

Museum für Deutsche Volkskunde
Im Winkel 6
tel. 83 20 31

Museum für Indische Kunst, Islamische Kunst und Ostasiatische Kunst
Lansstrasse 8
tel. 8 30 11

Museum für Verkehr und Technik
Trebbiner Strasse 9
tel. 25 48 40

Museum für Völkerkunde
Lansstrasse 8
tel. 8 30 11

Museum für Vor- und Frühgeschichte Langhansbau des Schloss Charlottenburg
Spandauer Damm
tel. 32 09 11

Museumsdorf Düppel
Chauertstrasse 11
tel. 8 02 66 71

Musikinstrumenten-Museum
Tiergartenstrasse 1
tel. 2 54 81 0

Nationalgalerie
Potsdamer Strasse 50
tel. 2 66 26 63/2

Nationalgalerie-Galerie der Romantik in Schloss Charlottenburg
Luisenplatz
tel. 32 01 12 04/5

Polizeihistorische Sammlung Polizeipräsidium
Platz der Luftbrücke 6
tel. 69 93 50 50

Reichstagsgebäude
Platz der Republik
tel. 39 77 0

Skulpturengalerie
Arnimallee 23– 27
tel. 8 30 11

Staatliche Kunsthalle Berlin
Budapester Strasse 43–44
tel. 2 61 70 67/68

Staatsbibliothek
Potsdamer Strasse 33
tel. 2 66 1

Teddy-Museum
Ku'damm Karree
tel. 8 81 41 71

Topographie des Terrors
Stresemannstrasse 110
tel. 25 48 67 03

Werkbund-Archiv im Martin-Gropius-Bau
Stresemannstrasse 110
tel. 25 48 60

Zille-Museum
Nollendorfplatz

Zitadelle Spandau
Zitadellenweg (am Juliusturm)

Zuckermuseum
Amrumer Strasse
tel. 31 42 75 20/1

Museums in East Berlin

Berliner Handwerksmuseum
Am Mühlendamm 5
tel. 21 71 33 09

Bodemuseum—Museumsinsel
entrance from Monbijou-Brücke between Weidendamm and Kupfergraben

Brecht-Haus Berlin
Chausseestrasse 124
tel. 2 82 99 16

Huguenottenmuseum
Platz der Akademie
tel. 2 29 17 60

Kunstgewerbemuseum
Schloss Köpenick
Schlossinsel Köpenick
tel. 6 57 26 51

Johannes-R.-Becher-Haus
Majakowskiring 34
tel. 4 82 61 62

Märkisches Museum
Am Köllnischen Park 5
tel. 2 75 49 02/24

Museum Berliner Arbeiterleben um 1900
Husemannstrasse 12
tel. 4 48 56 75

Museum für Deutsche Geschichte
Unter den Linden 2
tel. 2 00 05 91

Museum für Naturkunde
Invalidenstrasse 43
tel. 2 89 75 40

Nationalgalerie—Museumsinsel
entrance from Bodestrasse

Otto-Nagel-Haus
Märkisches Ufer 16–18
tel. 2 79 14 02

Pergamonmuseum—Museumsinsel
entrance via Kupfergraben Bridge

Postmuseum
Leipziger Strasse at corner of Mauerstrasse
tel. 23 41 22 02

Schinkelmuseum
in Friedrich-Werdersche Church

Staatliche Museen zu Berlin
Bodestrasse 1–3
tel. 2 20 03 81

Theaters. The following is a list of theaters in Berlin. Consult the listings in *Tip* or *Zitty* (both bi-monthly publications) or the monthly *Berlin-Programm* for performance schedules.

If you don't want to make a special trip to the theater to purchase tickets, try one of the ticket agencies. They charge a small handling fee, but can save you time. Your best bet is the tiny *Theaterkasse im Europa-Center*, Tauentzienstrasse 9, tel. 2 61 70 51/52, where the two men in charge both speak English and can offer recommendations. Other ticket offices include: *City-Center*, Kurfürstendamm 16, tel. 8 82 65 63; *KaDeWe*, Tauentzienstrasse 21, tel. 24 80 39; *Kiosk am Zoo*, Kantstrasse 3–4, tel. 8 81 36 03; *Wertheim*, Kurfürstendamm 231, tel. 8 82 53 54.

Theaters in West Berlin

Deutsche Oper Berlin
Bismarckstrasse 34–37
tel. 3 41 44 49

Freie Volksbühne
Schaperstrasse 24
tel. 8 81 37 42

Hansa-Theater
Alt-Moabit 47
tel. 3 91 44 60

Hebbel-Theater
Stresemannstrasse 29
tel. 2 51 04 06

Kleines Theater
Südwestkorso 64
tel. 8 21 30 30

Komödie
Kurfürstendamm 206
tel. 8 82 78 93

Renaissance-Theater
Hardenbergstrasse 6
tel. 3 12 42 02

Schaubühne am Lehniner Platz
Kurfürstendamm 153
tel. 89 00 23

Schiller-Theater
Bismarckstrasse 110
tel. 3 19 52 36

Schiller-Theater-Werkstätt
Bismarckstrasse 110
tel. 3 19 52 36

Schlosspark-Theater
41 Schloss-Strasse 48
tel. 7 91 12 13

Theater des Westens
Kantstrasse 24
tel. 8 81 37 42

Theater am Kurfürstendamm
Kurfürstendamm 206
tel. 8 82 37 89

Tribüne
Otto-Suhr-Allee 18– 20
tel. 3 41 26 00

Vaganten-Bühne
Kantstrasse 12a
tel. 3 12 45 39

Theaters in East Berlin

Berliner Ensemble
Am Bertolt-Brecht-Platz
tel. 28 80

Deutsche Staatsoper
Unter den Linden 7
tel. 2 07 18 28

Deutsches Theater Kammerspiele
Schumannstrasse 13a
tel. 2 87 12 25

Die Distel
Friedrichstrasse 101
tel. 29 15 79

Friedrichstadtpalast
Friedrichstrasse 107
tel. 2 28 26 0

Komische Oper
Behrenstrasse 55–57
tel. 2 20 27 61

Maxim Gorki Theater/Foyertheater
Am Festungsgraben 2
tel. 2 00 10

Metropol-Theater
Friedrichstrasse 101–102
tel 2 00 06 51

Schauspielhaus Berlin
Platz der Akademie
tel. 2 27 21 57

Volksbühne
Rosa-Luxemburg-Platz
tel. 2 82 59 21

Index

If more than one page number appears next to the name of the attraction, the boldface number indicates the page where the detailed description appears in the text.

Academic Center for Social Research, 47
Academy of Sciences, 108
Admiralspalast, 102
Ägyptisches Museum (Museum Island), 112, **115–116**
Ägyptisches Museum (Charlottenburg Palace), 54
Air Lift Memorial, 86
Air Lift Square, 85, **86**
Air Transport Ministry, 22
Akademie der Künste, 21, **39**
Alexanderplatz, 5, 22, 101, **118–121**
Allied Air-Traffic Control Center, 83
Allied Military Prison, 62
Altstadt-Café, 60
Alt-Berliner Weissbierstube, 90
Alte Bibliothek (Old Library), 103
Alte Fischerhütte, 65
Alter Krug, 76
Alter Marstall (Old Military Stable), 121
Altes Museum, 18, 110, **111–112**
Altes Palais (Old Palace), 103
Amerika Gedenkbibliothek (American Commemorative Library), 90–91
Amerika-Haus Berlin, 34
Anhalter Bahnhof, 90
Antikenmuseum (Antiquities Museum) (Charlottenburg Palace), 54–55
Antikensammlung (Antiquities Collection) (Museum Island), 113
Applied Art and Poster Collection, 33
Aquarium, 28
Archiv zur Geschichte der Max-Planck-Gesellschaft, 75

Art Library with the Museum of Architecture, Fashion Illustration and Graphic Design, 33
Arts' Academy, 21, **34–35**, 39
Askanischer Platz, 90
Asternplatz, 81
Ausflugslinie (excursion bus), 58, 62, 68, 72
Ausstellungs- und Messegelände, 56
Aviation Ministry, 107
Avus, 57

Bahnhof Zoologischer Garten "Bahnhof Zoo," **25**, 33
Ballerbau, 92
Baroque gardens, 52
Bauhaus-Archiv/Museum für Gestaltung (Bauhaus Archives and Museum for Design), 23, **48**
Bayerischer Platz, 84
Bebelplatz, 103, 104
Bellevue Palace, **40–41**, 49
Belvedere, 52
Berliner Dom (Berlin Cathedral), 19, **106–107**
Berliner Ensemble, 102
Berliner Forst (Berlin Forest), 97
Berliner Handwerksmuseum, 123
Berliner Porzellan Collection (Berlin Procelain Collection), 52
Berliner Schloss (Berlin Palace), 50
Berlinische Galerie (Berlin Gallery), 89
Berlin-Kinomuseum (Berlin Movie Museum), 91
Berlin Museum, 90
Berlin Philharmonic, **45**, 109

Index

Berlin Representation to the Assembly of German Cities, 37
Berlin Verkehrsamt, 25, 30
Berlin Wall, 43, 44, 82, 89, 99, 101
Bethlehemskirche (Bethlehem Church), 87
Bewag Building, 47
Blockhouse (Log Building), 73
Blücherplatz, 90
Bode-Museum, 110–111, **115–118**
Böhmisches Dorf, 87
Botanischer Garten (Botanical Gardens), 80–81
Bote & Bock, 35
Brandenburg Gate (Brandenburger Tor), 18, 40, **43–44,** 99–100
Breitscheidplatz, 29
British Council, 34
British Embassy, 101
Britz, 17
Broadcasting House, 56
Broadcasting Tower, 56
Bröhan Museum, 55
Brücke-Museum, 66
Bücherbogen, 31
Buckow, 17
Buddhist Temple, 98
Bundesverwaltungsgericht, 33
Business hours, 141
BVG information office, 25–26

Café Bauer, 102
Café Kranzler, 32
Carillon, 41–42
Casino (Schloss Klein-Glienicke), 73
Castle Restaurant, 61
Cemeteries:
    Dorotheenstädtischer, 126
    Schönhauser Allee, 126
    Weissensee, 126
Centrum, 119–120
Chalet Suisse, 66
Chamissoplatz, 92
Chapel of Saints Constantine and Helena, 98
Charlottenburg, 30, 35, 36
Charlottenburger Brücke (Bridge), 37
Charlottenburger Tor (gate), 37
Charlottenburg-Nord, 93
Charlottenburg Palace, 2, 5, 17, 18, **48–55**
Checkpoint Charlie, **89,** 99, 107
Children's Museum, 79
Church of Mary Queen of Martyrs, 94
Church of Saints Peter and Paul, 73
Climate, 134
Cöllner Fischmarkt, 122
Consulates, 136–137
Corbusier-Haus, 58
Currency, 141
Customs, 135–136

Dachsberg, 64
Dahlem Museen, 46, **77–81**
Dahlem Country Estate and Museum, 76
Dahlem-Dorf, 74, **75–76**
Das Panorama Berlin, 28
Department of Prints and Drawings (Dahlem Museum), 77, 79
Department of Prints and Drawings (Museum Island), 111–112
Deutsche Bundesbahn, 34
Deutsche Oper Berlin, 23, **36–37**
Deutscher Dom, 17, **109**
Deutsches Rundfunkmuseum (German Broadcasting Museum), 57
Deutsche Staatsoper (German State Opera), 23, 49, **103–104**
Deutschlandhalle, 57
Dianasee (Diana Lake), 67
Die Brücke, 46, 112
"Die Distel" ("The Thistle"), 102
"Die Stachelschweine" ("The Porcupines"), 30
Domäne Dahlem Landgut und Museum, 76
Domhotel, 22, 108
Düppel Forest, 2, **69–70**

Early Christian-Byzantine Collection, 116; see also 78–79

Egyptian Museum (Charlottenburg Palace), 54
Egyptian Museum (Museum Island), 112, **115–116**
Eisenbahn-Markthalle, 93
Elefantentor, **26,** 28
Embassies, 136–137
Emergency, 144
Emperor Frederick Memorial Church, 39
Emperor William Memorial Church, 29–30
English Garden, 38
Eosander Portal, 106
Ephraim-Palais (Ephraim Palace), 17, **123**
Equestrian Statue of Friedrich II, 103
Equestrian Statue of the Great Elector, 17, **50**
Ernst-Reuter-Haus (Ernst Reuter House), 37
Ernst-Reuter-Platz, **36,** 37
Ethnological Museum (Dahlem Museum), 77, **79**
Ethnological Museum (Museum Island), 113, **115**
Europa-Center, 5, 29, **30**
Evangelischer Oberkirchenrat (Protestant High Consistory), 33
Exhibition and Fair Grounds, 56

Falkenseer-Platz, 59
Far Eastern Collection, 115; see also 77, 80
Fasanerie Restaurant, 32
Federal Civil Court, 33
Fernsehturm, 5, **120**
Fischerinsel (Fisherman's Island), 122
Foreign Ministry, 105–106
Foreign Trade Ministry, 101
Forsthaus Paulsborn, 66
Forum Fridiricianum, 104
Französischer Dom, 17, **108–109**
Freedom Bell (Freiheitsglocke), 84
Freie Universität (Free University), 5, **74–75**
Mensa, 75
Freigelände (open-air gardens), 81
French Cathedral, 17, **108–109**
French Embassy, 101
Freunde der Domäne Dahlem (Friends of the Dahlem Domain), 76
Friedenau, 82
Friedhöfe, *see* cemeteries
Friedrichsbrücke, 111
Friedrichsfelde, 5
Friedrichstadtpalast, 102
Friedrich-Werdersche Church, 106
Frohnau, 97–98
Frühchristlich-byzantinische Sammlung (Early Christian-Byzantine Collection), 116; see also 78–79
Funkturm, 56
Funkturmrestaurant, 56–57

Galerie der Romantik (Gallery of Romantic Art), 51–52
Galerie Pels-Leusden, 32
Gartenstadt Frohnau, 98
Gedenkstätte Deutscher Widerstand, 47–48
Gedenkstätte Plötzensee, 94–96
Geheimes Staatsarchiv Preussischer Kulturbesitz, 76
Gemäldegalerie (Painting Gallery) (Dahlem Museum), 46, **77–78**
Gemäldegalerie (Painting Gallery) (Museum Island), 117
Gendarmenmarkt (Gendarme Market), 108
Georg-Kolbe-Grove, 58
Georg-Kolbe-Museum, 58
German Cathedral, 17, **109**
German Cultural Institute, 35
German Federal Railroad, 34
German Institute of Urban Studies, 37
German State Library, 5, 23, 44, 47, 102
German State Opera, 49, **103–104**
Gipsformerei der Staatlichen Museen, 55

160 Index

Glienicke Hunting Lodge, 73–74
Glienicker Brücke, 73
Glockenspiel (carillon), 73
Goethe-Institut, 35
Goldener Hirsch (Golden Stag), 84–85
Golden Gallery, 51
Golgotha, 91
Gouverneurshaus (Governor's House), 103
Grand Hotel, 102
Graphics Collection, 33
Great Curiosity, 73
Great Müggel Lake, 1
Greenhouse Displays, 80–81
Greenwichpromenade, 97
Griebnitzsee, 68
Gripstheater, 39
Grisebach Collection, 33
Gropiusstadt, 5
Grosser Stern, 39
Grosser Wannsee, 68, 69
Grosses Fenster (Big Window), 65
Grosse Steinlanke Bay, 64
Grosses Tropenhaus, 81
Grossfürstenplatz, 41
Grundkredit-Bank, 28
Grunewald, 1, 2, 31, 57, **62–65**
Grunewaldsee (Grunewald Lake), 62, 65, **66–67**
Grunewaldturm (Grunewald Tower), 1, **64**

Halbinsel Schildhorn, 63–64
Halensee, 67
Hammarskjöldplatz, 56
Handwerkbrunnen (Craftsmen's Fountain), 122
Hansaviertel, 5, **38–39**
Hardenbergplatz, 26
Haus am Checkpoint Charlie Museum, 89
Haus am Waldsee, 65
Haus der Kulturen der Welt (House of World Cultures), 41
Haus des Rundfunks (Broadcasting House), 56

Haus Sans Souci, 69
Havel, 1, 59, 60, 64, 65, 68, 69, 71, 73
Havelberg, 1
Havelchaussee, 2, 62, **63–64**
Heiligensee, 17, 97
Heimatmuseum Spandau, 61
Hellersdorf, 5
Henry-Ford-Bau (Henry Ford Building), 75
Herkulesbrücke, 48
Hermannplatz, 87, 88
Hermsdorf, 97
Herthasee, 67
Historical Rooms (Charlottenburg Palace), 50–51
Hochschule der Künste, 34–35
Hohenschönhausen, 5
Hohenzollern Crypt, 107
Hotels, 138–141
Hubertussee, 67
Hugenottenmuseum (Huguenot Museum), 108
Humboldt-Schloss Tegel (Humboldt Castle), 96–97
Humboldt-Universität, 102–103
Hundekehlefenn nature preserve, 67
Hundekehlesee, 63
Hungarian Embassy, 101

Information, 148–149
Information Gallery, 46
Informationszentrum, 120
Informationszentrum Berlin, 34
Innsbrucker Platz, 84
Institute for Applied Economic Research, 101
Insulaner, 85
International Congress Center (ICC), 30, 31, **57**
Internationales Handelszentrum (International Trade Center), 102
Ishtar Gate, 114
Islamisches Museum (Islamic Museum) (Museum Island), 113, **114**; see also 77, 80
Italian Embassy, 101

Index **161**

Jagdschloss Glienicke, 73–74
Jagdschloss Grunewald, 66
Joe am Ku'damm, 32
Jüdisches Gemeindehaus (Jewish Community Center), 35
Juliusturm (Julius Tower), 61
Jungfernheide forest, 52
Jürgenlanke Bay, 63

Kaiser-Friedrich Gedächtniskirche, 39
Kaiser-Wilhelm-Gedächtniskirche, 29–30
Kammergericht, 83, 90
Kammermusiksaal (Chamber Music Hall), 5, 23, 45
Karlsberg, 1, 64
Kasino (Schloss Klein-Glienicke), 73
Käthe-Kollwitz-Museum, 32
Kaufhaus des Westens (KaDeWe), 32
Kiepert Bookstore, 35
Kirchplatz, 121
Kleine Müggelberg, 125
Kleiner Wannsee, 68–69
Klein-Glienicke Palace, 18, **73–74**
Kleistpark, 83–84
Knoblauchhaus (Garlic House), 123
Koenigssee (Kings Lake), 67
Kohlhaas & Company, 32
Kolk, 59, 60
Köllnischer Park, 123
Komische Oper, 101–102
Kommandantenhaus (Commander's House), 61
Komödie, 31
Kongresshalle, 41
Königskolonnaden (King's Colonnade), 83
Kontrollratsgebäude, 83
Kottbusser, Brücke, 92
Kreuzberg, 1, 87, **91–93**
Kreuzberg Arts Center, 92–93
Kreuzberg City Hall, 90
Kreuzberg SO 36, 92

Kronprinzenpalais (Crown Prince's Palace), 104
Krumme Lanke, 2, 62, 65
Ku'damm Eck, 32
Ku'damm-Karree, 32
Kulturforum (Culture Forum), 5, **44–47**
Kunstbibliothek mit dem Museum für Architektur, Modebild und Grafik Design, 33
Kunst der DDR der Nationalgalerie (Art of the DDR from the National Gallery), 111
Kunstgewerbemuseum, 5, **45–46**, 89
Kunstgewerbemuseum im Schloss Köpenick (Handcrafts Museum in Kopenick Castle), 124
Künstlerhaus Bethanien, 92–93
Kupfergraben, 106
Küpferstichkabinett (Dahlem Museum), 46, 77, **79**
Küpferstichkabinett (Museum Island), 111–112
Kurfürstendamm "Ku'damm," 2, 20, **31–32**, 38, 67

Landwehr Kanal, 36, 37, 90, 92
Lange Brücke, 50
Lehniner Platz, 31
Lichtenrade, 86
Lichterfelde, 17
Lieper Bay, 64
Lietzenseepark, 30, 31
Lindwerder, 64
Lipperheid Costume Library, 33
Literaturhaus Berlin, 31–32
Löwentor, 26
Lübars, 98
Luise restaurant, 76

Maifeld parade grounds, 58
Marheineke Markt-Hall (Marheineke Market Hall), 92
Mariannenplatz, 92
Maria Regina Martyrum, 94
Mariendorf, 17, 86

162 Index

Marienfelde, 17, 86
Marienkirche (Church of St. Mary), 17, **120–121**
Mark Brandenburg Museum, 123–124
Market Gate of Miletus, 114
Märkisches Museum, 122, 123
Märkisches Viertel, 5
Martin-Gropius-Bau (Martin Gropius Building), 89–90
Marx-Engels-Brücke, 106
Marx-Engels-Forum, 121
Marx-Engels-Platz, 5, 100, 101, **106**, 111
Marzahn, 5
Matthäuskirche (Church of St. Matthew), 46
Mausoleum, 53
Maxim Gorki Theater, 105
Max Planck Society Historical Archives, 75
Mehringplatz, 90
Memorial to Foreign Minister Walter Rathenau, 67
Memorial to the German Resistance, 47–48
Memorial to the Victims of Fascism and Militarism, 105
Metropol Hotel, 102
Metropol Theater, 102
Ministry for Public Education, 101
Mittelgebirge, 1
Molkenmarkt (Dairy Market), 122
Monument to Elector Joachim II, 60
Monument to the Wars of Liberation, 91
Müggelberge, 1, 125
Müggelsee, 125
Müggelturm (Müggel Tower), 125
Mühlendammbrücke, 122
Münzkabinett (Coin Cabinet), 118
Museen Dahlem, 77–80
Museum für Deutsche Geschichte (Museum of German history), 17, **105**
Museum für Deutscher Völkerkunde (Museum of German Ethnology), 76
Museum für Indische Kunst (Museum of Indian Art), 77, **79–80**
Museum für Islamische Kunst (Museum of Islamic Art) (Dahlem Museum), 77, **80;** see also 113, 114
Museum für Naturkunde (Museum of Natural History), 124
Museum für Ostasiatische Kunst (Museum of Far Eastern Art), 77, **80;** see also 115
Museum für Ur- und Frühgeschichte (Museum of Prehistory and Early History) (Museum Island), 112, **117–118;** see also 53
Museum für Völkerkunde (Ethnological Museum) (Dahlem Museum), 77, **79**
Museum für Völkskunde (Ethnological Museum) (Museum Island), 113, **115**
Museum für Vor- und Frühgeschichte (Museum of Prehistory and Early History) (Charlottenburg Palace), 53; see also 112, 117–118
Museum of Applied Arts, 5, **45–46**, 89
Museum of Greek and Roman Antiquities, 54–55; see also 113
Museums, 152–155
Museumsinsel (Museum Island), 1, 106, 109, **110–118**
Musikinstrumenten-Museum (Museum of Musical Instruments), 5, **45**

Nationalgalerie (Kulturforum), 5, 23, **46–47**
Nationalgalerie (Museum Island), 19, 110, **112**
Near Eastern Museum, 113, **114**

Neptunbrunnen (Neptune Fountain), 121
Neuer Marstall (New Military Stable), 121
Neues Museum, 110, 111, **112**
Neue Wache, 18, 104–105
Neukölln, 3, 87–88
Neukölln Town Hall, 87
New Lake, 38
New Wing, 51–52
Nightlife, 148
Nikolaikirche (Church of St. Nicholas), 17
Nikolaikirche (Church of St. Nicholas) (Spandau), 60
Nikolaikirche (Church of St. Nicholas) (St. Nicholas Quarter), 122
Nikolaiviertel (St. Nicholas Quarter), 4, 17, **121–123**
Nikolassee, 57
Nikolskoe, 73
Nollendorfplatz, 21

Olympia Stadion, 22, 57, 58–59
Olympischer Platz, 58
Opera House, 18
Operncafé (Opera Café), 104
Ostasiatische Sammlung, 113, **115**; see also 77, 80
Otto-Hahn-Bau, 75
Otto-Nagel-Haus (Otto Nagel House), 123

Painting Gallery (Dahlem Museum), 46, **77–78**
Painting Gallery (Museum Island), 117
Palace Hotel, 30
Palais Unter den Linden, 104
Palas (Knight's Hall), 61
Palast der Republik (Palace of the Republic), 5, 22, 100, **106**
Pariser Platz, **100**, 101
Paul-Ernst-Park, 65
Peacock Island, 38, 68, 69, **70–72**
 aviary, 72
 Biedermeier Garden, 71
 Cavalier House, 72
 dairy, 71, 72
 cow stall, 72
 Frigate Shed, 72
 Jacob Well, 71–72
 Memorial Temple for Queen Luise, 72
 Otaheite Cabinet (Tahitian Room), 71
 Palace, 71–72
 Rose Garden, 71
 The Slide, 72
 spawning meadow, 72
 Steam Engine House, 72
 Winter House for Migratory Birds, 72
Pergamon Altar, 113
Pergamon-Museum, 111, **113–115**
Pfaueninsel, see Peacock Island
Pfaueninselchaussee, 69
Philharmonie (Philharmonic Hall), 5, 23, 44, **45**
Plaster Casting Workshop of the State Museums, 55
Platz der Akademie, 4, 17, 18, 22, **108**
Platz der Luftbrücke, 85, **86**
Platz der Republik, 39, 42
Pohlesee, 68
Polish Embassy, 101
Postage, 141, 144
Postmuseum, 107
Potsdam, 127–129
 Alter Markt, 128
 Altes Rathaus (Old City Hall), 128
 Brandenburger Tor (Brandeburg Gate), 129
 Cecilienhof Palace, 128
 Church of Saints Peter and Paul, 128
 film museum, 128
 Holländisches Viertel (Dutch Quarter), 129
 Informeion Office, 128
 Knobelsdorffbau, 128

164 Index

Potsdam (*continued*)
  Kulturhaus "Hans Marschwitza," 128
  Marstall (Stables), 128
  Nauener Tor (Nauen Gate), 129
  Nikolaikirche (Church of St. Nicholas), 128
  Platz der Einheit, 128
  Platz der Nationen, 129
Potsdamer Platz, 44
Potsdam Town Palace, 18
Prenzlauer Berg, 5
Prinz Eisenherz Bookshop, 31
Prinzessinnenpalais (Princess's Palace), 104
Processional Road from Babylon, 114

Quadriga, 43

Radio Free Berlin, 56
Railroad Market Hall, 93
Rathaus-Brücke, 121
Rathaus Neukölln, 87
Rathaus Schöneberg, 84
Ratskeller, 84
Reformationsplatz, 60
Reichstag, 19, **42–43**
Reisebüro-Hochhaus (Travel Bureau Skyscraper), 120
Reiterstandbild des Grossen Kurfürsten, 17, **50**
Rembrandt collection, 78
Renaissance Theater, 35
Resistance to National Socialism, 48
Restaurants, 146–148
RIAS (Radio in the American Sector), 85
Ribbeckhaus (Ribbeck House), 17, **121**
Richardplatz, 87
Richard-Wagner-Platz, 48
Riehmer's Hofgarten, 91
Riemenschneider Room, 79
Rixdorfer Höhe, 88
Romanisches Café, 20

Rose Garden, 38
Rotes Rathaus (Red City Hall), 19, **121**
Rubble Woman, 88, 121
Rudolph-Wilde-Park, 84
Rudow, 17
Russian Cemetery, 98
Russian Embassy, 101

St.-Annen-Kirche (Church of St. Anne), 17, **76**
St.-Ansgar-Kirche (Church of St. Ansgar), 39
St.-Hedwigs-Kathedrale, 104
Sammlung Ludwig Aachen, 111
Sanssouci, 18, **129–132**
  Charlottenhof Palace, 132
  Chinese Tea House, 131
  Communs, 132
  Drachenhaus (Dragon House), 131
  Gitterpavillon, 130
  Great Fountain, 129
  Grotto Hall, 132
  Marlygarten, 129
  Neue Kammern (New Chambers), 130
  Neues Palais (New Palace), 129, **131–132**
  Obeliskportal (Obelisk Portal), 129
  Orangerie, 131
  Park Charlottenhof, 132
  Römanische Bäder (Roman Baths), 132
  Ruinenberg, 130
  Schloss, 18, 103, **130–131**
  Sicilian Garden, 129
  Theater, 132
Savignyplatz, 30–31
Schäferberg, 1
Schaubühne Theater, 31
Schaugewächshäuser, 80–81
Schauspielhaus (Playhouse), 18, 21, **109**
Schildhorn Peninsula, 63–64

Schiller Monument, 108
Schiller-Oberschule Charlottenburg (Schiller Secondary School), 36
Schiller-Theater, 36
Schinkel Museum, 106
Schinkel Pavillon "Villa am Meer," 50, **52**
Schlachtensee, 2, 62, 65
Schleuse Spandau (Spandau Sluice), 60
Schloss Bellevue, **40–41**, 49
Schlossbrücke, 106
Schloss Charlottenburg, *see* Charlottenburg Palace
Schloss Friedrichsfelde (Friedrichsfelde Palace), 126
Schloss Klein-Glienicke, 73–74
Schmargendorf, 17
Scholzplatz, 62
Schöneberg, 3, **82**
Schöneberg City Hall, 84
Schrebergärten, 67
Schwanenwerder, 65
Sculpture Gallery, 46, 78–79, 117
Sculpture Garden, 47
Sculpture plaza (Kulturforum), 47
Secret Prussian State Cultural Heritage Archive, 76
Senate Library, 37
Sender Freies Berlin, 56
Shopping, 150–152
Siegessäule, 19, 37, **39–40**, 42
Skulpturengalerie mit Frühchristlich-Byzantischer Sammlung (Sculpture Gallery), 77, **78–79**, see also 117
Skulpturensammlung (Sculpture Collection), 117
Sommergarten (Summer Garden), 56
Sophie-Charlotte-Platz, 48
"Souvenir Strasse," 43
Sowjetisches Ehrenmal (Soviet Memorial), 44, 124–125
Spandau, 1, 2, 17, **59–62**
Spandau City Forest, 59
Spandauer Zitadelle, 60–61

Spielbank Berlin, 30
Spree, 1, 41, 52, 59
Spree-Ufer, 40, 121
Spreeweg, 40
Staatliche Kunsthalle Berlin, 29
Staatliche Porzellanmanufaktur, 37–38
Staatsbibliothek, 5, 23, 44, 47, 102
Staatsratsgebäude, 106
Stadt Berlin, 119
State Art Gallery, 29
State Council Building, 106
State Porcelain Factory, 37–38
Steinplatz, 35
Stölpchensee, 68
Stössensee, 1
Strandbad Wannsee, 2, **64–65**, 68, 69
Strasse des 17. Juni, **37**, 44, 101
Supreme Court of Justice, 83, 90
Synagoge Oranienburger Strasse, 125

Tanzendes Paar, 87–88
Tauentzien Strasse, 32
Technische Universität (Technical University), 5, **36**, 37
Tegel, 2, 96
Tegeler Fliess River, 98
Tegeler See, 1, 97
Telephones, 144
Television Tower, 5, **120**
Tempelhof, 85–87
Tempelhof Airport, 86–87
Tempelhofer Feld, 85
Teufelsberg, 1, 64
Teufelsee, 1, 63
Teufelsfenn, 63
Theater am Kurfürstendamm, 31
Theater am Schiffbauerdamm, 21
Theater des Westens (Theater of the West), 21, **30**
Theaters, 155–156
Theodor-Heuss-Platz, 55–56
Thomaskirche (Church of St. Thomas), 93

Tiergarten, 2, 5, **38**, 48
Tierpark Berlin in Friedrichsfelde (Zoo), 125–126
Time Zone, 135
Tomb of the Unknown Resistance Fighter, 105
Tomb of the Unknown Soldier, 105
Tourists' Bureau, 25, 30
Transportation:
    Air, 137–138
    Bus, 144–145
    Driving, 145–146
    Subway, 142–143, 144–145
    Taxi, 144
Travel Store, 35
Tribüne Theater, 37
Trödelmarkt (fleamarket), 37
Trümmerfrau, 88, 121
Turmstuben, 109

Uhr der fliessenden Zeit (Clock of Flowing Time), 30
Unter den Linden, 5, 18, 43, **100–106**, 109
U.S. Cultural Center, 34

Victory Column, 19, 37, **39–40**, 42
Vier Deutsche Strömen (Four German Rivers), 41
Viktoriapark, 91
Villa Borsig, 97
Villa Grisebach, 32
Villa von der Heydt, 48
Volkspark Hasenheide, 88
Volkspark Klein-Glienicke, 73
Vorderasiatisches Museum, 113, **114**

Waldbühne, 59
Wannsee, 1, 62, 67

Wannsee Beach, 2, **64–65**, 68, 69
Wannseebrücke, 69
Wannsee-Haus, 69
Wannseeterrassen Restaurant, 65
War Memorial (Spandau), 60
Wedding district, 96
Weidendammer Brücke, 102
Werderscher Markt, 106
Werkbund-Archiv, 89
White Hall, 51
Wilhelm-Foerster-Sternwarte (Observatory), 85
Wilmersdorf, 62
Winterfeldplatz, 83
Winterfeldplatz market, 83
Wissenschaftszentrum Berlin für Sozialforschung, 47
Wittenbergplatz, 32
Women's Federation Building, 103
World Chronometer, 120

Zehlendorf districts, 62
Zeiss-Planetarium, 85
Zentrales Haus der Deutsch-Sowjetischen Freundschaft (Central House of German-Soviet Friendship), 105
Zentralflughafen Tempelhof, 86–87
Zeughaus (Armory), 105
Zille-Hof flea market, 35
Zille Museum, 33
Zoologischer Garten (Zoological Garden), 26–28
Zuchthaus Plötzensee (Plötzensee Prison), 94–96
Zum lustigen Finken tavern, 98
Zum Nussbaum inn, 122